Design, Layout and Production

Bill Flies

Editors, Proof Readers

Bill Flies, Dianne Schjolberg, Ellen Hodgson Stewart

Copy Editor, Proof Reader

Susan Wandmacher

Cover Design

Bill Flies
Front Cover Picture: 1870 Frontenac Village
Back Cover Picture: 1870 Frontenac Point with Lakeside Hotel
Whitney Zimmerman, Photographers

Published by: Viriditas 2018, Frontenac, Minnesota.

Copyright © 2018 by Lorris Anne Wendland (USA), All Rights Reserved

ISBN-13: 978-0692920992 (Viriditas)
Library of Congress Control Number: 2017911592

Printed by CreateSpace, an Amazon company.

The information in this book is true and complete to the best of my knowledge.
It is offered with no guarantees on the part of the author.
Most of the pictures in this book were taken in the 19th century.
Age and 19th century technology affects the clarity of the pictures.

Communication welcome at:

19thCenturyFrontenac@gmail.com
Lorry Wendland, 28535 Lake Avenue Way, Frontenac Minnesota, 55026

Genealogy of a Village

The focus of this book is the genealogy of the pioneer families who created the village of Frontenac. Although this book is informative on its own, it is significantly complemented by its companion book, *19th Century Frontenac, Minnesota – The Rest of the Story,* which is filled with historic photographs and extensively researched facts that trace the roots of the early settlers, describe the homes they built, and follow their lives as they create the village.

My goal in this five-year project was to honor all the 19th century Frontenac settlers. The vital statistics on each settler and their family members, if found, were compiled using my genealogy software. This data is presented in family group sheets which give a concise visual recap that includes the name of the husband, wife, and children with their birth, marriage, and death information. Additional spouses of parents are recorded as well as children's spouses.

Uncovering previously unknown family relationships of many of these Frontenac settlers was especially interesting to me.

Ten transcribed census records from 1850 to 1900 list the Frontenac residents who lived in the village on the respective census dates. This helped determine when each pioneer arrived in the village and when their children were born.

The Garrard descendants understood the importance of their family documents and donated them to the Minnesota State University in Mankato, Minnesota. Two letters from that collection appear in this book: the 1858 letter Lewis Garrard wrote his mother Sarah Bella McLean and the 1859 letter from Israel to his brother Lewis.

Two 19th century photograph albums are also included in this book. The first, John Hull Underwood's album from 1885, a cherished archive at the Lake City, Minnesota Historical Society, is reprinted with their permission. The second album is a charming photograph and sketch album created by Lewis Garrard's two daughters, Edith and Anna, to commemorate their visit with their Uncle Israel in 1899.

With these two 19th Century Frontenac books, *Genealogy of a Village* and *The Rest of the Story*, I share the Frontenac story as it has never been told before, honoring all the 19th century settlers who lived in and created Frontenac.

Lorry Wendland

Table of Contents

5

Table of Contents

Table of Contents

Table of Contents

Table of Contents

Table of Contents

Minneapolis Tribune,   Thursday, July 6, 1916,   by Caryl B. Storrs

"Only Few Houses Left, With No Post Office, Stores or Factories
in Historic Old Frontenac, Facing Lake Pepin –
It Rests in Dignity, Peace and Beauty –
Founder was a Cincinnati Man Who Refused to Allow Railroad
to Build into Town –
Scene of first Attempt at Heavier than Air Flying; It Met with Failure.

Old Frontenac, Minn., July 6 – (Special) –

"Old Frontenac has looked quietly across Lake Pepin to the Wisconsin cliffs for more than half a century. New Frontenac, two miles away, has post office and railroad station, for they have neither in Old Town.

"You have to rub your eyes and pinch yourself when you arrive in Old Frontenac, two hours after leaving Minneapolis to believe you are in Minnesota at all.   It seems that you must have been traveling for days instead of hours, that the Mississippi must be the St. Lawrence and the region, that of Acadia or upper New Brunswick.

"There isn't a store in Old Frontenac, or a factory, or even a co-operative creamery. It is just a collection of old homes scattered along grass-grown roads, and if you ask where Mr. Hunecke lives, or Mr. Brunner, or Mr. Carlson, someone will tell you 'two or three lanes away.'

"Though the houses are old, they are well-kept, each has its carefully tended vegetable garden at one side, its syringas, roses and peonies in full bloom in front and the side-walks along the lanes are close trimmed turf of velvety green, thick spangled now with sweet clover. Everywhere are majestic oaks and venerable maples. Black-eyed Susan's, white yarrow and blue bells are the very rubbish of its fragrant alleys and byways.

Old Frontenac Undisturbed By Any Modern Strenuosity

"An unbelievable place is Old Frontenac in its dignity, peace and beauty, undisturbed by any suggestion of modern strenuosity save the subdued rumble of the Burlington freight trains on the Wisconsin shore, two miles across, the splashing of the stern-wheel packet up or down the river twice or thrice in a week, and the passing of an occasional automobile on its way to the Frontenac Inn.

"Frontenac has continued as it was started by General Israel Garrard who came to this heaven-on-earth from Cincinnati many years ago and bought the entire river front from Point-No-Point on the north to Point-au-Sabre on the south, a sweep of five miles. A clue to the general's character may be found in the fact that he emphatically refused the Milwaukee railroad's offer for a river frontage and compelled that line through what is called "the back valley", clear to Red Wing.

"One's first thought at looking at the old Garrard home at the top of the hill is that its builder must have come from much further South than Cincinnati. It is like "the big house" on a Virginia or Tennessee plantation. It is built with vertical, battened sides, dazzling white, with quaintly sloping roof, juts the right sort of big chimneys, and large two story porches, or galleries. The grounds show more care than the house, though everything is as neat as wax, and the giant trees need only to be live oaks hung with gray Spanish moss to make the illusion absolutely perfect.

"Here lived and died the eccentric general, famed for his lavish generosity and his dignified but obsessed riding of hobbies. The only bit of Old Frontenac that can be seen from a Milwaukee train is the red roofed tower of the Villa Maria, a retreat of Ursuline nuns standing in 100 acres of river frontage presented to them by General Garrard.

Good Books and Fast Sailing Boats His Hobby

"The general's best beloved hobbies were good books and fast sailing boats. He had a magnificent library, and back of his house is an old work shop filled to this day with fragmentary remnants of his models for fast sailing yachts and the masts, canvas, anchors, rudders and patent centerboards that once formed essential portions of the craft themselves. There is a legend in Old Frontenac that Herreshoff, the famous designer of some the American Cup defenders, once shamelessly stole and idea for a centerboard that was invented by General Garrard.

"General Garrard was not the only rich hobby rider in his family. He had a brother, Colonel Jeptha Garrard, who lived in Cincinnati, but who used to keep his pet hobby in his brother's ample and sympathetic stable at Old Frontenac. The hobby was heavier- than- air flying machines. which brings us, at last to the point of our rambling story.

"The delayed point of the story is this: that among the first experiments to be tried with heavier-than-air flying machines in this country, if not in the world, were those that took place at Point No Point on the Mississippi River, only about 60 miles below Minneapolis.

"Point No Point receives its curious name from its contour, which is such that is seems from every angle of view to be a sharp headland slanting 300 feet from wooded top to the river, but which really has no point at all, being merely a long cliff.

"On the side of this cliff a track was built to within 10 feet of the water, when it ran over the river and stopped.

First Aeroplane's Motive Power Was Cincinnati Man

"A car was placed on this track, and on the car was the flying machine, a light frame structure with broad canvas wings. The motive power was a man; a reckless balloonist secured somewhere around Cincinnati and brought north by Colonel Garrard. This indispensable idiot allowed himself to be placed in the machine, his arms attached to the wings and then the whole contrivance put upon the car. The car then ran down the steep side of Point No Point at a speed of something less than a million miles a minute, shot out over the water and dropped off the end of the track. As the car dropped from under him the indispensable idiot would shoot far out into the air and was supposed, by flapping his wings vigorously, to fly across to the Wisconsin shore. Tradition said that he made some startling flights, but he never got to Wisconsin; in fact, it was often with great difficulty that he succeeded in getting back to Minnesota.

"Of course all this was 30 or more years ago, long before the Wright brothers began their resultful work and long before the gasoline engine was a practicable possibility; and it was the want of some such portable engine that brought nothing out of Colonel Garrard's experiments other than a lot of fun for two lively old gentlemen, and a handsome salary and a succession of thrills to an indispensable idiot from the Ohio valley.

"Yet, it did bring something more; it filled a treasure house of endearing memories for the only survivor of these odd and premature experiments. This survivor is Edward Hunecke, who still lives in Old Frontenac, and does carpentry, gardening, and other gentle labor. Mr. Hunecke told me the main facts of this story with merry good nature, and one could see he still lives on the recollection of his intimate collaboration with the two Garrards, who must have been the most delightful and unusual gentlemen that ever lived in the Mississippi Valley, or any other valley.

Old Workshop Filed With Reminisces of 30 Years Ago.

"Mr. Hunecke took me into the old workshop, filled with the junk of 30 years ago, scraps and fragments that meant less than nothing to me, but from which he could reconstruct extinct species of boats, engines, flying machines and other prehistoric monsters as an archeologist rebuilds a complete megatherium from one lower tooth.

"Would that all archeologists were as entertaining as Mr. Hunecke; perhaps they might be if they had associated with their prehistoric monsters in life, as Mr. Hunecke did. Every wheel started wheels of pleasant and unusual narrative in his mind, every sail sent him on a voyage of reminiscence, every anchor brought him to rest in some pleasant harbor over which the last sun went down 30 years ago, but which he could again illuminate with the afterglow of happy memory.

"I don't know what I enjoyed more; the stories Mr. Hunecke told me, or the loving, tolerant, pride-tinged way in which they were told."

The following twenty pages are a duplication of the Section A information from the companion book:

19th Century Frontenac, Minnesota – The Rest of the Story.

This useful reference section is also included here to serve as an aid when reading this book. Because it includes village overlook photos, plat maps and legends with building identifiers, you will become acquainted with the layout of the 19th century Frontenac village and better understand each resident's place within it. Consider referring to this section while reading *The Rest of the Story.*

Overlook of 1870 Frontenac, Minnesota.

Taken from Garrard's Bluff by Joel E. Whitney, Whitney Zimmermann Photography Studio.

Joel Whitney's overlook picture of Frontenac is the anchor of the two 19th century Frontenac history books. This picture was undated, but research indicates that it was taken in the year 1870. A significant factor in determining the date was the presence of the Community Church and its bell tower. The church was built in 1862 and the bell tower and parsonage were built in 1863. The church burned in 1874, therefore, the photograph was taken between 1863 and 1874.

It is known that Whitney Zimmerman photographers took pictures in Goodhue County from 1868 to 1871 and the Minnesota Historical Society website states that most of their Frontenac photographs were taken in 1870. Therefore, the most likely date for the picture is the summer of 1870.

In *The Rest of the Story*, you, the reader, will become acquainted with every building in this picture and know the pioneers who lived in each of the houses.

1870 Whitney Zimmerman Studios.   Courtesy of Minnesota Historical Society
This overlook picture included Frontenac Point and the Lakeside Hotel Complex.

Graphic Designer Wendy Amundson digitally combined the two images
for a lovely view of the entire 1870 Frontenac village.

The Rest of the Story: **Book Organization**

A	Introduction	Book Organization
B	Setting the Stage	Factors Contributing to European Settlement
C	Understanding Early Frontenac.	Maps, Pictures, and Descriptions
D	Building the Village	Infrastructure and Commercial Development
E	Pioneers & Their Homes	House Details and their 19th Century Residents
F	Lakeside Hotel and Cottages	Development Progression on Frontenac Point
G	Village Life	Aspects of Social, Farming, and Religious Life
H	Lake Pepin & The Mississippi River	Influence of the Mississippi River
X	Appendices	Timeline, Acknowledgements, Descendants, Source Documents, Index

Section A: Reference Section

Section A assists the reader with identification and location of homes and buildings in the Village.

Frontenac Tour Guide

The "Frontenac Tour Guide" is reprinted at the end of this book. Consider removing the Tour Guide pages to create a convenient guide.

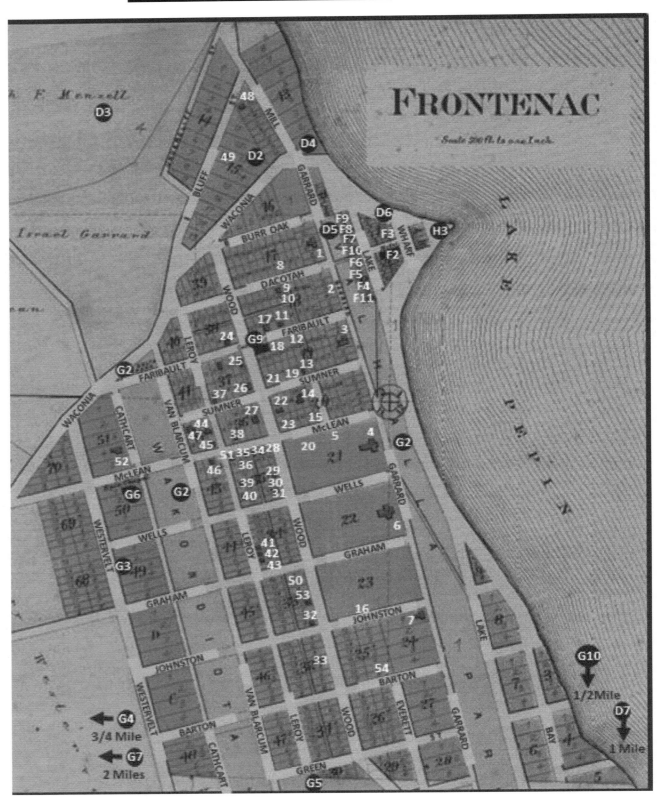

1894 Plat Map with Location Identifiers

1894 Plat of Frontenac with House, Park, and Business Location Identifiers

This 1894 Frontenac Plat map includes most of the village of Frontenac, Minnesota. The plat identifiers mark the location of houses, businesses, churches, parks, and places of village activity as well as book chapters, building locations on the overlook photos, and all other descriptions for each respective structure as noted below.

- *The Rest of the Story* Section D Identifiers show the location of businesses that helped build the village.
  - D2 - Saw Mill
  - D3 - Quarry
  - D4 - Lime Kiln
  - D5 - Brewery
  - D6 - Wharf
  - D7 - Flour Mill

- *The Rest of the Story* Section E Identifiers 1 - 54 (no preceding letter) show the location of the structures described in Section E. Each Section E structure has its own chapter and identifier number.

- *The Rest of the Story* Section F Identifiers show the location of buildings in the Lakeside Hotel complex.
  - F2 - Lakeside Hotel
  - F3 - Pavilion
  - F4 - Stable
  - F5 - Kittle House (Grapevine)
  - F6 - Virginia Cottage
  - F7 - Lakeside Shop
  - F8 – The Poplars Cottage
  - F9 - Fern Cottage
  - F10 - Pine Cottage
  - F11 - Support Buildings

- *The Rest of the Story* Section G Identifiers show the locations of businesses and public areas.
  - G2 - Frontenac Parks
  - G3 - Frontenac School
  - G4 - Waconia Farm
  - G5 - Frontenac Cemetery
  - G6 - Christ Episcopal Church
  - G7 - Dacotah Park – Race Track
  - G9 - German Methodist & Norwegian Lutheran Church
  - G10 - Villa Maria Academy

- *The Rest of the Story* Section H Identifiers show the location of Mississippi River and Lake Pepin structures.
  - H3 - Light House

1870 Frontenac Overlook with Location Identifiers

Numbers identify buildings and are the chapter numbers in Section E.

The following page honors some of the immigrants who lived in these homes.

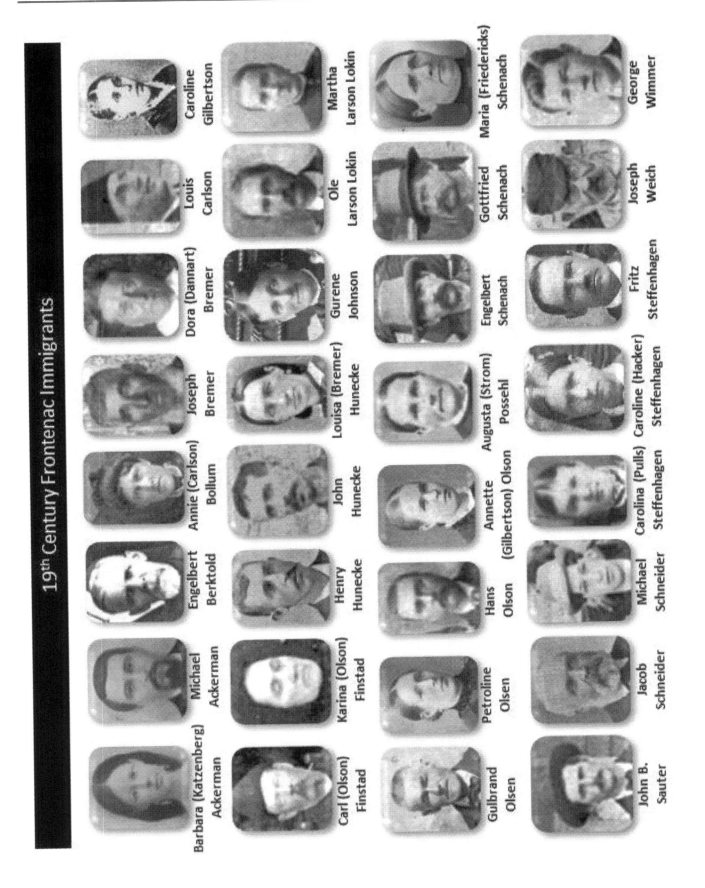

19th Century Frontenac Immigrants

Caroline Gilbertson
Martha Larson Lokin
Maria (Friedericks) Schenach
George Wimmer

Louis Carlson
Ole Larson Lokin
Gottfried Schenach
Joseph Weich

Dora (Dannart) Bremer
Gurene Johnson
Engelbert Schenach
Fritz Steffenhagen

Joseph Bremer
Louisa (Bremer) Hunecke
Augusta (Strom) Possehl
Caroline (Hacker) Steffenhagen

Annie (Carlson) Bollum
John Hunecke
Annette (Gilbertson) Olson
Carolina (Pulls) Steffenhagen

Engelbert Berktold
Henry Hunecke
Hans Olson
Michael Schneider

Michael Ackerman
Karina (Olson) Finstad
Petroline Olsen
Jacob Schneider

Barbara (Katzenberg) Ackerman
Carl (Olson) Finstad
Gulbrand Olsen
John B. Sauter

1870 Whitney Zimmerman Overlook – Buildings 1 - 14

Section E: Pioneers & Their Homes - Houses 1 - 14

E#	Block	Lots	2018 Status	House Name	2018 Addr	On Street	Between	1870 Owner	1870 Family Residents	1870 Profession	Born	Where born
1	17	1-13	Exists	Dacotah Cottage	28743	Garrard	Burr Oak / Dacotah	Sarah Bella McLean	Vacant			
1.1	18	2	Moved Exists		28819	Garrard	Dacotah / Faribault	Jacob Schneider 1861-1865	Already Moved		1831	Hessen-Darmstadt
2	18	7	Moved Gone	Pine Cottage	Mid Block	North side of Faribault	Manypenny / Garrard	Sarah Bella McLean	George Burmeister	Miller	1839	Prussia
3	19	1-9	Exists	Winona Cottage	28895	Garrard	Faribault / Sumner	Israel Garrard	Boarding House			
4	21	All	Exists	St. Hubert's Lodge	29055	Garrard	McLean / Wells	Israel Garrard	Israel Garrard / Hans Johnson	Lawyer / Laborer	1826 / 1842	Kentucky / Norway
5	21	NE corner	Moved Gone		29055	Garrard	McLean / Wells	Israel Garrard	Buildings on St. Hubert's block			
6	22	All	Exists	Locust Lodge	29133	Garrard	Wells / Graham	Evert Westervelt	Evert Westervelt	Farmer (1st yr)	1813	New York
7	24	1	Exists	Greystone	29277	Garrard	Johnston / Barton	Sarah Bella McLean	James Davidson	Lumber Man	1831	Pennsylvania
8	17	10	Gone		34921	Dacotah	Manypenny / Wood	Elam Miller	Elam Miller	Plasterer Mason	1836	Mississippi
9	18	23	Exists	Honey Bee	34962	Dacotah	Manypenny / Wood	Nicholaus Poppe	Nicholaus Poppe	Laborer	1824	Hanover
10	18	S 23	Gone		S. of 34962	Dacotah	Manypenny / Wood	Nicholaus Poppe	Christ Christianson	Laborer	1834	Norway
11	18	S 10-11	Exists		34921	Faribault	Manypenny / Wood	John Gerken	John Gerken	Laborer	1826	Hanover
12	19	22	Moved Gone	The Poplars	28891	Manypenny	Faribault / Sumner	Israel Garrard	Karsten Stuhr	Laborer	1837	Hanover
13	19	10, 11	Gone		E. of 34911	Sumner	Manypenny / Wood	Israel Garrard / Evert Westervelt	Community Buildings			
14	20	20-23	Exists	Parsonage	28597	Manypenny	McLean / Sumner	Sarah Bella McLean	Jacob Van Eschew	Clergy Man	1828	Switzerland

1870 Whitney Zimmerman Overlook – Buildings 15 - 28

Section E: Pioneers & Their Homes - Houses 15 - 28

E#	Block	Lots	2018 Status	House Name	2018 Addr	On Street	Between	1870 Owner	1870 Family Residents	1870 Profession	Born	Where born
15	20	10-13	Burned Gone	Community Church		N Side of McLean	Manypenny Wood	Sarah Bella McLean				
16	23		Gone		Mid Block	N Side of Johnston	Garrard Wood	Sarah Bella McLean	Nicholas Christ	Laborer	1843	Prussia
17	18	12	Burned Gone		34903	Faribault	Manypenny Wood	John Hunecke	John Hunecke	Tailor	1832	Westfalen, Prussia
18	19	20	Gone		Mid Block	S Side of Faribault	Manypenny Wood	August John Lubeck Heirs	Carl C. Steffenhagen	Retired	1803	Prussia
19	19	12	Exists		34911	Sumner	Manypenny Wood	Engelbert Schenach	Engelbert Schenach	Laborer	1832	Tyrol, Austria
20	21	West End	Gone			S Side McLean	Garrard Wood	Israel Garrard	St. Hubert's Shop			
21	19	14-16	Moved Exists	Kittle House	NE Corner	Sumner & Wood	Manypenny Wood	Israel Garrard	Ole Larson Loken / Carl Olson	Laborer / Laborer	1828 / 1838	Norway / Norway
22	20	17-19	Exists		28960	Wood	McLean Sumner	Englebert Haller	Engelbert Haller	Carpenter	1833	Wurtemberg
23	20	14-16	Moved Gone		34879	McLean	Manypenny Wood	Martin Schlunt	Boarding house / Martin Schlunt	Boarding	1828	Wurtemberg
24	38	1-3	Moved Exists		Mid Block	N Side of Faribault	Wood LeRoy	Israel Garrard	Christopher John Steffenhagen	Farmer	1824	Mecklenburg
25	37	10-12	Gone		Opposite 28900	Wood	Faribault Sumner	Henry Hunecke	Henry Hunecke	Carpenter	1834	Prussia
26	37	1-3	Exists		28929	Wood	Faribault Sumner	Michael Ackerman	Michael Ackerman	Carpenter	1835	Bavaria
27	36	1-2	Exists	Frontenac Hotel, aka Schneider Hotel	28971	Wood	McLean Sumner	Jacob Schneider	Jacob Schneider / Claus Hauschild / Christ Brinkman	Hotel keeper / Laborer / Laborer	1831 / 1832 / 1833	Hessen-Darmstadt / Hanover / Hanover
28	35	6	Gone		SW Corner	Wood & McLean	McLean Wells	John Hager	John Hager	Laborer	1833	Bavaria

1870 Whitney Zimmerman Overlook – Buildings 29 - 43

Section E: Pioneers & Their Homes - Houses 29 - 43

E#	Block	Lots	2018 Status	House Name	2018 Addr	On Street	Between	1870 Owner	1870 Family Residents	1870 Profession	Born	Where born
29	35	7,8	Exists	Post Office	29039	Wood	McLean Wells	Henry Lorentzen	Henry Lorentzen	Postmaster & Notary	1821	Hamburg
30	35	9	Gone		29055	Wood	McLean Wells	Henry Isensee	John Olson	Boot & Shoe Maker	1815	Norway
31	35	10	Exists		29065	Wood	McLean Wells	John Friedericks	John Friedericks / Johannes Gerken	Laborer / Laborer	1840 / 1824	Mecklenburg / Hanover
32	33	7-8	Exists		29255	Johnston	Wood LeRoy	John Seba	John Seba	Laborer	1829	Hanover
33	32	4	Moved Exists		29289	Wood	Johnston Barton	Israel Garrard	Josiah Batchelder	Boat Builder	1833	Maine
34	35	5	Exists		34844	McLean	Wood LeRoy	Gottfried Schenach	Gottfried Schenach	Blacksmith	1825	Tyrol, Austria
35	35	4	Exists		34832	McLean	Wood LeRoy	Emmanuel Schenach	Emmanuel Schenach	Wagon Maker	1825	Tyrol, Austria
36	35	2-3	Moved Gone		S. side McLean	West of Alley	Wood LeRoy	Henry Muller	Henry Muller	Laborer	1815	Mecklenburg
37	37	6	Exists		34805	Sumner	Wood LeRoy	Joseph Weich	Joseph Weich / John Vierengel	Carpenter / Musician	1804 / 1842	Baden / Bavaria
38	36	5	Gone		North side	McLean	Wood LeRoy	John Bahr	John Bahr	Turner of Wood	1811	Hanover
39	35	15	Gone		N. of 29050	LeRoy	McLean Wells	Joachim Koehn	Joachim Koehn	Laborer	1838	Mecklenburg
40	35	14	Exists		29050	Leroy	McLean Wells	Christ Friedericks	Christ Friedericks	Laborer	1827	Mecklenburg
41	34	12	Gone		N. of 29136	LeRoy	Wells Graham	John Markmann	John Markmann	Laborer	1841	Prussia
42	34	11	Gone		29136	LeRoy	Wells Graham	Wolfgang Schloerstein	Wolfgang Schloerstein	Laborer	1816	Austria
43	34	10	Gone		S. of 29136	LeRoy	Wells Graham	Mary Ann Sperl	Mary Ann Sperl	Housekeeper	1845	Austria

1870 Whitney Zimmerman Overlook – Buildings 44 - 54

Section E: Pioneers & Their Homes - Houses 44 - 54

E#	Block	Lots	2018 Status	House Name	2018 Addr	On Street	Between	1870 Owner	1870 Family Residents	1870 Profession	Born	Where born
44	42	N 1/2 of 1,2	Exists		34778	Sumner	Van Blarcum LeRoy	Carl Peters	Joachim Bremer	Laborer	1831	Mecklenburg
45	42	S 1/2 of 1,2	Gone		34783	McLean	Van Blarcum LeRoy	Israel Garrard	Barn			
46	43	3-4	Gone			South Side of McLean	Van Blarcum LeRoy	Charles F. Herder	Charles F. Herder	Farmer	1833	Prussia
47	42	3-4	Exists		28964	Van Blarcum	McLean Sumner	Frontenac Mission	Vacant			
48*	15	1-3, 11	Gone		28535	Lake Ave Way	Waconia Bluff	Ole (Larson) Loken	Ole (Larson) Loken	Quarryman	1828	Norway
49*	15	13	Moved Exists		W. of 28535	Lake Ave Way	Waconia Bluff	Evert Westervelt	James Lester Annie (Loken) Lester	Quarryman	1856 1861	Iowa Norway
50*	33	1,2	Gone		34850	Graham	Wood LeRoy	Hans Olson	Hans Olson	Quarryman	1860	Norway
51*	35	1,2	Exists		34808	McLean	Wood LeRoy	George Bartels, Jr	George Bartels, Jr	Carpenter	1862	Hanover
52*	51	4	Gone		34661	McLean (CR 2)	Cathcart Waconia	Nathanial Collins McLean	Nathanial Collins McLean	Stock Raiser	1818	Ohio
53*	33	6	Gone		28790	Wood	Johnston Graham	Ole Haga	Ole Haga	Quarryman	1847	Norway
54	25	7,8	Moved Exists	Virginia Cottage	Mid Block	N. Barton	Garrard Wood	James A. Owens	James A. Owens	Clerk for Garrards	1839	Pennsylvania

* 19th Century Frontenac Homes NOT on the 1870 Overlook Picture

1995 Aerial with 1870 Building and Shoreline Locations

Section D: Building the Village

ID	Status	NAME	Plat Map Location Description	2018 Street # (Approx)	2018 Street	Begin Year	End year	Yrs Exist in 2018
D2	Gone	Saw Mill	West of Mill Street, Between Waconia and Bluff	28589	Lake Avenue Way	1856	1871	15
D3	Gone	Quarry	NW of Undercliff Street		Frontenac State Park	1858	1920	62
D4	Gone	Lime Kiln	East of Garrard Avenue North of Waconia, Block 13	SE of Lake Ave Way Bridge	Lake Avenue Way	1858	1871	13
D5	Gone	Brewery	West of Lake Street, Block 11	SW of 28725	Lake Avenue Way	1860	1864	4
D6	Gone	Wharf	North Border of Block 1	28776	Lake Avenue Way	1867	1900	33
D7	Gone	Flour Mill	Head of Sand Point Trail	Near Hwy 61	County Road 2 Blvd	1866	1912	46

Section F: Lakeside Complex

ID	Status	NAME	Plat Map Location Description	2018 Street # (Approx)	2018 Street	Begin Year	End year	Yrs Exist in 2018
F2	Exists	Lakeside Hotel	South of Agate Street West of Wharf Street	28796	Lake Avenue Way	1858	*	160
F3	Gone	Pavilion	North of Agate Street West of Wharf Street	28793	Lake Avenue Way	1859	1997	138
F4	Gone	Stable	East of Lake Street	28813	Lake Avenue Way	1867	1976	109
F5	Exists	Kittle House (Grapevine)	West of Lake Street, Block 11	28775	Lake Avenue Way	1865	*	153
F6	Moved Exists	Virginia Cottage	West of Lake Street, Block 11	N. of 28775	Lake Avenue Way	1865	*	153
F7	Gone	Lakeside Shop	West of Lake Street, Block 11	28745	Lake Avenue Way	1869	1975	106
F8	Gone	Poplars Cottage	West of Lake Street, Block 11	S. of 28725	Lake Avenue Way	1863	1997	134
F9	Gone	Fern Cottage	West of Lake Street, Block 11	28725	Lake Avenue Way	1860	2009	149
F10	Gone	Pine Cottage	West of Lake Street, Block 11	28745	Lake Avenue Way	1858	1949	91

Aerial of Frontenac Plain from Lake Pepin Looking West

Section G: Village Life

Section H: Mississippi River & Lake Pepin

ID	Status	NAME	Plat Map Location Description	2018 Street # (Approx)	2018 Street	Begin Year	End year	Yrs Exist in 2018
G2		Frontenac Parks						
	Gone	Eclipse Park	Intersection of Waconia & Bluff. Area now in Frontenac State Park			1857	1859	2
	Exists	Delta Park	Bordered by Waconia, (N), Faribault (S), & Van Blarcum (W)		North of Wakondiota Park	1857	*	161
	Exists	Valhalla Park	Bordered by Waconia (N), Ludlow (S), Garrard (E), & Lake (W)		Garrard, Lake	1857	*	161
	Exists	Wakondiota Park	Bordered by Faribault (N), Winona (S), Van Blarcum (E), Cathcart (W)		Van Blarcum	1857	*	161
G3	Moved Exists	Frontenac School	Westervelt Avenue Way	29118	Westervelt Way	1869	1958	89
G4	Exists	Waconia Farm	McLean across from Waconia Cliff	29750	County Road #2	1850	*	168
G5	Exists	Frontenac Cemetery	West of Wood, South of Green St.		South Extension	1867	*	151
G6	Exists	Christ Episcopal Church	Southeast Corner of McLean and Westervelt Avenue	34660	McLean, County Road #2	1868	*	150
G7	Gone	Dakota Park	West of Territorial Rd		South of CR #2	1871	1941	70
G9	Gone	German Methodist & Norwegian Lutheran Church	SE Corner of Faribault & Wood	W. of 34894	Faribault	1888	1975	87
G10	Exists	Villa Maria Academy	South of Winona Avenue	29847	County Road #2	1891	2018	127
H3	Gone	Lighthouse	Frontenac Point, East of Block A & B			1871	1877	6

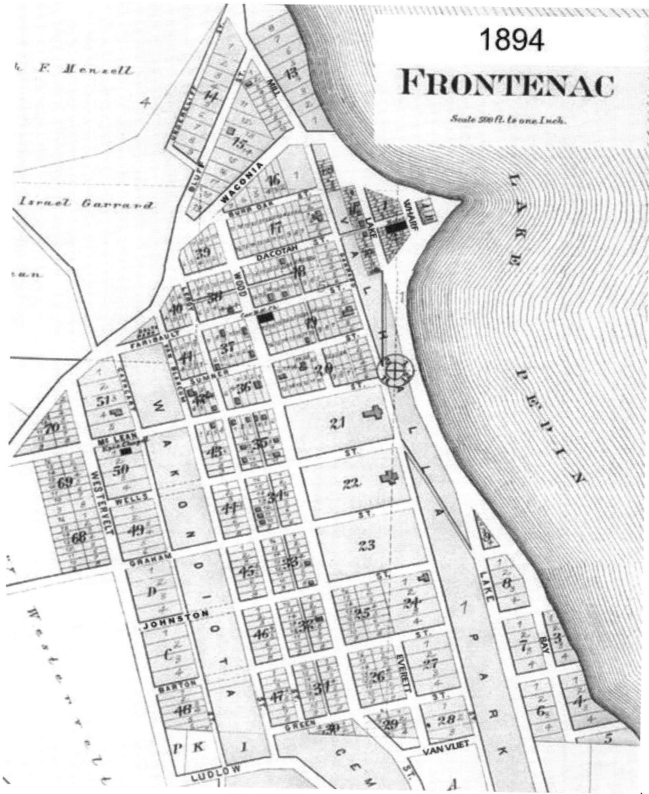

The 1894 Frontenac Plat Map

The locations of buildings are indicated on this map by
overhead view icons that approximate the size and shape of the buildings.

Family Group Sheets

~~~~~

19ᵗʰ Century Pioneers
And Their Families

Families are listed
alphabetically by the last name of the husband.
All names in the family group sheets are in the index.

Family Group Record   Johann Michael Ackerman & Barbara Katzenberger

Husband	Johann Michael Ackerman	
Born	12 Jul 1834	Nußdorf (BA. Landau), Bayern
Christened	20 Jul 1834	Nußdorf (BA. Landau), Bayern
Died	16 May 1911	Missoula, Missoula, Montana, USA
Buried	May 1911	Frontenac, Goodhue, Minnesota, USA
Address	Old Frontenac Cemetery, Frontenac, Minnesota	
Father	Jacob Ackerman (-)	
Mother	Annie Messenschmidt (-)	
Marriage	13 Jun 1860	Red Wing, Goodhue, Minnesota, USA
Other Spouse	Margaret Poppe (1827-1895)	18 Mar 1876 - Frontenac, Goodhue, Minnesota, USA

Wife	Barbara Katzenberger	
Born	17 Jan 1843	Mailes, , Königreich Bayern
Christened		
Died	17 Jan 1870	Frontenac, Goodhue, Minnesota, USA
Cause of Death	scarlet fever	
Buried	Jan 1870	Frontenac, Goodhue, Minnesota, USA
Address	Old Frontenac Cemetery, Frontenac, Minnesota	
Father	Michel Katzenberger (1806-Bef 1856)	
Mother	Dorothea Shale (1815-1887)	

Children		
1	F	Anna D. Ackerman
Born	1861	Frontenac, Goodhue, Minnesota, USA
Christened		
Died	9 Feb 1933	Missoula, Missoula, Montana, USA
Buried		
Spouse	Frank R. Trafford (1857-1926)	3 Sep 1890
2	M	Edward Michael Ackerman
Born	5 Feb 1863	Frontenac, Goodhue, Minnesota, USA
Christened		
Died	26 Apr 1944	Florence Township, Goodhue, Minnesota, USA
Buried	Apr 1944	Frontenac, Goodhue, Minnesota, USA
Address	Old Frontenac Cemetery, Frontenac, Minnesota	
Spouse	Lilly A. Menzel (1869-1947)	
Marr. Date	25 May 1893 - Frontenac, Goodhue, Minnesota, USA	
3	M	William Ackerman
AKA	Willie	
Born	14 Feb 1866	Frontenac, Goodhue, Minnesota, USA
Christened		
Died	20 May 1876	Frontenac, Goodhue, Minnesota, USA
Cause of Death	drowning	
Buried	May 1876	Frontenac, Goodhue, Minnesota, USA
Address	Old Frontenac Cemetery, Frontenac, Minnesota	
Spouse		

Family Group Record Johann Michael Ackerman & Margaret Poppe

Husband	Johann Michael Ackerman	
Born	12 Jul 1834	Nußdorf (BA. Landau), Bayern
Christened	20 Jul 1834	Nußdorf (BA. Landau), Bayern
Died	16 May 1911	Missoula, Missoula, Montana, USA
Buried	May 1911	Frontenac, Goodhue, Minnesota, USA
Address	Old Frontenac Cemetery, Frontenac, Minnesota	
Father	Jacob Ackerman (-)	
Mother	Annie Messenschmidt (-)	
Marriage	18 Mar 1876	Frontenac, Goodhue, Minnesota, USA
Other Spouse	Barbara Katzenberger (1843-1870)	13 Jun 1860 - Red Wing, Goodhue, Minnesota, USA

Wife	Margaret Poppe	
AKA	Mary Martha	
Born	23 Aug 1827	, , , Hanover
Christened		
Died	12 May 1895	Frontenac, Goodhue, Minnesota, USA
Buried	14 May 1895	Frontenac, Goodhue, Minnesota, USA
Address	Old Frontenac Cemetery, Frontenac, Minnesota	
Father	Poppe (-)	
Mother		

Children

Family Group Record Edward Michael Ackerman & Llily A. Menzel

Husband	Edward Michael Ackerman	
Born	5 Feb 1863	Frontenac, Goodhue, Minnesota, USA
Christened		
Died	26 Apr 1944	Florence Township, Goodhue, Minnesota, USA
Buried	Apr 1944	Frontenac, Goodhue, Minnesota, USA
Address	Old Frontenac Cemetery, Frontenac, Minnesota	
Father	Johann Michael Ackerman (1834-1911)	
Mother	Barbara Katzenberger (1843-1870)	
Marriage	25 May 1893	Frontenac, Goodhue, Minnesota, USA

Wife	Lilly A. Menzel	
Born	Aug 1869	Florence Township, Goodhue, Minnesota, USA
Christened		
Died	21 Mar 1947	Red Wing, Goodhue, Minnesota, USA
Buried	Mar 1947	Frontenac, Goodhue, Minnesota, USA
Address	Old Frontenac Cemetery, Frontenac, Minnesota	
Father	William Frederick Bernard Menzel (1847-1921)	
Mother	Elizabeth K. Keye (1851-1930)	

Children			
1	F	Irma Marie Ackerman	
Born		22 Sep 1895	Frontenac, Goodhue, Minnesota, USA
Christened			
Died		26 Nov 1950	St. Peter, Nicollet, Minnesota, USA
Buried		Nov 1950	Frontenac, Goodhue, Minnesota, USA
Address		Old Frontenac Cemetery, Frontenac, Minnesota	
Spouse		William Marshall Laidlaw (1884-1964)	Abt 1921

2	F	Bernice Emma Ackerman	
Born		4 Jul 1898	Frontenac, Goodhue, Minnesota, USA
Christened		5 Mar 1899	Frontenac Station, Goodhue, Minnesota, USA
Address		St. John's Ev. Lutheran Church, Frontenac Station, Minnesota	
Died		9 Dec 1967	Frontenac, Goodhue, Minnesota, USA
Buried		Dec 1967	Frontenac, Goodhue, Minnesota, USA
Address		Old Frontenac Cemetery, Frontenac, Minnesota	
Spouse		Did Not Marry	

Family Group Record John Wolfgang Bahr & Julianna Bahr

Husband	John Wolfgang Bahr	
Born	Nov 1810	, , , Saxony-Coburg
Christened		
Died	3 Oct 1884	Prior, Big Stone , Minnesota, USA
Buried	Oct 1884	Prior Township, Big Stone, Minnesota, USA
Address	Mathews Lakeside Cemetery, Big Stone County, Minnesota	
Marriage	Abt 1841	, , , Saxony

Wife	Juliana	
Born	1814	, , , Saxony-Meiningen
Christened		
Died	5 Sep 1904	Prior, Big Stone, Minnesota, USA
Buried		
Address	Mathews Lakeside Cemetery, Big Stone County, Minnesota	

Children		
1 F	**Fredericka Sophia Bahr**	
Born	1843	, , , Saxony
Christened		
Died		
Buried		
Spouse	Charles Sigloh (1835-)	
2 M	**Frederick Richard Bahr**	
Born	1849	, , , Saxony
Christened		
Died		
Buried		
Spouse	Martha (1853-)	
3 M	**Brutto (Plutto) Bahr**	
Born	1854	, , Wisconsin, USA
Christened		
Died		
Buried		
Spouse		

Family Group Record George Bartels Sr. & Katie Bartels

Husband	George Bartels Sr.	
Born	1827	, , , Hanover
Christened		
Died	22 Oct 1898	Frontenac, Goodhue, Minnesota, USA
Buried		
Marriage	Abt 1850	, , , Hanover

Wife	Katie	
Born	1828	, , , Hanover
Christened		
Died	Between 1885 and 1895	Frontenac, Goodhue, Minnesota, USA
Buried		

Children		
1 M	Jacob Bartels	
Born	27 Mar 1852	, , , Hanover
Christened		
Died	31 May 1927	Minneapolis, Hennepin, Minnesota, USA
Buried	3 Jun 1927	Minneapolis, Hennepin, Minnesota, USA
Spouse	Caroline W. (1858-1912)	Abt 1877
2 F	Anna G. Bartels	
Born	1856	, , , Hanover
Christened		
Died	1941	, Columbia, New York, USA
Buried	1941	Ghent, Columbia, New York, USA
Spouse	Arnold Wambach (1839-1900)	
3 F	Martha Bartels	
Born	May 1857	, , , Hanover
Christened		
Died	1935	
Buried	1935	Frontenac, Goodhue, Minnesota, USA
Address	Old Frontenac Cemetery, Frontenac, Minnesota	
Spouse	John J. Krelberg (1851-1918)	Abt 1878 - Kinderhook, Columbia, New York, USA
4 M	George E. Bartels Jr.	
Born	Apr 1862	, , , Hanover
Christened		
Died	21 May 1919	Frontenac, Goodhue, Minnesota, USA
Cause of Death	suicide	
Buried	24 May 1919	Frontenac, Goodhue, Minnesota, USA
Address	Old Frontenac Cemetery, Frontenac, Minnesota	
Spouse	Minnie Meyer (1869-1902)	25 Nov 1890 - Frontenac Station, Goodhue, Minnesota, USA
5 M	Henry Herman Bartels	
Born	Oct 1867	, , , Hanover
Christened		
Died	7 Mar 1939	St. Paul, Ramsey, Minnesota, USA
Buried		
Spouse	Wilhelmina Jeanetta Thiars (1869-)	22 Dec 1887 - Frontenac, Goodhue, Minnesota, USA

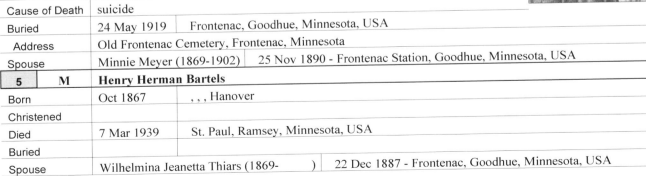

Family Group Record George E. Bartels Jr. & Minnie Meyer

Husband	George E. Bartels Jr.	
Born	Apr 1862	, , , Hanover
Died	21 May 1919	Frontenac, Goodhue, Minnesota, USA
Cause of Death	suicide	
Buried	24 May 1919	Frontenac, Goodhue, Minnesota, USA
Address	Old Frontenac Cemetery, Frontenac, Minnesota	
Father	George Bartels Sr. (1827-1898)	
Mother	Katie (1828-Between 1885/1895)	
Marriage	25 Nov 1890	Frontenac Station, Goodhue, Minnesota, USA

Wife	Minnie Meyer	
Born	Jul 1869	, , Illinois, USA
Died	21 Apr 1902	Frontenac, Goodhue, Minnesota, USA
Buried		
Father	Frederick Meyer (Abt 1840-Bef 1880)	
Mother	Minna (1840-1898)	

Children			
1	U	Baby #1 Bartels	
Born		Abt 1892	Frontenac, Goodhue, Minnesota, USA
Died		Abt 1892	Frontenac, Goodhue, Minnesota, USA
2	M	Rueben Georg Heinrich Bartels	
Born		17 Sep 1893	Frontenac, Goodhue, Minnesota, USA
Christened		1894	Frontenac Station, Goodhue, Minnesota, USA
Address		St. John's Ev. Lutheran Church, Frontenac Station, Minnesota	
Died		1952	
Buried		1952	Red Wing, Goodhue, Minnesota, USA
Address		Oakwood Cemetery, Red Wing, MN	
Spouse		Florence A. (1893-1981)	
3	U	Baby #2 Bartels	
Born		Abt 1896	Frontenac, Goodhue, Minnesota, USA
Died		Abt 1896	Frontenac, Goodhue, Minnesota, USA
4	M	Richmond Frederick John Bartels	
Born		5 Jan 1899	Frontenac, Goodhue, Minnesota, USA
Christened		5 Mar 1899	Frontenac Station, Goodhue, Minnesota, USA
Address		St. John's Ev. Lutheran Church, Frontenac Station, Minnesota	
Died		1938	
Buried		1938	Frontenac, Goodhue, Minnesota, USA
Address		Old Frontenac Cemetery, Frontenac, Minnesota	
Spouse		Anna M. (1898-1987)	

Family Group Record Henry Herman Bartels & Jeanetta Thiars

Husband	Henry Herman Bartels	
Born	Oct 1867	, , , Hanover
Christened		
Died	7 Mar 1939	St. Paul, Ramsey, Minnesota, USA
Buried		
Father	George Bartels Sr. (1827-1898)	
Mother	Katie (1828-Between 1885/1895)	
Marriage	22 Dec 1887	Frontenac, Goodhue, Minnesota, USA

Wife	Wilhelmina Jeanetta Thiars	
AKA	Nettie	
Born	Mar 1869	, , , Germany
Christened		
Died		
Buried		

Children		
1 F	Emilie Martha Bartels	
Born	24 Feb 1889	Frontenac, Goodhue, Minnesota, USA
Christened	28 Apr 1889	Frontenac Station, Goodhue, Minnesota, USA
Address	St. John's Ev. Lutheran Church, Frontenac Station, Minnesota	
Died		
Buried		
Spouse		
2 M	Harry Joh. Arthur Bartels	
Born	23 Nov 1891	Frontenac, Goodhue, Minnesota, USA
Christened	4 Mar 1892	Frontenac Station, Goodhue, Minnesota, USA
Address	St. John's Ev. Lutheran Church, Frontenac Station, Minnesota	
Died		
Buried		
Spouse	Margaret E. (-)	
3 F	Edna Bertha Anna Bartels	
Born	29 Mar 1894	Frontenac, Goodhue, Minnesota, USA
Christened	12 Mar 1895	Frontenac Station, Goodhue, Minnesota, USA
Address	St. John's Ev. Lutheran Church, Frontenac Station, Minnesota	
Died		
Buried		
Spouse		

Family Group Record Jacob Bartels & Caroline W. Bartels

Husband	Jacob Bartels	
Born	27 Mar 1852	, , , Hanover
Christened		
Died	31 May 1927	Minneapolis, Hennepin, Minnesota, USA
Buried	3 Jun 1927	Minneapolis, Hennepin, Minnesota, USA
Father	George Bartels Sr. (1827-1898)	
Mother	Katie (1828-Between 1885/1895)	
Marriage	Abt 1877	

Wife	Caroline W.	
Born	1858	, , , Prussia
Christened		
Died	10 Apr 1912	Frontenac, Goodhue, Minnesota, USA
Buried	Apr 1912	Frontenac, Goodhue, Minnesota, USA
Address	Old Frontenac Cemetery, Frontenac, Minnesota	

Children		
1 F	Martha Bartels	
Born	1879	Frontenac, Goodhue, Minnesota, USA
Christened		
Died		
Buried		
Spouse		
2 F	Annie Bartels	
Born	1881	Frontenac, Goodhue, Minnesota, USA
Christened		
Died		
Buried		
Spouse		
3 F	Katie Bartels	
Born	1887	Augsburg Township, Marshall , Minnesota, USA
Christened		
Died		
Buried		
Spouse		
4 F	Henrietta A. Bartels	
Born	1896	Augsburg Township, Marshall , Minnesota, USA
Christened		
Died		
Buried		
Spouse		

Family Group Record Josiah Q. Batchelder & Elizabeth Bowers

Husband	Josiah Q. Batchelder	
Born	30 May 1833	Wellington, Penobscot, Maine, USA
Christened		
Died	23 Jan 1913	Stillwater, Washington, Minnesota, USA
Buried	26 Jan 1913	Stillwater, Washington, Minnesota, USA
Address	Fairview Cemetery, Stillwater, Minnesota	
Father	Stephen Batchelder (-)	
Mother	Betsey Hutchings (-)	
Marriage	1859	Red Wing, Goodhue, Minnesota, USA

Wife	Elizabeth Bowers	
Born	17 Oct 1840	Decatur, Adams, Indiana, USA
Christened		
Died	8 Jun 1934	Great Falls, Cascade, Montana, USA
Buried	Jun 1934	Stillwater, Washington, Minnesota, USA
Address	Fairview Cemetery, Stillwater, Minnesota	

Children		
1 F	Jessie M. Batchelder	
Born	1863	Pleasant Valley, Pierce, Wisconsin, USA
Christened		
Died		
Buried		
Spouse	Frank H. Lunts (-)	26 Oct 1887 - River Falls, Pierce, Wisconsin, USA
2 M	Harry L. Batchelder	
Born	1869	Frontenac, Goodhue, Minnesota, USA
Christened		
Died		
Buried		
Spouse		
3 M	Dr. Edwin Josiah Batchelder	
Born	17 Apr 1875	Osceola, Polk, Wisconsin, USA
Christened		
Died	30 Sep 1920	Minneapolis, Hennepin, Minnesota, USA
Buried		
Spouse		
4 F	Maud B. Batchelder	
Born	6 Sep 1878	Bayport, Washington, Minnesota, USA
Christened		
Died	1956	Great Falls, Cascade, Montana, USA
Buried		
Spouse		

Family Group Record James J. Beals & Susan B. Greene

Husband	James J. Beals	
Born	1810	
Christened		
Died	Cir 1859	
Buried		
Marriage	Cir 1841	

Wife	Susan B. Greene	
Born	Oct 1823	, , Rhode Island, USA
Christened		
Died	19 Apr 1904	St. Paul, Ramsey, Minnesota, USA
Buried		Boston, Suffolk, Massachusetts, USA

Children		
1 F	Susan R. Beals	
Born	1844	Tonawanda, Erie, New York, USA
Christened		
Died		
Buried		
Spouse		
2 M	James Beals	
Born	1846	Tonawanda, Erie, New York, USA
Christened		
Died		
Buried		
Spouse		
3 F	Mary E. Beals	
Born	1847	Tonawanda, Erie, New York, USA
Christened		
Died		
Buried		
Spouse		
4 M	Samuel J. Beals	
Born	1849	Tonawanda, Erie, New York, USA
Christened		
Died		
Buried		
Spouse		
5 F	Carrie A. Beals	
Born	1857	Tonawanda, Erie, New York, USA
Christened		
Died		
Buried		
Spouse		

Family Group Record Engelbert John Berktold & Anna Daniels

Husband	Engelbert John Berktold	
Born	1 May 1845	Biberwier, , Tyrol, Austria
Christened		
Died	21 May 1936	Lake City, Wabasha, Minnesota, USA
Buried	25 May 1936	Bellechester, Goodhue, Minnesota, USA
Address	St. Marys Cemetery, Bellechester, MN	
Father	Berktold (-)	
Mother		
Marriage	7 Jan 1868	Red Wing, Goodhue, Minnesota, USA

Wife	Anna Kathleen Daniels	
AKA	Daniels	
Born	4 Jul 1848	Luxenbourg, Belgium
Christened		
Died	28 Jun 1928	Lake City, Wabasha, Minnesota, USA
Buried	4 Jul 1928	Bellechester, Goodhue, Minnesota, USA
Address	St. Marys Cemetery, Bellechester, MN	
Father	Frank Daniels (-)	
Mother	Katherine (-)	

Children			
1	M	Adolph Berktold	
Born		1869	Mt Pleasant Township, Wabasha, Minnesota, USA
Christened			
Died		9 Aug 1880	Mt Pleasant Township, Wabasha, Minnesota, USA
Cause of Death		typhoid fever	
Buried		Aug 1880	Bellechester, Goodhue, Minnesota, USA
Address		St. Marys Cemetery, Bellechester, MN	
Spouse			

2	F	Kathleen Berktold	
Born		1872	Mt Pleasant Township, Wabasha, Minnesota, USA
Christened			
Died			
Buried			
Spouse		John J. Miller (1864-)	

3	M	John Matthias Berktold	
Born		1874	Mt Pleasant Township, Wabasha, Minnesota, USA
Christened			
Died		22 Nov 1947	Lake City, Wabasha, Minnesota, USA
Buried		Nov 1947	Lake City, Wabasha, Minnesota, USA
Address		St. Mary's Cemetery, Lake City, MN	
Spouse		Mary M. (Maime) Horrigan (1869-1967)	

Family Group Record Engelbert John Berktold & Anna Daniels

Children (cont.)			
4	**F**	**Philleomena Berktold**	
Born		9 Aug 1874	Mt Pleasant Township, Wabasha, Minnesota, USA
Christened			
Died		22 May 1953	Los Angeles, Los Angeles, California, USA
Buried			
Spouse		George Marshesseault (-)	
5	**M**	**Frank Berktold**	
Born		1876	Mt Pleasant Township, Wabasha, Minnesota, USA
Christened			
Died		1877	Mt Pleasant Township, Wabasha, Minnesota, USA
Buried		1877	Bellechester, Goodhue, Minnesota, USA
Address		St. Marys Cemetery, Bellechester, MN	
Spouse			
6	**M**	**Theodore Anthony Berktold**	
Born		4 May 1880	Mt Pleasant Township, Wabasha, Minnesota, USA
Christened			
Died		31 Oct 1955	Mt Pleasant Township, Wabasha, Minnesota, USA
Buried		Nov 1955	Lake City, Wabasha, Minnesota, USA
Address		St. Mary's Cemetery, Lake City, MN	
Spouse		Anna Catharine Giles (1882-1974)	
7	**F**	**Marie M. Berktold**	
Born		31 May 1881	Mt Pleasant Township, Wabasha, Minnesota, USA
Christened			
Died		1 Nov 1915	Donnybrook, Ward, North Dakota, USA
Buried		Nov 1915	Lake City, Wabasha, Minnesota, USA
Address		St. Mary's Cemetery, Lake City, MN	
Spouse		Edward M. Gregoire (1879-1958)	
8	**F**	**Roseanna Harrit Berktold**	
Born		23 Mar 1885	Mt Pleasant Township, Wabasha, Minnesota, USA
Christened			
Died		31 Oct 1971	
Buried		31 Oct 1971	Lake City, Wabasha, Minnesota, USA
Address		St. Mary's Cemetery, Lake City, MN	
Spouse		Anthony Giles (1884-1938)	1 Jun 1910 - Lake City, Wabasha, Minnesota, USA

Family Group Record Johan Hinrich Bohmbach & Fredericka Friedericks Lubeck

Husband	Johan Hinrich Bohmbach	
AKA	Henry	
Born	17 Jun 1822	Bargstadt, , , Hanover
Died	7 Jan 1917	Red Wing, Goodhue, Minnesota, USA
Buried	Jan 1917	Red Wing, Goodhue, Minnesota, USA
Address	St. John's Evangelical Cemetery, Red Wing, Minnesota	
Marriage	18 Feb 1865	Red Wing, Goodhue, Minnesota, USA
Other Spouse	Catherina Margareth Tomhafe (Abt 1823-Abt 1861)	21 Mar 1848 - , , , Hannover

Wife	Fredericka Lisetta Friedericks	
Born	8 May 1832	, , , Mecklenburg
Died	7 Nov 1911	Red Wing, Goodhue, Minnesota, USA
Buried	Nov 1911	Red Wing, Goodhue, Minnesota, USA
Address	St. John's Evangelical Cemetery, Red Wing, Minnesota	
Father	Johann Christian Friedericks (Abt 1805-)	
Mother	Maria Frederica Volkert (Abt 1805-)	
Other Spouse	August John Lubeck (1827-Abt 1864)	Abt 1857 - . Goodhue, Minnesota, USA

Children		
1	M	William J. Bohmbach
Born	25 Nov 1865	Red Wing, Goodhue, Minnesota, USA
Died	3 Nov 1950	Red Wing, Goodhue, Minnesota, USA
Buried	Nov 1950	Red Wing, Goodhue, Minnesota, USA
Address	Burnside Cemetery, Red Wing, MN	
Spouse	Minnie Tyler (-)	
2	M	Ludwig Peter Friederick Bohmbach
AKA	Louis	
Born	28 Apr 1867	Hay Creek Township, Goodhue, Minnesota, USA
Died	1874	, Goodhue, Minnesota, USA
3	F	Anna Lisette Bohmbach
Born	18 Mar 1868	Red Wing, Goodhue, Minnesota, USA
Died	1917	
4	M	Dr. Christ John Bohmbach
Born	17 Feb 1871	Red Wing, Goodhue, Minnesota, USA
Died	1953	Red Wing, Goodhue, Minnesota, USA
Buried	1953	Red Wing, Goodhue, Minnesota, USA
Address	Oakwood Cemetery, Red Wing, MN	

Family Group Record Ole Jacob Oyen Bollum & Inge Mathilde Karlsdatter

Husband	Ole Jacob Oyen Bollum	
Born	5 Dec 1862	Belvidere, Goodhue, Minnesota, USA
Christened		
Died	18 Sep 1946	Redwood Falls, Redwood, Minnesota, USA
Buried	Sep 1946	Belvidere Mills, Goodhue, Minnesota, USA
Address	Hoff Norwegian Lutheran Church Cemetery, Belvidere Mills, Minnesota	
Father	Ole Johnson Bollum (1823-1899)	
Mother	Helena Halvorsdatter Oppergaard (1825-1913)	
Marriage	26 May 1886	Belvidere, Goodhue, Minnesota, USA

Wife	Inga Mathilde Karlsdatter	
AKA	Annie, Carlson, Finstad	
Born	18 Jul 1866	Eidsvoll, Akershus, Norway
Christened	11 Nov 1866	Eidsvoll, Akershus, Norway
Address	Eidsvoll Parish Church, Eidvoll, Akershus,, Norway	
Died	26 Oct 1954	Redwood Falls, Redwood, Minnesota, USA
Buried	Oct 1954	Belvidere Mills, Goodhue, Minnesota, USA
Address	Hoff Norwegian Lutheran Church Cemetery, Belvidere Mills, Minnesota	
Father	Karl Olson Finstad (1837-1907)	
Mother	Berthe Karine Larsdatter Loken (1827-1893)	

Children		
1	M	Claude Oleander Bollum
Born	5 Feb 1888	Belvidere, Goodhue, Minnesota, USA
Christened		
Died	18 Apr 1889	Belvidere Township, Goodhue, Minnesota, USA
Buried	Apr 1889	Belvidere Mills, Goodhue, Minnesota, USA
Address	Hoff Norwegian Lutheran Church Cemetery, Belvidere Mills, Minnesota	
Spouse		
2	M	Chester Orin Bollum
Born	6 Jun 1889	Belvidere, Goodhue, Minnesota, USA
Christened		
Died	29 Jul 1913	Redwood Falls, Redwood, Minnesota, USA
Cause of Death	electrocuted while working on telephone line	
Buried		
Spouse		
3	M	Edwin Herbert Bollum
Born	13 Aug 1894	Boyd, Lac qui Parle, Minnesota, USA
Christened		
Died	12 Jun 1977	Redwood Falls, Redwood, Minnesota, USA
Buried	15 Jun 1977	Redwood Falls, Redwood, Minnesota, USA
Address	Redwood Falls Cemetery, Redwood Falls, MN	
Spouse	Inez Margaret Werder (1896-1979)	
Marr. Date	17 Feb 1918 - Camp Cody, Luna, New Mexico, USA	

Children (cont.)			
4	**F**	**Edith Carroll Bollum**	
Born	13 Aug 1894	Boyd, Lac qui Parle, Minnesota, USA	
Christened			
Died	5 Sep 1956	Redwood Falls, Redwood, Minnesota, USA	
Buried	7 Sep 1956	Redwood Falls, Redwood, Minnesota, USA	
Address	Redwood Falls Cemetery, Redwood Falls, MN		
Spouse	Gilbert Hugh MacDougall (-)		

Family Group Record Joachim Christian Friedrich Bremer & Sophia Christiana Elizabeth Schueler

Husband	Joachim Christian Friedrich Bremer	
Born	26 May 1804	Borow, Luebz, , Mecklenburg-Schwerin
Christened		
Died	1874	
Buried		
Marriage	21 Nov 1828	Burow, Luebz, , Mecklenburg

Wife	Sophia Christina Elizabeth Schueler	
Born	1808	, , , Grand Duchy of Mecklenburg
Christened		
Died	1848	, , , Grand Duchy of Mecklenburg
Buried		

Children		
1 **F**	**Louisa Margaret Henrietta Bremer**	
AKA	Elizabeth, Lizzie	
Born	17 Mar 1829	, , , Mecklenburg
Christened		
Died	17 Sep 1893	Frontenac, Goodhue, Minnesota, USA
Buried	Sep 1893	Frontenac, Goodhue, Minnesota, USA
Address	Old Frontenac Cemetery, Frontenac, Minnesota	
Spouse	Henrich Bernhard Hunecke (1831-1907)	
Marr. Date	1856 - Winona, Wabashaw County, Territory of Minnesota	

2 **M**	**Christian Johann Bremer**	
Born	21 Nov 1830	Bobzin, Parish of Lubz, Gustrow, Grand Duchy of Mecklenburg
Christened		
Died	1885	Lyons, Wayne, New York, USA
Buried	1885	Lyons, Wayne, New York, USA
Spouse	Mary (1827-1879)	1856

3 **M**	**Joachim (Joseph) Bremer**	
Born	2 Sep 1834	, , , Mecklenburg
Christened		
Died	12 Jan 1914	Frontenac, Goodhue, Minnesota, USA
Cause of Death	cancer	
Buried	15 Jan 1914	Frontenac, Goodhue, Minnesota, USA
Address	Old Frontenac Cemetery, Frontenac, Minnesota	
Spouse	Dora (Dorothea) Joanna Dannart (1841-1908)	
Marr. Date	Oct 1868 - Frontenac, Goodhue, Minnesota, USA	

4 **F**	**Caroline Friederika Dorothea Bremer**	
Born	1 Mar 1835	, , , Mecklenburg
Christened		
Died	5 Nov 1901	Frontenac, Goodhue, Minnesota, USA
Buried		
Spouse	Johann Bernhard Huneke (1834-1905)	
Marr. Date	27 Dec 1859 - Frontenac, Goodhue, Minnesota, USA	

Family Group Record Joachim (Joseph) Bremer & Dora Dannart

Husband	Joachim (Joseph) Bremer	
Born	2 Sep 1834	, , , Mecklenburg
Christened		
Died	12 Jan 1914	Frontenac, Goodhue, Minnesota, USA
Cause of Death	cancer	
Buried	15 Jan 1914	Frontenac, Goodhue, Minnesota, USA
Address	Old Frontenac Cemetery, Frontenac, Minnesota	
Father	Joachim Christian Friedrich Bremer (1804-1874)	
Mother	Sophia Christina Elizabeth Schueler (1808-1848)	
Marriage	Oct 1868	Frontenac, Goodhue, Minnesota, USA

Wife	Dora (Dorothea) Joanna Dannart	
AKA	Doris	
Born	Sep 1841	, , , Mecklenburg
Christened		
Died	23 Nov 1908	Frontenac, Goodhue, Minnesota, USA
Cause of Death	cancer	
Buried	24 Nov 1908	Frontenac, Goodhue, Minnesota, USA
Address	Old Frontenac Cemetery, Frontenac, Minnesota	
Father	Dannart (-)	
Mother		

Children		
1	M	Fredrick D. Lubeck Bremer
Born	23 Sep 1872	Frontenac, Goodhue, Minnesota, USA
Christened		
Died	8 Nov 1932	
Buried		
Spouse	Ida Steffenhagen (1878-1944)	
Marr. Date	6 Jan 1896 - Red Wing, Goodhue, Minnesota, USA	

Family Group Record Fredrick D. Lubeck Bremer & Ida Steffenhagen

Husband	Fredrick D. Lubeck Bremer	
Born	23 Sep 1872	Frontenac, Goodhue, Minnesota, USA
Christened		
Died	8 Nov 1932	
Buried		
Father	Joachim (Joseph) Bremer (1834-1914)	
Mother	Dora (Dorothea) Joanna Dannart (1841-1908)	
Father	John August Friedrich Lubeck (1821-1911)	
Mother	Auguste Dannart (1851-1923)	
Marriage	6 Jan 1896	Red Wing, Goodhue, Minnesota, USA

Wife	Ida Steffenhagen	
AKA	Etta	
Born	14 Aug 1878	Frontenac, Goodhue, Minnesota, USA
Christened		
Died	14 Jun 1944	Red Wing, Goodhue, Minnesota, USA
Cause of Death	actue cardiac dilation, myocarditis & nephritis//acute arthritis	
Buried	Jun 1944	Red Wing, Goodhue, Minnesota, USA
Address	Oakwood Cemetery, Red Wing, MN	
Father	Johann Friedrich August Steffenhagen (1845-1930)	
Mother	Friedrike Sophie Caroline Hacker (1847-1883)	
Other Spouse	Charles J. F. Kepke (1876-1961)	7 Dec 1899 - Frontenac, Goodhue, Minnesota, USA

Children			
1	F	Lillian (Lillie) Anna Marie Bremer Kepke	
Born		20 Aug 1896	Frontenac, Goodhue, Minnesota, USA
Christened		18 Sep 1896	Frontenac Station, Goodhue, Minnesota, USA
Address		St. John's Ev. Lutheran Church, Frontenac Station, Minnesota	
Died		28 Jul 1949	Rochester, Olmsted, Minnesota, USA
Buried		Jul 1949	Frontenac, Goodhue, Minnesota, USA
Address		Old Frontenac Cemetery, Frontenac, Minnesota	
Spouse		Charles F. C. Steffenhagen (1882-)	

54

Family Group Record John Brunner & Louisa Henrietta Hunecke

Husband	John Brunner	
Born	21 Sep 1855	, Zurich, Switzerland
Christened		
Died	19 Aug 1935	, Goodhue, Minnesota, USA
Cause of Death	apoplexy	
Buried	21 Aug 1935	Frontenac, Goodhue, Minnesota, USA
Address	Old Frontenac Cemetery, Frontenac, Minnesota	
Marriage	24 Jun 1890	Frontenac, Goodhue, Minnesota, USA

Wife	Louisa Henrietta Hunecke	
Born	Jul 1863	Frontenac, Goodhue, Minnesota, USA
Christened		
Died	28 Nov 1934	Red Wing, Goodhue, Minnesota, USA
Buried	1 Dec 1934	Frontenac, Goodhue, Minnesota, USA
Address	Old Frontenac Cemetery, Frontenac, Minnesota	
Father	Henrich Bernhard Hunecke (1831-1907)	
Mother	Louisa Margaret Henrietta Bremer (1829-1893)	

Children

1	F	Adelheite (Adela) Wilhelmina Brunner	
Born		2 Jul 1891	La Crosse, La Crosse, Wisconsin, USA
Christened			
Died		15 Dec 1983	Red Wing, Goodhue, Minnesota, USA
Buried		Dec 1983	Red Wing, Goodhue, Minnesota, USA
Address		Oakwood Cemetery, Red Wing, MN	
Spouse		Ludwig Adolph Alfred Possehl (1884-1946)	
Marr. Date		9 Oct 1909 - Frontenac, Goodhue, Minnesota, USA	

2	F	Anna Louise Brunner	
Born		16 Aug 1893	La Crosse, La Crosse, Wisconsin, USA
Christened			
Died		31 Mar 1971	, Goodhue, Minnesota, USA
Buried		Apr 1971	Frontenac, Goodhue, Minnesota, USA
Address		Old Frontenac Cemetery, Frontenac, Minnesota	
Spouse		John Rudolph Peper (1894-1947)	Abt 1925 - , Goodhue, Minnesota, USA

3	M	Edward Carl Brunner	
Born		19 Feb 1897	Wayzata, Hennepin, Minnesota, USA
Christened		8 Apr 1903	Frontenac Station, Goodhue, Minnesota, USA
Address		St. John's Ev. Lutheran Church, Frontenac Station, Minnesota	
Died		11 Oct 1950	Red Wing, Goodhue, Minnesota, USA
Cause of Death		brain tumor	
Buried		Oct 1950	Frontenac, Goodhue, Minnesota, USA
Address		Old Frontenac Cemetery, Frontenac, Minnesota	
Spouse		Edna Dorothy Peper (1901-1970)	Abt 1925 - , Goodhue, Minnesota, USA

Family Group Record Jonathan Bullard & Polly Whiting

Husband	Jonathan Bullard	
Born	14 Sep 1781	Holliston, Middlesex, Massachusetts, USA
Christened		
Died	11 Feb 1842	
Buried	Feb 1842	Denmark, Lee, Iowa, USA
Address	Denmark Cemetery, Denmark, Iowa	
Father	Asa Bullard (-)	
Mother	Hannah Cook (-)	
Marriage	3 Oct 1806	Holliston, Middlesex, Massachusetts, USA

Wife	Polly Whiting	
AKA	Mary	
Born	28 Nov 1784	Medway, Norfolk, Massachusetts, USA
Christened		
Died	Sep 1844	Denmark, Lee, Iowa, USA
Buried	Sep 1844	Denmark, Lee, Iowa, USA
Address	Denmark Cemetery, Denmark, Iowa	
Father	Elias Whiting (-)	
Mother	Susannah Hall (-)	

Children		
1 M	Captain Edward Bullard	
Born	27 May 1810	Franklin, Norfolk, Massachusetts, USA
Christened		
Died	14 Jan 1872	Red Wing, Goodhue, Minnesota, USA
Buried	Jan 1872	Red Wing, Goodhue, Minnesota, USA
Address	Oakwood Cemetery, Red Wing, MN	
Spouse	Angeline Raymond (1811-1886)	Abt 1840
2 M	David Whiting Bullard	
Born	9 Jul 1811	Franklin, Norfolk, Massachusetts, USA
Christened		
Died		
Buried		
Spouse		
3 F	Juliann (Julia A.) Bullard	
AKA	Julia Ann	
Born	23 Jul 1812	Holliston, Middlesex, Massachusetts, USA
Christened		
Died	11 Apr 1901	Frontenac, Goodhue, Minnesota, USA
Cause of Death	old age	
Buried	13 Apr 1901	Frontenac, Goodhue, Minnesota, USA
Address	Old Frontenac Episcopal Church Cemetery, Frontenac, Minnesota	
Spouse	Evert V. Westervelt (1813-1888)	7 Jun 1845 - Boston, Suffolk, Massachusetts, USA

Family Group Record Jonathan Bullard & Polly Whiting

Children (cont.)

4	M	Jonathan Bullard Jr.	
Born	25 Aug 1816	Holliston, Middlesex, Massachusetts, USA	
Christened			
Died	11 Sep 1877		
Buried	Sep 1877	Denmark, Lee, Iowa, USA	
Address	Denmark Cemetery, Denmark, Iowa		
Spouse			

5	F	Mary E. Bullard	
Born	6 Oct 1817	Holliston, Middlesex, Massachusetts, USA	
Christened			
Died	28 Apr 1894	Emporia, Lyon, Kansas, USA	
Buried	Apr 1894	Emporia, Lyon, Kansas, USA	
Spouse	Stephen Perry Loomis (1813-1901)	8 Jun 1840 - Denmark, Lee, Iowa, USA	

6	F	Harriet Bullard	
Born	19 Apr 1820	Holliston, Middlesex, Massachusetts, USA	
Christened			
Died			
Buried			
Spouse			

7	M	George Wilkins Bullard	
Born	1 Dec 1827	Holliston, Middlesex, Massachusetts, USA	
Christened			
Died	Cir 1862		
Buried			
Spouse	Lavina Caroline (1827-)	Cir 1849	

Family Group Record Charles E. Bullard & Molly Schunk

Husband	Charles E. Bullard	
Born	5 Feb 1850	Fort Madison, Lee, Iowa, USA
Christened		
Died	19 May 1892	, Goodhue, Minnesota, USA
Buried	May 1892	Red Wing, Goodhue, Minnesota, USA
Address	Oakwood Cemetery, Red Wing, MN	
Father	Captain Edward Bullard (1810-1872)	
Mother	Angeline Raymond (1811-1886)	
Marriage	29 May 1875	, Goodhue, Minnesota, USA

Wife	Molly Schunk	
Born	21 Sep 1853	Hay Creek Township, Goodhue, Minnesota, USA
Christened		
Died	18 Mar 1884	
Buried	Mar 1884	Red Wing, Goodhue, Minnesota, USA
Address	Oakwood Cemetery, Red Wing, MN	

Children		
1 F	Julia M. Bullard	
Born	1879	Hay Creek Township, Goodhue, Minnesota, USA
Christened		
Died	30 Nov 1898	, Goodhue, Minnesota, USA
Buried	Dec 1898	Red Wing, Goodhue, Minnesota, USA
Address	Oakwood Cemetery, Red Wing, MN	
Spouse		

Family Group Record George Wilkins Bullard & Lavina Caroline Bullard

Husband	George Wilkins Bullard	
Born	1 Dec 1827	Holliston, Middlesex, Massachusetts, USA
Christened		
Died	Cir 1862	
Buried		
Father	Jonathan Bullard (1781-1842)	
Mother	Polly Whiting (1784-1844)	
Marriage	Cir 1849	

Wife	Lavina Caroline	
Born	1827	, , Ohio, USA
Christened		
Died		
Buried		
Other Spouse	Mohammon Onum (Dunn) (1834-)	28 Jun 1863 - , Goodhue, Minnesota, USA

Children		
1 M	George P. Bullard	
Born	3 Nov 1851	Waconia, Wabashaw County, Territory of Minnesota
Christened		
Died	20 Nov 1851	Waconia, Wabashaw County, Territory of Minnesota
Buried	20 Nov 1851	Waconia, Wabashaw County, Territory of Minnesota
Address	Wacouta Township Cemetery, Wacouta, MN	
Spouse		
2 F	Carrie H. Bullard	
Born	1857	Wacouta, Goodhue, Minnesota Territory
Christened		
Died		
Buried		
Spouse	Edwin Bostock (-)	3 Sep 1877 - , Goodhue, Minnesota, USA
3 M	George Bullard	
Born	28 Oct 1859	Wacouta, Goodhue, Minnesota, USA
Christened		
Died	28 Oct 1859	Wacouta, Goodhue, Minnesota, USA
Buried	Oct 1859	Wacouta, Goodhue, Minnesota, USA
Address	Wacouta Township Cemetery, Wacouta, MN	
Spouse		
4 F	Harriet N. Bullard	
AKA	Hatti	
Born	1863	Wacouta, Goodhue, Minnesota, USA
Christened		
Died		
Buried		
Spouse	Ambrose D. Phillips (-)	22 Feb 1881 - Wacouta, Goodhue, Minnesota, USA

Family Group Record Ole Ludweg (Louis) Carlson & Caroline Augusta Scherf

Husband	Ole Ludweg (Louis) Carlson	
AKA	Lewis, Lucy, Louis Carlson, Finstad	
Born	19 Jul 1863	Eidsvoll, Akershus, Norway
Christened	13 Sep 1863	Eidsvoll, Akershus, Norway
Address	Eidsvoll Parish Church, Eidvoll, Akershus,, Norway	
Died	14 Mar 1935	Frontenac, Goodhue, Minnesota, USA
Cause of Death	pneumonia	
Buried	16 Mar 1935	Frontenac, Goodhue, Minnesota, USA
Address	Old Frontenac Episcopal Church Cemetery, Frontenac, Minnesota	
Father	Karl Olson Finstad (1837-1907)	
Mother	Berthe Karine Larsdatter Loken (1827-1893)	
Marriage	14 Jan 1892	Frontenac, Goodhue, Minnesota, USA

Wife	Carolyn Augusta Scherf	
AKA	Carrie, Caroline	
Born	18 Apr 1870	Cameron, Clinton, Missouri, USA
Christened	7 Apr 1885	Frontenac, Goodhue, Minnesota, USA
Address	Christ Episcopal Church, Old Frontenac, Minnesota	
Died	23 Aug 1953	Red Wing, Goodhue, Minnesota, USA
Cause of Death	stroke	
Buried	25 Aug 1953	Frontenac, Goodhue, Minnesota, USA
Address	Old Frontenac Episcopal Church Cemetery, Frontenac, Minnesota	
Father	Herman Scherf (1842-1918)	
Mother	Carolina Johanna Maria Steffenhagen (1853-1927)	

Children		
1 M	Raymond Louis Carlson	
Born	21 Mar 1896	Frontenac, Goodhue, Minnesota, USA
Christened	14 Jun 1896	Frontenac, Goodhue, Minnesota, USA
Address	Christ Episcopal Church, Old Frontenac, Minnesota	
Died	29 Mar 1962	, Goodhue, Minnesota, USA
Buried	Mar 1962	Frontenac, Goodhue, Minnesota, USA
Address	Old Frontenac Cemetery, Frontenac, Minnesota	
Spouse	Katherine M. Hackett (1895-1975)	Abt 1920 - , Goodhue, Minnesota, USA
2 M	Winfred Franklin Carlson	
AKA	Winnie	
Born	28 Mar 1899	Frontenac, Goodhue, Minnesota, USA
Christened		
Died	11 Aug 1967	Red Wing, Goodhue, Minnesota, USA
Cause of Death	heart attack	
Buried	14 Aug 1967	Red Wing, Goodhue, Minnesota, USA
Address	Oakwood Cemetery, Red Wing, MN	
Spouse	Florence Fern (Dolly) Johnson (1905-2000)	7 Feb 1929 - , , Minnesota, USA

Family Group Record Ole Andreas Carstenson (Carsten) & Oline Margaretha Olsdatter

Husband	Ole Andreas Carstenson (Carsten)	
Born	25 Apr 1828	, , , Norway
Died	26 Dec 1913	Frontenac, Goodhue, Minnesota, USA
Cause of Death	pneumonia	
Buried	29 Dec 1913	Frontenac, Goodhue, Minnesota, USA
Address	Old Frontenac Cemetery, Frontenac, Minnesota	
Father	Karste Aucter Theraldson (Abt 1800-)	
Mother	Nors Olsdatter (Abt 1800-)	
Marriage	14 Apr 1854	Nes, Akershus, Norway

Wife	Oline Margaretha Olsdatter	
Born	Jun 1829	, , , Norway
Died	15 Feb 1918	Chippewa Falls, Chippewa, Wisconsin, USA
Cause of Death	valvular heart disease//asthma	
Buried	18 Feb 1918	Frontenac, Goodhue, Minnesota, USA
Address	Old Frontenac Cemetery, Frontenac, Minnesota	
Father	Ole Olson (-)	
Mother		

Children

1	F	Carolina Andreasdatter (Carsten)	
Born		Aug 1859	Nes, Akershus, Norway
Spouse		William Lester (1856-)	Dec 1881 - Frontenac, Goodhue, Minnesota, USA

2	F	Julie Andreasdatter (Carsten)	
Born		24 Oct 1860	Nes, Akershus, Norway
Christened		18 Nov 1860	Nes, Akershus, Norway
Died		12 Jan 1905	
Buried		Jan 1905	Frontenac, Goodhue, Minnesota, USA
Address		Old Frontenac Cemetery, Frontenac, Minnesota	
Spouse		Herman J. Friedericks (1865-1907)	24 Sep 1890 - Frontenac, Goodhue, Minnesota, USA

3	F	Sevena (Ellen) Andreasdatter (Carsten)	
Born		1861	Nes, Akershus, Norway
Died		1952	
Buried		1952	Frontenac, Goodhue, Minnesota, USA
Address		Old Frontenac Cemetery, Frontenac, Minnesota	
Spouse		Did Not Marry	

4	M	Jens Casper Carstenson (Carsten)	
AKA		Casper Oleson	
Born		26 Jun 1863	Nes, Akershus, Norway
Christened		23 Aug 1863	Nes, Akershus, Norway
Died		29 Nov 1942	Frontenac, Goodhue, Minnesota, USA
Cause of Death		coronary thrombosis	
Buried		1 Dec 1942	Frontenac, Goodhue, Minnesota, USA
Address		Old Frontenac Cemetery, Frontenac, Minnesota	
Spouse		Lena Maria (Mary) Poppe (1867-1929)	29 Dec 1898 - , Goodhue, Minnesota, USA

5	F	Anna Andreasdatter	
Born		2 Oct 1863	Verdal, Nord-Trondelag, Norway
Died		2 Oct 1863	Verdal, Nord-Trondelag, Norway

Family Group Record Ole Andreas Carstenson (Carsten) & Oline Margaretha Olsdatter

Children (cont.)

6	F	**Mina Ovidia Ole Andreasdatter**	
Born	7 Dec 1865	Nes, Akershus, Norway	
Christened	31 Dec 1865	Nes, Akershus, Norway	
Died	1 Feb 1943		
Buried	Feb 1943	Frontenac, Goodhue, Minnesota, USA	
Address	Old Frontenac Cemetery, Frontenac, Minnesota		
Spouse	Edward Michael Herder (1866-1918)		
Marr. Date	Abt 1890 - Frontenac, Goodhue, Minnesota, USA		

7	M	**Thorvald (Tarvel) Carstenson (Carsten)**	
AKA	Tarvel Oleson		
Born	31 Dec 1868	Nes, Akershus, Norway	
Christened	14 Feb 1869	Nes, Akershus, Norway	
Died		, , , USA	
Spouse	Did Not Marry		

8	M	**John Carstenson (Carsten)**	
Born	Mar 1872	, , Wisconsin, USA	
Died	1965		
Buried	1965	Frontenac, Goodhue, Minnesota, USA	
Address	Old Frontenac Cemetery, Frontenac, Minnesota		
Spouse	Did Not Marry		

Husband	Thomas Jefferson Cates	
AKA	Gates	
Born	8 Sep 1833	Tonawanda, Erie, New York, USA
Died	22 Nov 1898	Long Prairie, Todd, Minnesota, USA
Father	Samuel Cates (-)	
Mother	Dilly Nokes (-)	
Marriage	4 Nov 1860	Frontenac, Goodhue, Minnesota, USA

Wife	Eleanor Caroline Westervelt	
Born	28 Oct 1843	, , Iowa, Northwest Territory
Died	1915	, , Minnesota, USA
Buried		
Father	Evert V. Westervelt (1813-1888)	
Mother	Dicey W. Smelly (Abt 1813-Abt 1843)	

Children				
1	F	Dilly Dicey Cates		
Born		7 Jun 1863	Wacouta, Goodhue, Minnesota Territory	
Spouse		Edwin Chadwick (-)		
2	F	Nellie A. Cates		
Born		1866	Long Prairie, Todd, Minnesota, USA	
3	M	Edmund M. B. Cates		
Born		Oct 1867	Long Prairie, Todd, Minnesota, USA	
4	F	Katie M. Cates		
Born		1870	Long Prairie, Todd, Minnesota, USA	
5	F	Eva Edna Cates		
Born		Dec 1872	Long Prairie, Todd, Minnesota, USA	
Died		1901	Long Prairie, Todd, Minnesota, USA	
Spouse		Herbert William Attlesley (1867-1936)		

Family Group Record Nicholas Crist & Victoria Hiley

Husband	Nicholas Crist	
AKA	Crist	
Born	May 1842	Berlin, , , Prussia
Died	1 Feb 1920	Fargo, Cass, North Dakota, USA
Cause of Death	brights disease//old age	
Buried		
Marriage	27 Mar 1867	Red Wing, Goodhue, Minnesota, USA

Wife	Victoria Ewerz (Hillig)	
AKA	Dora	
Born	21 Dec 1850	Tyrol, , Austria
Died	10 Jul 1927	Grand Rapids, LaMoure, North Dakota, USA
Cause of Death	old age	
Buried		
Father	Augustus Hillig (1815-)	
Mother	Aloisia Ursula (Lois) Ewerz (Cir 1826-)	

Children				
1	M	Harry Crist		
	Born	Dec 1867	Florence Township, Goodhue, Minnesota, USA	
	Died	1940		
2	M	Nicholas Alfred Crist		
	Born	Jan 1869	Florence Township, Goodhue, Minnesota, USA	
	Died	1938		
3	M	Edward William Crist		
	Born	1871	Florence Township, Goodhue, Minnesota, USA	
	Died	1951		
4	F	Alida Louise Crist		
	Born	1873	Florence Township, Goodhue, Minnesota, USA	
	Died	1930		
5	M	John C. Herbert Crist		
	Born	Mar 1876	Florence Township, Goodhue, Minnesota, USA	
	Died	1938		
6	F	Bertha Elizabeth Crist		
	Born	Mar 1880	Florence Township, Goodhue, Minnesota, USA	
	Died	1941		
7	F	Emma Ernestine Crist		
	Born	12 Nov 1882	Florence Township, Goodhue, Minnesota, USA	
	Died	1974		
8	F	Lois Mabel Crist		
	Born	24 Mar 1887	Grand Rapids, LaMoure, North Dakota, USA	
	Died	18 Jul 1887		
9	M	Albert Frank Crist		
	Born	Dec 1889	Grand Rapids, LaMoure, North Dakota, USA	

Family Group Record Christian (Christ) Christiansen & Sarah Christiansen

Husband	Christian (Christ) Christiansen	
Born	1839	, , , Norway
Marriage	Abt 1869	, Goodhue, Minnesota, USA

Wife	Sara	
Born	1849	, , , Mecklenburg

Children

1	F	**Katie Christiansen**	
Born		1871	Frontenac, Goodhue, Minnesota, USA
Christened			Frontenac, Goodhue, Minnesota, USA
Address		Christ Episcopal Church, Old Frontenac, Minnesota	
2	M	**William Christiansen**	
Born		16 Nov 1872	Frontenac, Goodhue, Minnesota, USA
Christened			Frontenac, Goodhue, Minnesota, USA
Address		Christ Episcopal Church, Old Frontenac, Minnesota	
3	M	**Benjamin Christiansen**	
Born		11 Mar 1875	Frontenac, Goodhue, Minnesota, USA
Christened			Frontenac, Goodhue, Minnesota, USA
Address		Christ Episcopal Church, Old Frontenac, Minnesota	
4	F	**Nellie Christiansen**	
Born		1877	Frontenac, Goodhue, Minnesota, USA
Christened			Frontenac, Goodhue, Minnesota, USA
Address		Christ Episcopal Church, Old Frontenac, Minnesota	
5	F	**Lena Christiansen**	
Born		1879	Frontenac, Goodhue, Minnesota, USA
Christened			Frontenac, Goodhue, Minnesota, USA
Address		Christ Episcopal Church, Old Frontenac, Minnesota	
6	F	**Elsie May Christiansen**	
Born		10 Jun 1884	Frontenac, Goodhue, Minnesota, USA
Christened		31 Aug 1884	Frontenac, Goodhue, Minnesota, USA
Address		Christ Episcopal Church, Old Frontenac, Minnesota	

Family Group Record Cord Dammann & Anna Wiegersen

Husband	Cord Dammann	
Born	Abt 1801	Bliedersdorf, , Stade, Hanover
Christened		
Died		
Buried		
Marriage	21 Jun 1840	Neukloster-Hedendorf, Stade, Hanover

Wife	Anna Wiegersen	
Born	29 Jul 1806	Neukloster-Hedendorf, Stade, Hanover
Christened		
Died	Abt 1886	, Goodhue, Minnesota, USA
Buried		

Children

1	M	Hinrich (Henry) Dammann	
Born		30 Mar 1841	Neukloster-Hedendorf, Stade, Hanover
Christened			
Died		8 Jun 1907	Frontenac, Goodhue, Minnesota, USA
Cause of Death		lung fever	
Buried		11 Jun 1907	Frontenac, Goodhue, Minnesota, USA
Address		Old Frontenac Cemetery, Frontenac, Minnesota	
Spouse		Katharena Tigdeman (1846-1935)	Abt 1870 - , Goodhue, Minnesota, USA

2	M	Hein Dammann	
Born		28 Jun 1846	Hedendorf, Stade, Hanover
Christened			
Died		1917	Goodhue Village, Goodhue, Minnesota, USA
Buried		1917	Goodhue Village, Goodhue, Minnesota, USA
Address		St. John's Evangelical Lutheran Cemetery, Goodhue,, Minnesota	
Spouse		Rebekka Lytje (1843-1917)	Abt 1871 - . Goodhue, Minnesota, USA

3	M	Peter Dammann	
Born		12 Mar 1847	Neukloster-Hedendorf, Stade, Hanover
Christened			
Died		25 Nov 1925	Frontenac, Goodhue, Minnesota, USA
Buried		28 Nov 1925	Frontenac, Goodhue, Minnesota, USA
Address		Old Frontenac Cemetery, Frontenac, Minnesota	
Spouse		Rebecca Wilshusen (1834-1914)	23 Oct 1873 - , Goodhue, Minnesota, USA

4	M	Johannes (John) E. Dammann	
Born		Apr 1848	Neukloster-Hedendorf, Stade, Hanover
Christened			
Died		19 Jan 1929	Frontenac, Goodhue, Minnesota, USA
Buried		Jan 1929	Frontenac, Goodhue, Minnesota, USA
Address		Old Frontenac Cemetery, Frontenac, Minnesota	
Spouse		Anna (1859-1929)	Abt 1878 - , Stade, Hanover

Family Group Record   Peter Dammann & Rebecca Wilshusen Poppe

Husband	Peter Dammann	
Born	12 Mar 1847	Neukloster-Hedendorf, Stade, Hanover
Christened		
Died	25 Nov 1925	Frontenac, Goodhue, Minnesota, USA
Buried	28 Nov 1925	Frontenac, Goodhue, Minnesota, USA
Address	Old Frontenac Cemetery, Frontenac, Minnesota	
Father	Cord Dammann (Abt 1801-)	
Mother	Anna Wiegersen (1806-Abt 1886)	
Marriage	23 Oct 1873	, Goodhue, Minnesota, USA

Wife	Rebecca Wilshusen	
AKA	Relhausen	
Born	Jul 1834	, , , Hanover
Christened		
Died	27 Oct 1914	Frontenac, Goodhue, Minnesota, USA
Buried	Oct 1914	Frontenac, Goodhue, Minnesota, USA
Address	Old Frontenac Cemetery, Frontenac, Minnesota	
Other Spouse	Nicolaus (Claus) Deidrich Poppe (1822-1871)	Abt 1857 - New York City, New York, New York, USA

Children

Family Group Record Hein Dammann & Rebekka Lytje

Husband	Hein Dammann	
Born	28 Jun 1846	Hedendorf, Stade, Hanover
Christened		
Died	1917	Goodhue Village, Goodhue, Minnesota, USA
Buried	1917	Goodhue Village, Goodhue, Minnesota, USA
Address	St. John's Evangelical Lutheran Cemetery, Goodhue,, Minnesota	
Father	Cord Dammann (Abt 1801-)	
Mother	Anna Wiegersen (1806-Abt 1886)	
Marriage	Abt 1871	. Goodhue, Minnesota, USA

Wife	Rebekka Lytje	
Born	May 1843	, , , Germany
Christened		
Died	8 Jul 1917	Goodhue Village, Goodhue, Minnesota, USA
Buried	Jul 1917	Goodhue Village, Goodhue, Minnesota, USA
Address	St. John's Evangelical Lutheran Cemetery, Goodhue,, Minnesota	
Father	Matthus Lytje (-)	
Mother	Adelheit Valters (-)	

Children		
1 F	Anna M. Dammann	
Born	1872	Goodhue Village, Goodhue, Minnesota, USA
Christened		
Died		
Buried		
Spouse		

Family Group Record Hinrich (Henry) Dammann & Katharena Tigdeman

Husband	Hinrich (Henry) Dammann	
Born	30 Mar 1841	Neukloster-Hedendorf, Stade, Hanover
Christened		
Died	8 Jun 1907	Frontenac, Goodhue, Minnesota, USA
Cause of Death	lung fever	
Buried	11 Jun 1907	Frontenac, Goodhue, Minnesota, USA
Address	Old Frontenac Cemetery, Frontenac, Minnesota	
Father	Cord Dammann (Abt 1801-)	
Mother	Anna Wiegersen (1806-Abt 1886)	
Marriage	Abt 1870	, Goodhue, Minnesota, USA

Wife	Katharena Tigdeman	
Born	18 Jan 1846	, , , Hanover
Christened		
Died	27 Apr 1935	, Goodhue, Minnesota, USA
Buried	Apr 1935	Frontenac, Goodhue, Minnesota, USA
Address	Old Frontenac Cemetery, Frontenac, Minnesota	

Children			
1	M	John Dammann	
Born		1871	Florence Township, Goodhue, Minnesota, USA
Christened			
Died		29 Mar 1945	, Goodhue, Minnesota, USA
Buried		Mar 1945	Frontenac, Goodhue, Minnesota, USA
Address		Old Frontenac Cemetery, Frontenac, Minnesota	
Spouse		Katharina A. Fahring (1875-1945)	
2	M	Henry Dammann	
Born		1872	Florence Township, Goodhue, Minnesota, USA
Christened			
Died		1 Nov 1942	, Wabasha, Minnesota, USA
Buried		Nov 1942	Frontenac, Goodhue, Minnesota, USA
Address		Old Frontenac Cemetery, Frontenac, Minnesota	
Spouse		Did Not Marry	
3	M	Charles Dammann	
Born		1874	Florence Township, Goodhue, Minnesota, USA
Christened			
Died		20 Sep 1952	, Goodhue, Minnesota, USA
Buried		Sep 1952	Frontenac, Goodhue, Minnesota, USA
Address		Old Frontenac Cemetery, Frontenac, Minnesota	
Spouse		Did Not Marry	

Family Group Record Hinrich (Henry) Dammann & Katharena Tigdeman

Children (cont.)			
4	**F**	**Mary Dammann**	
Born	Aug 1876	Florence Township, Goodhue, Minnesota, USA	
Christened			
Died	1952	, Goodhue, Minnesota, USA	
Buried	1952	Frontenac, Goodhue, Minnesota, USA	
Address	Old Frontenac Cemetery, Frontenac, Minnesota		
Spouse	Joseph Gerken (1863-1938)	3 Jun 1897 - Frontenac, Goodhue, Minnesota, USA	

Family Group Record Johannes (John) E. Dammann & Anna Dammann

Husband	Johannes (John) E. Dammann	
Born	Apr 1848	Neukloster-Hedendorf, Stade, Hanover
Died	19 Jan 1929	Frontenac, Goodhue, Minnesota, USA
Buried	Jan 1929	Frontenac, Goodhue, Minnesota, USA
Address	Old Frontenac Cemetery, Frontenac, Minnesota	
Father	Cord Dammann (Abt 1801-)	
Mother	Anna Wiegersen (1806-Abt 1886)	
Marriage	Abt 1878	, Stade, Hanover

Wife	Anna	
Born	Oct 1859	Neukloster-Hedendorf, Stade, Hanover
Died	1929	Florence Township, Goodhue, Minnesota, USA
Buried	1929	Frontenac, Goodhue, Minnesota, USA
Address	Old Frontenac Cemetery, Frontenac, Minnesota	

Children			
1	M	Henry Dammann	
Born		1881	Neukloster-Hedendorf, Stade, Hanover
2	M	Harris Dammann	
Born		1883	Neukloster-Hedendorf, Stade, Hanover
3	F	Anna Dora Dammann	
Born		22 Feb 1885	Frontenac, Goodhue, Minnesota, USA

4	F	Mary Dammann	
Born		Jan 1887	Frontenac, Goodhue, Minnesota, USA

5	F	Emma Dammann	
Born		Mar 1890	Frontenac, Goodhue, Minnesota, USA

Husband	Dannart	
Born		
Christened		
Died .		
Buried		
Marriage		

Wife		
Born		
Christened		
Died		
Buried		

Children			
1	**F**	**Dora (Dorothea) Joanna Dannart**	
AKA		Doris	
Born		Sep 1841	, , , Mecklenburg
Christened			
Died		23 Nov 1908	Frontenac, Goodhue, Minnesota, USA
Cause of Death		cancer	
Buried		24 Nov 1908	Frontenac, Goodhue, Minnesota, USA
Address		Old Frontenac Cemetery, Frontenac, Minnesota	
Spouse		Joachim (Joseph) Bremer (1834-1914)	Oct 1868 - Frontenac, Goodhue, Minnesota, USA
2	**F**	**Auguste Dannart**	
Born		Feb 1851	, , , Mecklenburg
Christened			
Died		12 Apr 1923	Frontenac, Goodhue, Minnesota, USA
Buried		1923	Frontenac, Goodhue, Minnesota, USA
Address		Old Frontenac Cemetery, Frontenac, Minnesota	
Spouse		John August Friedrich Lubeck (1821-1911)	21 Jun 1872 - , Goodhue, Minnesota, USA

Family Group Record William J. Eisenbrand & Caroline C. Zirkelbach

Husband	William J. Eisenbrand	
Born	19 May 1834	, , , Germany
Christened		
Died	1 Oct 1891	
Buried	Oct 1891	Red Wing, Goodhue, Minnesota, USA
Address	Oakwood Cemetery, Red Wing, MN	
Marriage		

Wife	Caroline C. Zirkelbach	
Born	18 Sep 1844	, , , Germany
Christened		
Died	13 Jul 1903	Red Wing, Goodhue, Minnesota, USA
Buried	Jul 1903	Red Wing, Goodhue, Minnesota, USA
Address	Oakwood Cemetery, Red Wing, MN	

Children		
1 F	Teresa Eisenbrand	
Born	Dec 1861	Red Wing, Goodhue, Minnesota, USA
Christened		
Died		
Buried		
Spouse	Frederick Meyer (1863-)	Abt 1884
2 F	Carolyn Marie Eisenbrand	
Born	Jan 1876	Red Wing, Goodhue, Minnesota, USA
Christened		
Died	29 Jul 1945	Red Wing, Goodhue, Minnesota, USA
Buried		
Spouse	Frank Morley (-Bef 1900)	1 Dec 1897 - , Goodhue, Minnesota, USA
Spouse	Erik Iverson (1880-)	10 Nov 1905 - St. Paul, Ramsey, Minnesota, USA
3 F	Hattie C. Eisenbrand	
Born	Jul 1882	Red Wing, Goodhue, Minnesota, USA
Christened		
Died	1961	
Buried	1961	Red Wing, Goodhue, Minnesota, USA
Address	Oakwood Cemetery, Red Wing, MN	
Spouse	Bernard Melvin Boxrud (1879-1947)	

Family Group Record Even Evensen & Lena Larsdatter Loken

Husband	Even Evensen	
Born	1833	, , Norway
Christened		
Died	1 Apr 1892	Frontenac, Goodhue, Minnesota, USA
Cause of Death	suicide by poison	
Buried	4 Apr 1892	Frontenac, Goodhue, Minnesota, USA
Address	Old Frontenac Cemetery, Frontenac, Minnesota	
Marriage	Abt 1860	, , , Norway

Wife	Lena Larsdatter Loken	
Born	25 May 1834	Eidsvoll, Akershus, Norway
Christened		
Died	4 Feb 1882	Frontenac, Goodhue, Minnesota, USA
Buried	Feb 1882	Frontenac, Goodhue, Minnesota, USA
Address	Old Frontenac Cemetery, Frontenac, Minnesota	
Father	Lars Larson Loken (Abt 1799-Bef 1865)	
Mother	Johanna Olsdatter (1799-Cir 1870)	

Children			
1	M	Louis Evensen	
Born		1865	Norway
Christened			
Died		5 May 1901	, , Minnesota, USA
Buried			
Spouse			
2	M	Ole Evensen	
Born		1874	Frontenac, Goodhue, Minnesota, USA
Christened			
Died			
Buried			
Spouse			

Family Group Record Henry Evert & Augusta Keye

Husband	Henry Evert	
Born	1848	, , , Mecklenburg
Christened		
Died	1913	Argyle, Marshall, Minnesota, USA
Buried		
Marriage	Abt 1876	, Goodhue, Minnesota, USA

Wife	Augusta Keye	
Born	1860	Florence Township, Goodhue, Minnesota, USA
Christened		
Died	1939	Argyle, Marshall, Minnesota, USA
Buried		
Father	Andrew Ferdinand Keye (1814-1904)	
Mother	Friderike Uda (1825-1887)	

Children			
1	F	Emma Evert	
Born		21 Nov 1877	Frontenac, Goodhue, Minnesota, USA
Christened			
Died		15 Apr 1958	, Marshall, Minnesota, USA
Buried			
Spouse			
2	F	May Evert	
Born		1881	, , Minnesota, USA
Christened			
Died		1963	, Marshall, Minnesota, USA
Buried			
Spouse			
3	F	Natalie Evert	
Born		1883	, , Minnesota, USA
Christened			
Died		1959	, Marshall, Minnesota, USA
Buried			
Spouse			
4	M	Benjamin Evert	
Born		1885	, , Minnesota, USA
Christened			
Died		1965	
Buried		1965	, Marshall, Minnesota, USA
Spouse			
5	M	Harry S. Evert	
Born		5 Jan 1894	, Marshall, Minnesota, USA
Christened			
Died		20 Jun 1960	
Buried			, Marshall, Minnesota, USA
Spouse			

Family Group Record Karl Olson Finstad & Bertha Karine Larsdatter Loken

Husband	Karl Olson Finstad	
AKA	Carl Oleson Finstad, Oleson	
Born	Dec 1837	, , Akershus, Norway
Christened		
Died	28 Jun 1907	Frontenac, Goodhue, Minnesota, USA
Buried	Jun 1907	Frontenac, Goodhue, Minnesota, USA
Address	Old Frontenac Cemetery, Frontenac, Minnesota	
Father	Ole Jenson (-)	
Mother		
Marriage	17 Jul 1863	Eidsvoll prestegaard, Akershus County, Norway

Wife	Berthe Karine Larsdatter Loken	
AKA	Carrie, Karine, Corine Finstad	
Born	Jan 1827	Eidsvoll, Akershus, Norway
Christened		
Died	9 Sep 1893	Frontenac, Goodhue, Minnesota, USA
Cause of Death	Rheumatism	
Buried	11 Sep 1893	Frontenac, Goodhue, Minnesota, USA
Address	Old Frontenac Episcopal Church Cemetery, Frontenac, Minnesota	
Father	Lars Larson Loken (Abt 1799-Bef 1865)	
Mother	Johanna Olsdatter (1799-Cir 1870)	

Children			
1	M	Ole Ludweg (Louis) Carlson	
AKA		Lewis, Lucy, Louis Carlson, Finstad	
Born		19 Jul 1863	Eidsvoll, Akershus, Norway
Christened		13 Sep 1863	Eidsvoll, Akershus, Norway
Address		Eidsvoll Parish Church, Eidvoll, Akershus,, Norway	
Died		14 Mar 1935	Frontenac, Goodhue, Minnesota, USA
Cause of Death		pneumonia	
Buried		16 Mar 1935	Frontenac, Goodhue, Minnesota, USA
Address		Old Frontenac Episcopal Church Cemetery, Frontenac, Minnesota	
Spouse		Carolyn Augusta Scherf (1870-1953)	14 Jan 1892 - Frontenac, Goodhue, Minnesota, USA
2	F	Inga Mathilde Karlsdatter	
AKA		Annie, Carlson, Finstad	
Born		18 Jul 1866	Eidsvoll, Akershus, Norway
Christened		11 Nov 1866	Eidsvoll, Akershus, Norway
Address		Eidsvoll Parish Church, Eidvoll, Akershus,, Norway	
Died		26 Oct 1954	Redwood Falls, Redwood, Minnesota, USA
Buried		Oct 1954	Belvidere Mills, Goodhue, Minnesota, USA
Address		Hoff Norwegian Lutheran Church Cemetery, Belvidere Mills, Minnesota	
Spouse		Ole Jacob Oyen Bollum (1862-1946)	26 May 1886 - Belvidere, Goodhue, Minnesota, USA

Children (cont.)		
3	**F**	**Ragna Caroline Karlsdatter**

AKA	Carlson, Finstad	
Born	11 Aug 1870	Frontenac, Goodhue, Minnesota, USA
Christened		
Died	10 Nov 1959	Frontenac, Goodhue, Minnesota, USA
Cause of Death	old age//heart disease	
Buried	12 Nov 1959	Frontenac, Goodhue, Minnesota, USA
Address	Old Frontenac Episcopal Church Cemetery, Frontenac, Minnesota	
Spouse	Edward Everett Westervelt (1853-1937)	
Marr. Date	28 May 1890 - Stockholm, Pepin, Wisconsin, USA	

Family Group Record Johann Christian Friedericks & Maria Frederica Volkert

Husband	Johann Christian Friedericks	
Born	Abt 1805	Waren, Muritz, Mecklenburg
Marriage	Abt 1825	, , , Mecklenburg

Wife	Maria Frederica Volkert	
Born	Abt 1805	Waren, Muritz, Mecklenburg

Children

1	M	Christian (Christ) Friedericks	
Born		1830	Waren, Muritz, Mecklenburg
Died		1884	Frontenac, Goodhue, Minnesota, USA
Buried		1884	Frontenac, Goodhue, Minnesota, USA
Address		Old Frontenac Cemetery, Frontenac, Minnesota	
Spouse		Sophia Schmidt (1827-1912)	Abt 1856 - , , , Mecklenburg

2	F	Fredericka Lisetta Friedericks	
Born		8 May 1832	, , , Mecklenburg
Died		7 Nov 1911	Red Wing, Goodhue, Minnesota, USA
Buried		Nov 1911	Red Wing, Goodhue, Minnesota, USA
Address		St. John's Evangelical Cemetery, Red Wing, Minnesota	
Spouse		August John Lubeck (1827-Abt 1864)	Abt 1857 - . Goodhue, Minnesota, USA
Spouse		Johan Hinrich Bohmbach (1822-1917)	
Marr. Date		18 Feb 1865 - Red Wing, Goodhue, Minnesota, USA	

3	M	Fredrich (Fritz) Friedericks	
AKA		Fritz	
Born		May 1834	Waren, Muritz, Mecklenburg
Died		Abt 1906	Minneapolis, Hennepin, Minnesota, USA
Spouse		Elisabeth (Lissetta) C. Lipkock (1847-1925)	1864

4	F	Maria (Mary) Sophia Henrietta Friedericks	
AKA		Marg	
Born		27 Feb 1838	Waren, Muritz, Mecklenburg
Died		15 Jan 1913	Frontenac, Goodhue, Minnesota, USA
Cause of Death		acute bronchities	
Buried		Jan 1913	Frontenac, Goodhue, Minnesota, USA
Address		Old Frontenac Cemetery, Frontenac, Minnesota	
Spouse		Engelbert Schenach (1832-1922)	Apr 1861 - , Goodhue, Minnesota, USA

5	M	Johann C. Friedericks	
Born		24 May 1840	Waren, Muritz, Mecklenburg
Died		10 Feb 1908	Red Wing, Goodhue, Minnesota, USA
Buried		13 Feb 1908	
Spouse		Rebecca Gerken (1844-1898)	Abt 1865 - Frontenac, Goodhue, Minnesota, USA

Family Group Record Christian (Christ) Friedericks & Sophia Schmidt

Husband	Christian (Christ) Friedericks	
Born	1830	Waren, Muritz, Mecklenburg
Died	1884	Frontenac, Goodhue, Minnesota, USA
Buried	1884	Frontenac, Goodhue, Minnesota, USA
Address	Old Frontenac Cemetery, Frontenac, Minnesota	
Father	Johann Christian Friedericks (Abt 1805-)	
Mother	Maria Frederica Volkert (Abt 1805-)	
Marriage	Abt 1856	, , , Mecklenburg

Wife	Sophia Schmidt	
Born	Dec 1827	, , , Mecklenburg
Died	11 Dec 1912	Frontenac, Goodhue, Minnesota, USA
Buried	Dec 1912	Frontenac, Goodhue, Minnesota, USA
Address	Old Frontenac Cemetery, Frontenac, Minnesota	
Father	Schmidt (-)	
Mother	Doris (1803-)	

Children		
1 F	**Caroline Friedericks**	

Born	23 Aug 1858	, , , Mecklenburg
Died	24 May 1915	
Buried	May 1915	Frontenac, Goodhue, Minnesota, USA
Address	Old Frontenac Cemetery, Frontenac, Minnesota	
Spouse	Herman William Gustav Risch (1851-1933)	16 Dec 1879 - Frontenac, Goodhue, Minnesota, USA

2 U	**Unknown child #1 Friedericks**	
Born	Abt 1860	, , , Mecklenburg
Died	Bef 1865	, , , Mecklenburg

3 U	**Unknown child #2 Friedericks**	
Born	Abt 1862	, , , Mecklenburg
Died	Bef 1865	, , , Mecklenburg

4 M	**Herman J. Friedericks**	
Born	21 Jan 1865	, , , Mecklenburg
Died	6 Sep 1907	, Wabasha, Minnesota, USA
Buried	Sep 1907	Frontenac, Goodhue, Minnesota, USA
Address	Old Frontenac Cemetery, Frontenac, Minnesota	
Spouse	Julie Andreasdatter (Carsten) (1860-1905)	24 Sep 1890 - Frontenac, Goodhue, Minnesota, USA

5 M	**William Friedericks**	
Born	12 Feb 1868	Frontenac, Goodhue, Minnesota, USA
Died	1868	Frontenac, Goodhue, Minnesota, USA
Buried	1868	Frontenac, Goodhue, Minnesota, USA
Address	Old Frontenac Cemetery, Frontenac, Minnesota	

Family Group Record Fredrich (Fritz) Friedericks & Elisabeth Lipkock

Husband	Fredrich (Fritz) Friedericks	
AKA	Fritz	
Born	May 1834	Waren, Muritz, Mecklenburg
Christened		
Died	Abt 1906	Minneapolis, Hennepin, Minnesota, USA
Buried		
Father	Johann Christian Friedericks (Abt 1805-)	
Mother	Maria Frederica Volkert (Abt 1805-)	
Marriage	1864	

Wife	Elisabeth (Lissetta) C. Lipkock	
Born	Jul 1847	, , , Mecklenburg
Christened		
Died	4 Apr 1925	Minneapolis, Hennepin, Minnesota, USA
Buried		
Father	Charles Lipkock (-)	
Mother		

Children		

Family Group Record Johann C. Friedericks & Rebecca Gerken

Husband	Johann C. Friedericks	
Born	24 May 1840	Waren, Muritz, Mecklenburg
Died	10 Feb 1908	Red Wing, Goodhue, Minnesota, USA
Buried	13 Feb 1908	
Father	Johann Christian Friedericks (Abt 1805-)	
Mother	Maria Frederica Volkert (Abt 1805-)	
Marriage	Abt 1865	Frontenac, Goodhue, Minnesota, USA

Wife	Rebecca Gerken	
Born	1844	, , , Hanover
Died	19 Jun 1898	Red Wing, Goodhue, Minnesota, USA
Father	John Gerken # 2 (1821-1900)	
Mother	Anna (Abt 1821-Abt 1860)	

Children

1	M	John Friedericks		
Born		1866	Frontenac, Goodhue, Minnesota, USA	
Spouse		Anna Charlotte (-)	Cir 1885 - , Goodhue, Minnesota, USA	
2	F	Fredricka Friedericks		
Born		1868	Frontenac, Goodhue, Minnesota, USA	
3	M	Henry Friedericks		
Born		8 Apr 1871	Frontenac, Goodhue, Minnesota, USA	
Spouse		Hilda T (1874-)	Abt 1895 - Frontenac, Goodhue, Minnesota, USA	
4	F	Anna Bertha Margaret Friedericks		
Born		1 Oct 1875	Frontenac, Goodhue, Minnesota, USA	
Died		2 Oct 1911	Red Wing, Goodhue, Minnesota, USA	
Cause of Death		kidney disease		
Buried		Oct 1911	Frontenac, Goodhue, Minnesota, USA	
Address		Old Frontenac Cemetery, Frontenac, Minnesota		
Spouse		Frank B. Dahling (-)		
5	M	Charles Friedericks		
Born		10 Oct 1880	Frontenac, Goodhue, Minnesota, USA	
6	M	Emil Peter Friedericks		
Born		8 Jul 1883	Hay Creek Township, Goodhue, Minnesota, USA	
Christened		11 Jul 1883	Frontenac Station, Goodhue, Minnesota, USA	
Address		St. John's Ev. Lutheran Church, Frontenac Station, Minnesota		
Died		18 Jan 1935	St. Paul, Ramsey, Minnesota, USA	
Spouse		Josephine (-)		

Family Group Record Jeptha Dudley Garrard & Sarah Bella Ludlow

Husband	Jeptha Dudley Garrard	
Born	5 Dec 1802	Fairfield, Bourbon, Kentucky, USA
Christened		
Died	26 Jan 1837	Cincinnati, Hamilton, Ohio, USA
Buried	Jan 1837	Cincinnati, Hamilton, Ohio, USA
Address	Spring Grove Cemetary, Cincinnati, Ohio	
Father	General James Douglas Garrard (1773-1838)	
Mother	Ann Coyers (Nancy) Lewis (1774-1838)	
Marriage	25 Jun 1824	Cincinnati, Hamilton, Ohio, USA

Wife	Sarah Bella Ludlow	
Born	1802	Cumminsville, Hamilton, Ohio, USA
Christened		
Died	13 Jan 1882	Cincinnati, Hamilton, Ohio, USA
Cause of Death	cholera morbus//exhaustion	
Buried	15 Jan 1882	Cincinnati, Hamilton, Ohio, USA
Address	Spring Grove Cemetary, Cincinnati, Ohio	
Father	Col Israel Ludlow (1765-1804)	
Mother	Charlotte Chambers (1768-1821)	
Other Spouse	Justice John B. McLean (1785-1861)	11 May 1843 - Cincinnati, Hamilton, Ohio, USA

Children		
1	M	Brevet Brigadier General Israel Ludlow Garrard
Born	22 Oct 1825	Lexington, Fayette, Kentucky, USA
Christened		
Died	21 Sep 1901	Frontenac, Goodhue, Minnesota, USA
Buried	24 Sep 1901	Frontenac, Goodhue, Minnesota, USA
Address	Old Frontenac Cemetery, Frontenac, Minnesota	
Spouse	Catherine (Kate) Wood (1827-1867)	
Marr. Date	21 May 1856 - Manhattan, New York, New York, USA	

2	M	Brevet Brigadier General Kenner Dudley Garrard
Born	21 Sep 1827	Fairfield, Bourbon, Kentucky, USA
Christened		
Died	15 May 1879	Cincinnati, Hamilton, Ohio, USA
Cause of Death	hernia	
Buried	17 May 1879	Cincinnati, Hamilton, Ohio, USA
Address	Spring Grove Cemetary, Cincinnati, Ohio	
Spouse	Did Not Marry	

3	M	Dr. Lewis Hector Garrard
Born	15 Jun 1829	Cincinnati, Hamilton, Ohio, USA
Christened		
Died	7 Jul 1887	Lakewood, Chautauqua, New York, USA
Cause of Death	paralysis	
Buried	9 Jul 1887	Cincinnati, Hamilton, Ohio, USA
Address	Spring Grove Cemetary, Cincinnati, Ohio	
Spouse	Florence Minerva Van Vliet (1844-1897)	22 Oct 1862

Children (cont.)			
4	**M**	**Brevet Brigadier General Jeptha Dudley Garrard**	
AKA	Colonel		
Born	21 Apr 1836	Cincinnati, Hamilton, Ohio, USA	
Christened			
Died	16 Dec 1915	Cincinnati, Hamilton, Ohio, USA	
Cause of Death	angina pectoris		
Buried	20 Dec 1915	Cincinnati, Hamilton, Ohio, USA	
Address	Spring Grove Cemetary, Cincinnati, Ohio		
Spouse	Anna R. Knapp (1830-1887)	4 Oct 1864 - Auburn, Cayuga, New York, USA	

Family Group Record Brevet Brigadier General Israel Ludlow Garrard & Catherine Wood

Husband	Brevet Brigadier General Israel Ludlow Garrard	
Born	22 Oct 1825	Lexington, Fayette, Kentucky, USA
Christened		
Died	21 Sep 1901	Frontenac, Goodhue, Minnesota, USA
Buried	24 Sep 1901	Frontenac, Goodhue, Minnesota, USA
Address	Old Frontenac Cemetery, Frontenac, Minnesota	
Father	Jeptha Dudley Garrard (1802-1837)	
Mother	Sarah Bella Ludlow (1802-1882)	
Marriage	21 May 1856	Manhattan, New York, New York, USA

Wife	Catherine (Kate) Wood	
Born	16 Sep 1827	Chesterfield, Burlington, New Jersey, USA
Christened		
Died	12 Jan 1867	Frontenac, Goodhue, Minnesota, USA
Buried	16 Jan 1867	Frontenac, Goodhue, Minnesota, USA
Address	Old Frontenac Cemetery, Frontenac, Minnesota	
Father	George Wood (1789-1860)	
Mother	Mary Ewetse Kip (1800-1870)	

Children		
1 F	Margaret Hills Garrard	
Born	17 Mar 1857	Tonawanda, Erie, New York, USA
Christened		
Died	1934	Bellport, Suffolk, New York, USA
Buried	1934	Bellport, Suffolk, New York, USA
Address	Woodland Cemetery, Bellport, New York	
Spouse	Did Not Marry	
2 M	George Wood Garrard	
Born	18 Aug 1863	Peekskill, Westchester, New York, USA
Christened		
Died	25 Mar 1928	
Buried	Mar 1928	Frontenac, Goodhue, Minnesota, USA
Address	Old Frontenac Cemetery, Frontenac, Minnesota	
Spouse	Virginia Colden Hoffman (1864-1961)	
Marr. Date	31 Oct 1889 - Manhattan, New York, New York, USA	
3 M	K. Wood Garrard	
Born	12 Jan 1867	Frontenac, Goodhue, Minnesota, USA
Christened		
Died	Feb 1867	Frontenac, Goodhue, Minnesota, USA
Buried	Feb 1867	Frontenac, Goodhue, Minnesota, USA
Address	Old Frontenac Cemetery, Frontenac, Minnesota	
Spouse		

Family Group Record George Wood Garrard & Virginia Hoffman

Husband	George Wood Garrard	
Born	18 Aug 1863	Peekskill, Westchester, New York, USA
Christened		
Died	25 Mar 1928	
Buried	Mar 1928	Frontenac, Goodhue, Minnesota, USA
Address	Old Frontenac Cemetery, Frontenac, Minnesota	
Father	Brevet Brigadier General Israel Ludlow Garrard (1825-1901)	
Mother	Catherine (Kate) Wood (1827-1867)	
Marriage	31 Oct 1889	Manhattan, New York, New York, USA

Wife	Virginia Colden Hoffman	
Born	27 Feb 1864	New York, New York, New York, USA
Christened		
Died	21 Feb 1961	
Buried	26 Feb 1961	Frontenac, Goodhue, Minnesota, USA
Father	Lindley Murray Hoffman (1832-1897)	
Mother	Margaret Leggett Mott (1818-1888)	

Children

1	F	Beulah Murray Garrard	
	Born	7 Jan 1893	Tonawanda, Erie, New York, USA
	Christened	17 Aug 1902	Frontenac, Goodhue, Minnesota, USA
	Address	Christ Episcopal Church, Old Frontenac, Minnesota	
	Died	1965	Hampstead, London, , England
	Buried		
	Spouse	Major Leonard Charles Beecroft (1887-1953)	Abt 1922

2	F	Evelyn Stuart Garrard	
	Born	21 Jul 1895	Frontenac, Goodhue, Minnesota, USA
	Christened	17 Aug 1902	Frontenac, Goodhue, Minnesota, USA
	Address	Christ Episcopal Church, Old Frontenac, Minnesota	
	Died	2 Feb 1991	
	Buried	Feb 1991	Arlington, Arlington, Virginia, USA
	Address	Arlington National Cemetery, Arlington, Virginia	
	Spouse	Lewis Hans Starnes (-)	22 Apr 1915 - Frontenac, Goodhue, Minnesota, USA
	Spouse	Lieutenant Emanuel Chester Beck (Abt 1897-)	7 Nov 1927 - Pensacola, Escambia, Florida, USA

3	F	Catherine Wood Garrard	
	Born	15 Dec 1897	Frontenac, Goodhue, Minnesota, USA
	Christened	17 Aug 1902	Frontenac, Goodhue, Minnesota, USA
	Address	Christ Episcopal Church, Old Frontenac, Minnesota	
	Died	8 Apr 1968	
	Buried	Apr 1968	Frontenac, Goodhue, Minnesota, USA
	Address	Old Frontenac Cemetery, Frontenac, Minnesota	
	Spouse	Vice Admiral Frederick William McMahon (1898-1986)	
	Marr. Date	23 Jun 1923 - Los Angeles, Los Angeles, California, USA	

Family Group Record Dr. Lewis Hector Garrard & Florence Van Vleit

Husband	Dr. Lewis Hector Garrard	
Born	15 Jun 1829	Cincinnati, Hamilton, Ohio, USA
Christened		
Died	7 Jul 1887	Lakewood, Chautauqua, New York, USA
Cause of Death	paralysis	
Buried	9 Jul 1887	Cincinnati, Hamilton, Ohio, USA
Address	Spring Grove Cemetary, Cincinnati, Ohio	
Father	Jeptha Dudley Garrard (1802-1837)	
Mother	Sarah Bella Ludlow (1802-1882)	
Marriage	22 Oct 1862	

Wife	Florence Minerva Van Vliet	
Born	1844	Charlotte, Chittenden, Vermont, USA
Christened		
Died	2 Oct 1897	Bellport, Suffolk, New York, USA
Cause of Death	heart failure	
Buried	6 Oct 1897	Cincinnati, Hamilton, Ohio, USA
Address	Spring Grove Cemetary, Cincinnati, Ohio	
Father	Deacon Eli Van Vliet (1817-1874)	
Mother	Jane Walling (1821-)	

Children		
1	M	Frederick Garrard
Born	10 Aug 1863	Frontenac, Goodhue, Minnesota, USA
Christened		
Died	10 Aug 1863	Frontenac, Goodhue, Minnesota, USA
Buried	Aug 1863	Frontenac, Goodhue, Minnesota, USA
Spouse		
2	M	Winfred Garrard
Born	21 Apr 1865	Frontenac, Goodhue, Minnesota, USA
Christened		
Died	15 Nov 1869	Frontenac, Goodhue, Minnesota, USA
Cause of Death	diphtheria or scalet fever	
Buried	Nov 1869	Frontenac, Goodhue, Minnesota, USA
Address	Old Frontenac Cemetery, Frontenac, Minnesota	
Spouse		
3	F	Edith Garrard
AKA	Auny, Onie	
Born	7 Jun 1867	Frontenac, Goodhue, Minnesota, USA
Christened		
Died	12 Sep 1953	Old Fort, McDowell, North Carolina, USA
Buried	15 Sep 1953	Menomonie, Dunn, Wisconsin, USA
Address	Evergreen Cemetery, Menomonie, Wisconsin	
Spouse	Thomas Blair Wilson Jr. (1864-1936)	
Marr. Date	7 Jun 1906 - Menomonie, Dunn, Wisconsin, USA	

Family Group Record Dr. Lewis Hector Garrard & Florence Van Vleit

Children (cont.)			
4	**M**	**Van Vliet Garrard**	
Born	3 Sep 1869	Frontenac, Goodhue, Minnesota, USA	
Christened			
Died	5 Nov 1869	Frontenac, Goodhue, Minnesota, USA	
Cause of Death	diphtheria or scarlet fever		
Buried	Nov 1869	Frontenac, Goodhue, Minnesota, USA	
Address	Old Frontenac Cemetery, Frontenac, Minnesota		
Spouse			
5	**F**	**Anna Knapp Garrard**	
Born	13 Jun 1874	Lake City, Wabasha, Minnesota, USA	
Christened			
Died	31 Aug 1954	Frontenac, Goodhue, Minnesota, USA	
Buried	Sep 1954	Menomonie, Dunn, Wisconsin, USA	
Address	Evergreen Cemetery, Menomonie, Wisconsin		
Spouse	Paul Carlton Wilson (1869-1950)		
Marr. Date	26 Feb 1902 - Cincinnati, Hamilton, Ohio, USA		

Husband	Brevet Brigadier General Jeptha Dudley Garrard	
AKA	Colonel	
Born	21 Apr 1836	Cincinnati, Hamilton, Ohio, USA
Christened		
Died	16 Dec 1915	Cincinnati, Hamilton, Ohio, USA
Cause of Death	angina pectoris	
Buried	20 Dec 1915	Cincinnati, Hamilton, Ohio, USA
Address	Spring Grove Cemetary, Cincinnati, Ohio	
Father	Jeptha Dudley Garrard (1802-1837)	
Mother	Sarah Bella Ludlow (1802-1882)	
Marriage	4 Oct 1864	Auburn, Cayuga, New York, USA

Wife	Anna R. Knapp	
Born	1830	Auburn, Cayuga, New York, USA
Christened		
Died	18 May 1887	Cincinnati, Hamilton, Ohio, USA
Cause of Death	uraemia	
Buried	21 May 1887	Cincinnati, Hamilton, Ohio, USA
Address	Spring Grove Cemetary, Cincinnati, Ohio	
Father	Jehu Knapp (-)	
Mother	Louisa J. Vanderheyden (-)	

Children

Family Group Record   Johann Gerken # 1 & Margaretta Wichern

Husband	Johann Gerken # 1	
Born	12 Dec 1824	Mulsum, , , Hanover
Christened		
Died	19 Sep 1871	Frontenac, Goodhue, Minnesota, USA
Buried	Sep 1871	Frontenac, Goodhue, Minnesota, USA
Address	Old Frontenac Cemetery, Frontenac, Minnesota	
Father	Jost Gerken (-)	
Mother	Alheit Meyer (-)	
Marriage	9 May 1862	Hanover, Lower Saxony, Prussia

Wife	Margaretta E. Wichern	
Born	1 Jun 1833	Mulsum, Hanover, Lower Saxony, Prussia
Christened		
Died	22 Mar 1916	Frontenac, Goodhue, Minnesota, USA
Buried	Mar 1916	Frontenac, Goodhue, Minnesota, USA
Address	Old Frontenac Cemetery, Frontenac, Minnesota	
Father	Carston Wichern Sr (1803-1892)	
Mother	Anna Wiebusch (1807-1846)	
Other Spouse	John Gerken # 2 (1821-1900)	Abt 1875 - Frontenac, Goodhue, Minnesota, USA

Children		
1 M	Joseph Gerken	
AKA	John Gercken	
Born	Jul 1863	Hanover, Lower Saxony, Prussia
Christened		
Died	1938	, Goodhue, Minnesota, USA
Buried	1938	Frontenac, Goodhue, Minnesota, USA
Address	Old Frontenac Cemetery, Frontenac, Minnesota	
Spouse	Mary Dammann (1876-1952)	3 Jun 1897 - Frontenac, Goodhue, Minnesota, USA

Family Group Record John Gerken # 2 & Anna Gerken

Husband	John Gerken # 2	
Born	22 Apr 1821	, , , Hanover
Christened		
Died	2 Mar 1900	Frontenac, Goodhue, Minnesota, USA
Buried	Mar 1900	Frontenac, Goodhue, Minnesota, USA
Address	Old Frontenac Cemetery, Frontenac, Minnesota	
Father	Gerken (-)	
Mother	Anna (-)	
Marriage	Abt 1842	, , , Hanover
Other Spouse	Margaretta E. Wichern (1833-1916)	Abt 1875 - Frontenac, Goodhue, Minnesota, USA

Wife	Anna	
Born	Abt 1821	, ; , Hanover
Christened		
Died	Abt 1860	, , , Hanover
Buried		

Children		
1 F	Rebecca Gerken	
Born	1844	, , , Hanover
Christened		
Died	19 Jun 1898	Red Wing, Goodhue, Minnesota, USA
Buried		
Spouse	Johann C. Friedericks (1840-1908)	Abt 1865 - Frontenac, Goodhue, Minnesota, USA

Family Group Record   John Gerken # 2 & Margaretta Wichern

Husband	John Gerken # 2	
Born	22 Apr 1821	, , , Hanover
Christened		
Died	2 Mar 1900	Frontenac, Goodhue, Minnesota, USA
Buried	Mar 1900	Frontenac, Goodhue, Minnesota, USA
Address	Old Frontenac Cemetery, Frontenac, Minnesota	
Father	Gerken (-)	
Mother	Anna (-)	
Marriage	Abt 1875	Frontenac, Goodhue, Minnesota, USA
Other Spouse	Anna (Abt 1821-Abt 1860)	Abt 1842 - , , , Hanover

Wife	Margaretta E. Wichern	
Born	1 Jun 1833	Mulsum, Hanover, Lower Saxony, Prussia
Christened		
Died	22 Mar 1916	Frontenac, Goodhue, Minnesota, USA
Buried	Mar 1916	Frontenac, Goodhue, Minnesota, USA
Address	Old Frontenac Cemetery, Frontenac, Minnesota	
Father	Carston Wichern Sr (1803-1892)	
Mother	Anna Wiebusch (1807-1846)	
Other Spouse	Johann Gerken # 1 (1824-1871)	9 May 1862 - Hanover, Lower Saxony, Prussia

Children	

91

Family Group Record Hans Petter Gulbrandsen (Gilbertson) & Linas Caroline Nilsdatter

Husband	Hans Petter Gulbrandsen (Gilbertson)	
AKA	Peter Gilbertson	
Born	23 Jul 1859	Aker, Christiania, Akershus, Norway
Christened	18 Sep 1859	Vestre Aker Parish, Akershus, Oslo County, Norway
Died	22 Jul 1910	Chippewa Falls, Chippewa, Wisconsin, USA
Cause of Death	burns from powder explosion at quarry	
Buried	26 Jul 1910	Frontenac, Goodhue, Minnesota, USA
Address	Old Frontenac Cemetery, Frontenac, Minnesota	
Father	Gulbrand Olsen (1815-1901)	
Mother	Petroline Larsdatter (1828-Cir 1897)	
Marriage	22 May 1883	Red Wing, Goodhue, Minnesota, USA

Wife	Linas Caroline Nilsdatter (Nielsen)	
AKA	Lina	
Born	28 Mar 1860	, , , Norway
Christened		
Died	15 Mar 1929	Red Wing, Goodhue, Minnesota, USA
Cause of Death	heart attack	
Buried	18 Mar 1929	Frontenac, Goodhue, Minnesota, USA
Address	Old Frontenac Cemetery, Frontenac, Minnesota	
Father	Nils Erickson (-)	
Mother	Karen Andersdatter (-)	

Children		
1 M	Hjalmer (Elmer) Cornelius Gilbertson	
AKA	Hjalmer	
Born	1 Jan 1884	Frontenac, Goodhue, Minnesota, USA
Christened		
Died	18 Sep 1955	Lake City, Wabasha, Minnesota, USA
Buried	21 Sep 1955	Lake City, Wabasha, Minnesota, USA
Address	Oakwood Cemetery, Lake City, MN	
Spouse	Edelia Ethel Brostrom (1889-1969)	
Marr. Date	3 Dec 1906 - Stockholm, Pepin, Wisconsin, USA	
2 F	Nettie Gilbertson	
Born	18 Jul 1887	Frontenac, Goodhue, Minnesota, USA
Christened		
Died	1889	Frontenac, Goodhue, Minnesota, USA
Buried	1889	Mass Grave, Wells Creek Cemetery
Spouse		
3 M	Arthur Henry Gilbertson	
Born	12 Feb 1889	Frontenac, Goodhue, Minnesota, USA
Christened		
Died	13 Oct 1956	Brodhead, Green, Wisconsin, USA
Buried	Oct 1956	Frontenac, Goodhue, Minnesota, USA
Address	Old Frontenac Cemetery, Frontenac, Minnesota	
Spouse	Geneva Elvira Hehr (-)	28 Nov 1911

Family Group Record Hans Petter Gulbrandsen (Gilbertson) & Linas Caroline Nilsdatter

Children (cont.)			
4	F	**Lily Gilbertson**	
Born		7 Nov 1892	Frontenac, Goodhue, Minnesota, USA
Christened			
Died		22 Dec 1929	Tacoma, Pierce, Washington, USA
Buried		Dec 1929	Tacoma, Pierce, Washington, USA
Spouse		Lars Larsen Gammersvik (1880-1969)	Cir 1917

5	F	**Edna Rose Gilbertson**	
Born		17 Feb 1894	Frontenac, Goodhue, Minnesota, USA
Christened			
Died		6 Jun 1977	Minneapolis, Hennepin, Minnesota, USA
Buried		Jun 1977	Minneapolis, Hennepin, Minnesota, USA
Address		Sunset Memorial Park Cemetery, Minneapolis, MN	
Spouse		Norman M. Wethe (1891-1977)	Cir 1907

6	F	**Linda E. Gilbertson**	
Born		10 Mar 1897	Frontenac, Goodhue, Minnesota, USA
Christened			
Died		7 Apr 1934	St. Paul, Ramsey, Minnesota, USA
Buried		Apr 1934	Frontenac, Goodhue, Minnesota, USA
Address		Old Frontenac Cemetery, Frontenac, Minnesota	
Spouse		Harry Lewis (1889-)	

7	M	**Raymond Clarence Gilbertson**	
Born		10 Mar 1897	Frontenac, Goodhue, Minnesota, USA
Christened			
Died		8 Sep 1945	Minneapolis, Hennepin, Minnesota, USA
Buried		Sep 1945	Frontenac, Goodhue, Minnesota, USA
Address		Old Frontenac Cemetery, Frontenac, Minnesota	
Spouse		Emma M. Prinze (1897-)	

Family Group Record Charles F. Gohrke & Wilhelmina D. Sepke

Husband	Charles F. Gohrke	
Born	Jan 1863	, , , Pommerania
Christened		
Died	1939	, Goodhue, Minnesota, USA
Buried	1939	Frontenac, Goodhue, Minnesota, USA
Address	Old Frontenac Cemetery, Frontenac, Minnesota	
Father	Helmuth (Herman) Gohrke (Abt 1830-)	
Mother	Marie Sophie Friedrike Christine Steffenhagen (1838-1913)	
Marriage	15 Apr 1890	Red Wing, Goodhue, Minnesota, USA

Wife	Wilhelmina D. Sepke	
AKA	Minnie	
Born	Jun 1869	Berlin, , Brandenburg, Prussia
Christened		
Died	1962	, Goodhue, Minnesota, USA
Buried	1962	Frontenac, Goodhue, Minnesota, USA
Address	Old Frontenac Cemetery, Frontenac, Minnesota	
Father	Carl Frederick Sepke (1847-1889)	
Mother	Fredericka Bietz (1849-1887)	

Children		
1	F	Lillian Maria Martha Gohrke
Born	12 Jan 1891	Frontenac, Goodhue, Minnesota, USA
Christened	19 Apr 1891	Frontenac Station, Goodhue, Minnesota, USA
Address	St. John's Ev. Lutheran Church, Frontenac Station, Minnesota	
Died	1953	
Buried	1953	Frontenac, Goodhue, Minnesota, USA
Address	Old Frontenac Cemetery, Frontenac, Minnesota	
Spouse	Did Not Marry	

2	F	Louise Wilhelmina Catherine Gohrke
AKA	Lizzy	
Born	19 Feb 1893	Frontenac, Goodhue, Minnesota, USA
Christened	21 May 1893	Florence Township, Goodhue, Minnesota, USA
Died	19 Aug 1982	, Wabasha, Minnesota, USA
Buried	Aug 1982	Frontenac, Goodhue, Minnesota, USA
Address	Old Frontenac Cemetery, Frontenac, Minnesota	
Spouse	Did Not Marry	

Family Group Record Captain Duncan Graham & Susanne 'Istag Iwin Hazahotawin' Pennishon

Husband	Captain Duncan Graham	
Born	1772	Argyllshire , , Scotland
Died	5 Dec 1847	Mendota, , Minnesota Territory
Buried	6 Dec 1847	Mendota, , Minnesota Territory
Marriage	Abt 1796	Fort Snelling, , Northwest Territory

Wife	Susanne 'Istag Iwin Hazahotawin' Pennishon	
Born	Abt 1784	Would one day be Minnesota
Died	2 Mar 1848	Mendota, , Minnesota Territory
Buried		
Father	Antoine Gregare (Giguiere) (-)	
Mother	Daughter of Wapasha 1 (-)	

Children

1	F	Mary Elizabeth Graham	
Born	15 Jul 1805	Lake Pepin, Mississippi River, Louisiana Purchase	
Died	8 Apr 1876	Elizabeth, Otter Tail, Minnesota, USA	
Buried	Apr 1876	Faribault, Rice, Minnesota, USA	
Address	Calvary Cemetery, Faribault, MN		
Spouse	Alexander Faribault (1806-1882)	1 Nov 1825 - Mendota, , Louisiana Purchase	

2	F	Lucy Nancy 'Mary' Graham	
Born	Sep 1806	Mendota, , Minnesota Territory	
Died			
Buried			
Spouse	Joseph Buisson (-)		

3	F	Jennie (Sarah) Marie Graham	
Born	Abt 1811	, , Louisiana Purchase, USA	
Died	1841	Cratt's Landing (later Wabasha), Mississippi River	
Buried			
Spouse	Oliver Cratte (1801-1884)	4 Oct 1831 - Mendota, , Louisiana Purchase	

4	F	Jane Graham	
Born	Cir 1817	Prairie du Chien, Mississippi River, Louisiana Purchase	
Died	1881	Fort Snelling, , Minnesota, USA	
Buried			
Spouse	James (Bully) Wells (1806-1864)		
Marr. Date	12 Sep 1836 - Fort Snelling, , Louisiana Purchase		

5	M	Alexander Graham	
Born	15 Oct 1821	Prairie du Chien, Mississippi River, Louisiana Purchase	
Died	1866	Faribault, Rice, Minnesota, USA	
Buried			
Spouse	Helen Penishon (1823-1845)	1842 - Mendota, , Louisiana Purchase	
Spouse	Blosoom Quaike (-)	1846	

Family Group Record Ole Olson Haga & Albertine Larsdatter Elstad

Husband	Ole Olson Haga	
Born	14 Apr 1847	Eidsvoll, Akershus, Norway
Died	17 Mar 1931	Red Wing, Goodhue, Minnesota, USA
Buried	Mar 1931	Red Wing, Goodhue, Minnesota, USA
Address	Oakwood Cemetery, Red Wing, MN	
Father	O. O. Olson (-)	
Mother	Engibor Larson (-)	
Marriage	Abt 1869	, , , Norway

Wife	Albertine Larsdatter Elstad	
Born	Apr 1850	Eidsvoll, Akershus, Norway
Died	8 Jun 1924	Red Wing, Goodhue, Minnesota, USA
Buried	Jun 1924	Red Wing, Goodhue, Minnesota, USA
Address	Oakwood Cemetery, Red Wing, MN	
Father	Lars Elstad (-)	
Mother		

Children				
1	M	Lars Haga		
Born		Jan 1875	Eidsvoll, Akershus, Norway	
2	M	Martin Haga		
Born		1880	, , , Norway	
Died		1886	, Goodhue, Minnesota, USA	
3	M	Ole Martin Haga		
Born		21 Nov 1883	Frontenac, Goodhue, Minnesota, USA	
Died		4 Mar 1969	Zumbrota, Goodhue, Minnesota, USA	
Buried		Mar 1969	Zumbrota, Goodhue, Minnesota, USA	
Address		Zumbrota Cemetery, Zumbrota, MN		
Spouse		Gena E. Landsrud (1883-1952)		
4	F	Anna May Haga		
Born		1885	Frontenac, Goodhue, Minnesota, USA	
5	F	Mathilda Amelia Haga		
Born		3 May 1889	Frontenac, Goodhue, Minnesota, USA	
Died		12 Aug 1972	Red Wing, Goodhue, Minnesota, USA	
Buried		Aug 1972	Red Wing, Goodhue, Minnesota, USA	
Address		Oakwood Cemetery, Red Wing, MN		
Spouse		Walter Ellis Smith (1889-1966)	1903 - , Goodhue, Minnesota, USA	

Family Group Record John N. Hager & Ursula Hager

Husband	John N. Hager	
Born	22 Jun 1835	, , , Bavaria
Died	25 Apr 1905	Maiden Rock, Pierce, Wisconsin, USA
Buried	Apr 1905	Maiden Rock, Pierce, Wisconsin, USA
Address	Maiden Rock Cemetery, Maiden Rock, Pierce County, Wisconsin	
Marriage	Abt 1865	, Goodhue, Minnesota, USA

Wife	Ursula	
Born	Dec 1832	, , , Bavaria
Died	1910	Maiden Rock, Pierce, Wisconsin, USA
Buried	1910	Maiden Rock, Pierce, Wisconsin, USA
Address	Maiden Rock Cemetery, Maiden Rock, Pierce County, Wisconsin	

Children		
1	F	**Justina Hager**
Born	1862	, , , Bavaria
2	M	**John F. Hager**
Born	1866	Frontenac, Goodhue, Minnesota, USA
Died	1870	Frontenac, Goodhue, Minnesota, USA
3	M	**Engelbret B. Hager**
Born	1868	
Died	1936	
Buried	1936	Maiden Rock, Pierce, Wisconsin, USA
Address	Maiden Rock Cemetery, Maiden Rock, Pierce County, Wisconsin	
4	F	**Margaret C. Hager**
Born	8 Nov 1870	Frontenac, Goodhue, Minnesota, USA
Died	3 Oct 1955	
Buried	Oct 1955	Maiden Rock, Pierce, Wisconsin, USA
Address	Maiden Rock Cemetery, Maiden Rock, Pierce County, Wisconsin	
5	M	**John F. Hager**
Born	Jan 1873	Frontenac, Goodhue, Minnesota, USA
6	M	**Charles N. (Alexander) Hager**
Born	1874	Frontenac, Goodhue, Minnesota, USA

Family Group Record Engelbert Haller & Margaretha Katzenberger

Husband	Engelbert Haller	
Born	1832	Oberteuringen, Bodensee, Wurttemberg
Christened		
Died	27 Jun 1890	, Ramsey, Minnesota, USA
Buried	Jun 1890	St. Paul, Ramsey, Minnesota, USA
Address	Calvary Cemetery, St. Paul, Minnesota	
Marriage	4 Nov 1865	St. Paul, Ramsey, Minnesota, USA

Wife	Margaretha Grace Katzenberger	
Born	21 May 1844	Mailes, , Königreich Bayern
Christened		
Died	29 Dec 1869	Frontenac, Goodhue, Minnesota, USA
Buried	31 Dec 1869	Frontenac, Goodhue, Minnesota, USA
Address	Old Frontenac Cemetery, Frontenac, Minnesota	
Father	Michel Katzenberger (1806-Bef 1856)	
Mother	Dorothea Shale (1815-1887)	

Children		
1 F	Caroline G. Haller	
AKA	Carrie	
Born	Feb 1868	Frontenac, Goodhue, Minnesota, USA
Christened		
Died	5 Oct 1949	St. Paul, Ramsey, Minnesota, USA
Buried		
Spouse	Max Wittman (1867-1932)	28 Jun 1898 - St. Paul, Ramsey, Minnesota, USA
2 M	Alfred E. Haller	
Born	Feb 1869	Frontenac, Goodhue, Minnesota, USA
Christened		
Died	28 May 1953	St. Paul, Ramsey, Minnesota, USA
Buried	May 1953	St. Paul, Ramsey, Minnesota, USA
Address	Calvary Cemetery, St. Paul, Minnesota	
Spouse	Philomena Lauer (1874-)	Abt 1902

Family Group Record Valentini Hassemer & Margaretha Kollsch

Husband	Valentini Hassemer	
Born		
Christened		
Died		
Buried		
Marriage		

Wife	Margaretha Kollsch	
Born	Dec 1811	, , Hessen-Darmstadt
Christened		
Died	8 Feb 1896	
Buried	Feb 1896	Bloomer, Chippewa, Wisconsin, USA
Address	Saint Catherine Cemetery, Bloomer, WI	

Children

1 M Nicholas John Hassemer

Born	8 Apr 1835	, Dieburger, Hessen-Darmstadt
Christened	10 Apr 1835	Gau-Algesheim, Rheinhessen, Hessen-Darmstadt
Address	KATHOLISCH, GAU-ALGESHEIM, RHEINHESSEN, Hesse-Darmstadt	
Died	29 Jan 1898	Red Wing, Goodhue, Minnesota, USA
Buried	31 Jan 1898	Red Wing, Goodhue, Minnesota, USA
Address	Calvary Cemetery, Red Wing, Minnesota	
Spouse	Anna Francis Krause (1841-1897)	Abt 1861 - , Goodhue, Minnesota, USA

2 M John Hassemer

Born	13 Jul 1837	, Rheinhessen, Hessen-Darmstadt
Christened	14 Jul 1837	Gau-Algesheim, Rheinhessen, Hessen-Darmstadt
Died	18 Apr 1917	Bloomer, Chippewa, Wisconsin, USA
Buried	Apr 1917	Bloomer, Chippewa, Wisconsin, USA
Address	St. Paul & St. Jude Catholic Cemetery, Bloomer, WI	
Spouse		

Family Group Record Nicholas John Hassemer & Anna Francis Krause

Husband	Nicholas John Hassemer	
Born	8 Apr 1835	, Dieburger, Hessen-Darmstadt
Died	29 Jan 1898	Red Wing, Goodhue, Minnesota, USA
Buried	31 Jan 1898	Red Wing, Goodhue, Minnesota, USA
Address	Calvary Cemetery, Red Wing, Minnesota	
Father	Valentini Hassemer (-)	
Mother	Margaretha Kollsch (1811-1896)	
Marriage	Abt 1861	, Goodhue, Minnesota, USA

Wife	Anna Francis Krause	
Born	27 Dec 1841	, , , Bavaria
Died	30 Jan 1897	Red Wing, Goodhue, Minnesota, USA
Buried	Feb 1897	Red Wing, Goodhue, Minnesota, USA
Address	Calvary Cemetery, Red Wing, Minnesota	

Children		
1 **F**	**Anna Francis Hassemer**	
Born	Apr 1862	, Goodhue, Minnesota, USA
Died	1933	, Dakota, Minnesota, USA
Buried	1933	Hastings, Dakota, Minnesota, USA
Address	St. Elizabeth Cemetery, Hastings, MN	
Spouse	Mathias Berns (-)	
2 **F**	**Kathryn Hassemer**	
Born	1864	, Goodhue, Minnesota, USA
Died		
Buried		
Spouse	William Ninnov (-)	
3 **F**	**Margaretha Hassemer**	
Born	10 Mar 1865	, Goodhue, Minnesota, USA
Died	23 Dec 1867	, Goodhue, Minnesota, USA
Buried	Dec 1867	Red Wing, Goodhue, Minnesota, USA
Address	Calvary Cemetery, Red Wing, Minnesota	
Spouse		
4 **F**	**Mary L. Hassemer**	
Born	1869	Hay Creek Township, Goodhue, Minnesota, USA
Died	4 Sep 1917	Minneapolis, Hennepin, Minnesota, USA
Buried		
Spouse	Isadore J. Chiquet (1862-)	7 Jun 1893 - Red Wing, Goodhue, Minnesota, USA
5 **F**	**Teresa Hassemer**	
Born	1877	, Goodhue, Minnesota, USA
Died		
Buried		
Spouse		

Family Group Record Carl Martin Hausman & Katherine Hausman

Husband	Carl Martin Hausman	
Born	Nov 1823	, , , Wurttemberg
Died		
Buried		
Marriage	Abt 1852	Tonawanda, Erie, New York, USA

Wife	Katherine	
Born	Sep 1826	, , , Germany
Died		
Buried		

Children			
1	F	Eva Hausman	
Born		Nov 1852	Tonawanda, Erie, New York, USA
Died			
Buried			
Spouse			
2	F	Charlotte Hausman	
Born		1853	Albany, Albany, New York, USA
Died			
Buried			
Spouse			
3	M	Henry Hausman	
Born		1854	Albany, Albany, New York, USA
Died			
Buried			
Spouse			
4	M	Gottlieb Hausman	
Born		1856	Albany, Albany, New York, USA
Died			
Buried			
Spouse			
5	M	Edward Hausman	
Born		1858	Albany, Albany, New York, USA
Died			
Buried			
Spouse			
6	F	Catherine Hausman	
Born		1869	Tonawanda, Erie, New York, USA
Died			
Buried			
Spouse		J. W. Hoben (-)	16 Jan 1895 - Frontenac, Goodhue, Minnesota, USA

Family Group Record Ole Hawkinson & Ellen Hawkinson

Husband	Ole Hawkinson	
Born	1842	, , , Sweden
Marriage	Cir 1868	, , , Sweden

Wife	Ellen K.	
Born	3 Apr 1838	, , , Sweden
Died	1 Apr 1886	Frontenac, Goodhue, Minnesota, USA
Buried	Apr 1886	Frontenac, Goodhue, Minnesota, USA
Address	Old Frontenac Cemetery, Frontenac, Minnesota	

Children			
1	F	Mary Hawkinson	
Born		1870	, , , Sweden
2	M	Andrew Hawkinson	
Born		1873	, , , Sweden
3	M	Eddie Hawkinson	
Born		1876	, , , Sweden
4	M	Alfred Hawkinson	
Born		1879	Frontenac, Goodhue, Minnesota, USA
Died		26 Jun 1885	Frontenac, Goodhue, Minnesota, USA
Buried		Jun 1885	Frontenac, Goodhue, Minnesota, USA
Address		Old Frontenac Cemetery, Frontenac, Minnesota	

5	U	F. N. K. Hawkinson	
Born		16 Jan 1880	Frontenac, Goodhue, Minnesota, USA
Died		6 Feb 1880	Frontenac, Goodhue, Minnesota, USA

Family Group Record Charles Frederick Herder & Maria Dorothea Strenge

Husband	Charles Frederick Herder	
Born	26 Oct 1832	Magdeburg, , Saxony, Prussia
Died	3 Jul 1913	Frontenac, Goodhue, Minnesota, USA
Cause of Death	bronchia pneumonia induced by fracture	
Buried	6 Jul 1913	Frontenac, Goodhue, Minnesota, USA
Address	Old Frontenac Cemetery, Frontenac, Minnesota	
Father	Helmut Christian Herder (1787-1842)	
Mother	Maria Louise Busse (1789-)	
Marriage	3 Nov 1857	, Cook, Illinois, USA

Wife	Maria Dorothea Strenge	
Born	3 Nov 1830	Woelln, Havelberg, Sachen-Anhalt, Prussia
Died	9 Feb 1910	
Buried	Feb 1910	Frontenac, Goodhue, Minnesota, USA
Address	Old Frontenac Cemetery, Frontenac, Minnesota	

Children			
1	F	Emma Hannah Herder	
Born		Nov 1857	Chicago, Cook, Illinois, USA
Died			
Buried			
Spouse		Daniel Kukuk (Kookok) (1855-1923)	16 Mar 1877 - Frontenac, Goodhue, Minnesota, USA
2	M	Frederick Louis Herder	
Born		18 Nov 1859	Frontenac, Goodhue, Minnesota, USA
Died			Red Deer, , Quebec, Canada
Buried			
Spouse		Augusta Ernestina Haling (1864-1930)	20 Sep 1888 - Rochester, Olmsted, Minnesota, USA
3	F	Caroline Herder	
Born		1862	Frontenac, Goodhue, Minnesota, USA
Died			
Buried			
Spouse		Sinki (-Bef 1910)	
4	M	William Benjamin Herder	
Born		7 Apr 1864	Frontenac, Goodhue, Minnesota, USA
Died		27 Sep 1953	Medical Lake, Spokane, Washington, USA
Buried			
Spouse		Did Not Marry	
5	M	Edward Michael Herder	
Born		Nov 1866	Frontenac, Goodhue, Minnesota, USA
Died		28 Sep 1918	, Goodhue, Minnesota, USA
Cause of Death		suicide by gun shot	
Buried		Sep 1918	Frontenac, Goodhue, Minnesota, USA
Address		Old Frontenac Cemetery, Frontenac, Minnesota	
Spouse		Mina Ovidia Ole Andreasdatter (1865-1943)	
Marr. Date		Abt 1890 - Frontenac, Goodhue, Minnesota, USA	

Children (cont.)			
6	**F**	**Emelia Herder**	
Born		1869	Frontenac, Goodhue, Minnesota, USA
Died		29 Mar 1934	, Mendocino, California, USA
Buried			
Spouse			
7	**M**	**Herman Paul Herder**	
Born		25 Jun 1874	Frontenac, Goodhue, Minnesota, USA
Died		4 Jun 1950	, Los Angeles, California, USA
Buried			
Spouse		Mary F. Anderson (-)	
8	**F**	**Lydia Herder**	
Born		28 Nov 1878	Frontenac, Goodhue, Minnesota, USA
Died		1964	
Buried			
Spouse		Rolland Anderson (1881-1940)	

Family Group Record William Hofmeister & Amilia Percig

Husband	William Hofmeister	
Born	1828	, , , Mecklenburg
Christened		
Died		
Buried		
Marriage	Abt 1854	

Wife	Amilia Percig	
Born	1834	, , , Saxe-Weimer
Christened		
Died		
Buried		

Children		
1	F	Caroline Hofmeister
Born	1855	, , Wisconsin, USA
Christened		
Died		
Buried		
Spouse		
2	M	William A. Hofmeister
Born	Oct 1858	Frontenac, Goodhue, Minnesota, USA
Christened		
Died	18 Jan 1942	St. Paul, Ramsey, Minnesota, USA
Buried		
Spouse		
3	M	Edward Hofmeister
Born	1868	Winona, Winona, Minnesota, USA
Christened		
Died		
Buried		
Spouse		

Family Group Record Casper Heinrich Huneke & Elisabeth Schulte

Husband	Casper Heinrich Huneke	
Born	27 Jun 1790	, Erwitte, Westfalen, Prussia
Christened		
Died		, , , Prussia
Buried		
Marriage	31 Oct 1821	, Erwitte, Westfalen, Prussia

Wife	Anna Mar. Cathr. Elisabeth Schulte	
AKA	Eliz Schulenberg	
Born	1 Feb 1796	, Erwitte, Westfalen, Prussia
Christened	3 Feb 1796	, Erwitte, Westfalen, Prussia
Died	17 Sep 1850	, Erwitte, Westfalen, Prussia
Buried		
Father	Gaudens Gaudentius Schulte (Cir 1760-)	
Mother	Eva Gertrude Poepelbaum (Cir 1760-)	

Children		
1 **M**	**Frans Caspar Adolph Huneke**	
Born	7 Dec 1820	Vollinghausen, Erwitt, Westfalen, Prussia
Christened	9 Dec 1820	, Erwitte, Westfalen, Prussia
Address	Sankt Laurentius Roemisch-Katholische Church, Erwitte, Westfalen, Prussia	
Died	3 Jan 1822	Vollinghausen, Erwitt, Westfalen, Prussia
Buried		
Spouse		
2 **F**	**Anna Maria Elizabeth Huneke**	
Born	30 Nov 1822	Vollinghausen, Erwitt, Westfalen, Prussia
Christened	1 Dec 1822	, Erwitte, Westfalen, Prussia
Address	Sankt Laurentius Roemisch-Katholische Church, Erwitte, Westfalen, Prussia	
Died		
Buried		
Spouse		
3 **M**	**Joseph Caspar Theodore Huneke**	
Born	10 Nov 1824	Vollinghausen, Erwitt, Westfalen, Prussia
Christened	12 Nov 1824	, Erwitte, Westfalen, Prussia
Address	Sankt Laurentius Roemisch-Katholische Church, Erwitte, Westfalen, Prussia	
Died		
Buried		
Spouse	Marie Sibille Hense (-)	4 Mar 1857 - , Erwitte, Westfalen, Prussia
4 **M**	**Frans Casparus Huneke**	
Born	1 Jan 1827	Vollinghausen, Erwitt, Westfalen, Prussia
Christened	2 Jan 1827	, Erwitte, Westfalen, Prussia
Address	Sankt Laurentius Roemisch-Katholische Church, Erwitte, Westfalen, Prussia	
Died	1 Jul 1830	Vollinghausen, Erwitt, Westfalen, Prussia
Buried		
Spouse		

Family Group Record Casper Heinrich Huneke & Elisabeth Schulte

Children (cont.)			
5	**F**	**Maria Theresia Antonette Huneke**	
Born		9 May 1829	Vollinghausen, Erwitt, Westfalen, Prussia
Christened		10 May 1829	, Erwitte, Westfalen, Prussia
Address		Sankt Laurentius Roemisch-Katholische Church, Erwitte, Westfalen, Prussia	
Died			
Buried			
Spouse			
6	**M**	**Henrich Bernhard Hunecke**	
AKA		Henry, Huneke	
Born		22 Sep 1831	Vollinghausen, Erwitt, Westfalen, Prussia
Christened		23 Sep 1831	, Erwitte, Westfalen, Prussia
Address		Sankt Laurentius Roemisch-Katholische Church, Erwitte, Westfalen, Prussia	
Died		30 Nov 1907	Frontenac, Goodhue, Minnesota, USA
Buried		2 Dec 1907	Frontenac, Goodhue, Minnesota, USA
Address		Old Frontenac Cemetery, Frontenac, Minnesota	
Spouse		Louisa Margaret Henrietta Bremer (1829-1893)	
Marr. Date		1856 - Winona, Wabashaw County, Territory of Minnesota	
Spouse		Mary Ahlers (1844-1925)	14 Sep 1896 - Red Wing, Goodhue, Minnesota, USA
7	**M**	**Johann Bernhard Huneke**	
Born		Jul 1834	Vollinghausen, Erwitt, Westfalen, Prussia
Christened		6 Jul 1834	, Erwitte, Westfalen, Prussia
Address		Sankt Laurentius Roemisch-Katholische Church, Erwitte, Westfalen, Prussia	
Died		20 Dec 1905	Florence Township, Goodhue, Minnesota, USA
Buried			
Spouse		Caroline Friederika Dorothea Bremer (1835-1901)	
Marr. Date		27 Dec 1859 - Frontenac, Goodhue, Minnesota, USA	
8	**F**	**Franciscus Huneke**	
Born		12 Aug 1837	Vollinghausen, Erwitt, Westfalen, Prussia
Christened		13 Aug 1837	, Erwitte, Westfalen, Prussia
Address		Sankt Laurentius Roemisch-Katholische Church, Erwitte, Westfalen, Prussia	
Died		19 May 1838	Vollinghausen, Erwitt, Westfalen, Prussia
Buried			
Spouse			

Family Group Record Henrich Bernhard Hunecke & Louisa M. H. Bremer

Husband	Henrich Bernhard Hunecke	
AKA	Henry, Huneke	
Born	22 Sep 1831	Vollinghausen, Erwitt, Westfalen, Prussia
Christened	23 Sep 1831	, Erwitte, Westfalen, Prussia
Address	Sankt Laurentius Roemisch-Katholische Church, Erwitte, Westfalen, Prussia	
Died	30 Nov 1907	Frontenac, Goodhue, Minnesota, USA
Buried	2 Dec 1907	Frontenac, Goodhue, Minnesota, USA
Address	Old Frontenac Cemetery, Frontenac, Minnesota	
Father	Casper Heinrich Huneke (1790-)	
Mother	Anna Mar. Cathr. Elisabeth Schulte (1796-1850)	
Marriage	1856	Winona, Wabashaw County, Territory of Minnesota
Other Spouse	Mary Ahlers (1844-1925)	14 Sep 1896 - Red Wing, Goodhue, Minnesota, USA

Wife	Louisa Margaret Henrietta Bremer	
AKA	Elizabeth, Lizzie	
Born	17 Mar 1829	, , , Mecklenburg
Christened		
Died	17 Sep 1893	Frontenac, Goodhue, Minnesota, USA
Buried	Sep 1893	Frontenac, Goodhue, Minnesota, USA
Address	Old Frontenac Cemetery, Frontenac, Minnesota	
Father	Joachim Christian Friedrich Bremer (1804-1874)	
Mother	Sophia Christina Elizabeth Schueler (1808-1848)	

Children

1	F	Maria Caroline (Lena) Hunecke	
AKA		Lena	
Born		19 May 1858	Red Wing, Goodhue, Territory of Minnesota
Christened			
Died		3 Nov 1923	Synnes, Stevens, Minnesota, USA
Buried		Nov 1923	Morris, Stevens, Minnesota, USA
Address		Calvary Cemetery, Morris, Stevens County, Minnesota	
Spouse		Joseph William M. Sauter (1857-1930)	6 Jun 1882 - Red Wing, Goodhue, Minnesota, USA

2	F	Elizabeth Marie Hunecke	
AKA		Lizzie	
Born		2 Feb 1860	Frontenac, Goodhue, Minnesota, USA
Christened			
Died		16 Oct 1869	Frontenac, Goodhue, Minnesota, USA
Buried		Oct 1869	Frontenac, Goodhue, Minnesota, USA
Address		Old Frontenac Cemetery, Frontenac, Minnesota	
Spouse			

3	F	Caroline Marie Hunecke	
Born		4 Dec 1861	Frontenac, Goodhue, Minnesota, USA
Christened			
Died		Dec 1861	Frontenac, Goodhue, Minnesota, USA
Buried		Dec 1861	Frontenac, Goodhue, Minnesota, USA
Spouse			

Family Group Record Henrich Bernhard Hunecke & Louisa M. H. Bremer

Children (cont.)				
4	**F**	**Louisa Henrietta Hunecke**		
Born		Jul 1863	Frontenac, Goodhue, Minnesota, USA	
Christened				
Died		28 Nov 1934	Red Wing, Goodhue, Minnesota, USA	
Buried		1 Dec 1934	Frontenac, Goodhue, Minnesota, USA	
Address		Old Frontenac Cemetery, Frontenac, Minnesota		
Spouse		John Brunner (1855-1935)	24 Jun 1890 - Frontenac, Goodhue, Minnesota, USA	
5	**M**	**Edward Frederick Hunecke**		
Born		16 Jul 1865	Frontenac, Goodhue, Minnesota, USA	
Christened				
Died		16 Nov 1937	Frontenac, Goodhue, Minnesota, USA	
Buried		18 Nov 1937	Frontenac, Goodhue, Minnesota, USA	
Address		Old Frontenac Cemetery, Frontenac, Minnesota		
Spouse		Catherina (Katie) Poppe (1865-1943)		
Marr. Date		28 Sep 1892 - Frontenac, Goodhue, Minnesota, USA		
6	**M**	**Frederick H. Hunecke**		
Born		3 Mar 1868	Frontenac, Goodhue, Minnesota, USA	
Christened				
Died		23 Sep 1868	Frontenac, Goodhue, Minnesota, USA	
Buried		Sep 1868	Frontenac, Goodhue, Minnesota, USA	
Address		Old Frontenac Cemetery, Frontenac, Minnesota		
Spouse				

Family Group Record Henrich Bernhard Hunecke & Mary Ahlers

Husband	Henrich Bernhard Hunecke	
AKA	Henry, Huneke	
Born	22 Sep 1831	Vollinghausen, Erwitt, Westfalen, Prussia
Christened	23 Sep 1831	, Erwitte, Westfalen, Prussia
Address	Sankt Laurentius Roemisch-Katholische Church, Erwitte, Westfalen, Prussia	
Died	30 Nov 1907	Frontenac, Goodhue, Minnesota, USA
Buried	2 Dec 1907	Frontenac, Goodhue, Minnesota, USA
Address	Old Frontenac Cemetery, Frontenac, Minnesota	
Father	Casper Heinrich Huneke (1790-)	
Mother	Anna Mar. Cathr. Elisabeth Schulte (1796-1850)	
Marriage	14 Sep 1896	Red Wing, Goodhue, Minnesota, USA
Other Spouse	Louisa Margaret Henrietta Bremer (1829-1893)	
Date	1856 - Winona, Wabashaw County, Territory of Minnesota	

Wife	Mary Ahlers	
AKA	Ahlens, Allers	
Born	Jan 1844	, , , Germany
Christened		
Died	Jun 1925	
Buried		
Other Spouse	August Bucholze (-)	13 Jul 1857 - Red Wing, Goodhue, Minnesota, USA

Children

Family Group Record Johann Bernhard Huneke & Caroline Bremer

Husband	Johann Bernhard Huneke	
Born	Jul 1834	Vollinghausen, Erwitt, Westfalen, Prussia
Christened	6 Jul 1834	, Erwitte, Westfalen, Prussia
Address	Sankt Laurentius Roemisch-Katholische Church, Erwitte, Westfalen, Prussia	
Died	20 Dec 1905	Florence Township, Goodhue, Minnesota, USA
Buried		
Father	Casper Heinrich Huneke (1790-)	
Mother	Anna Mar. Cathr. Elisabeth Schulte (1796-1850)	
Marriage	27 Dec 1859	Frontenac, Goodhue, Minnesota, USA

Wife	Caroline Friederika Dorothea Bremer	
Born	1 Mar 1835	, , , Mecklenburg
Christened		
Died	5 Nov 1901	Frontenac, Goodhue, Minnesota, USA
Buried		
Father	Joachim Christian Friedrich Bremer (1804-1874)	
Mother	Sophia Christina Elizabeth Schueler (1808-1848)	

Children

Family Group Record Edward Frederick Hunecke & Catherina Poppe

Husband	Edward Frederick Hunecke	
Born	16 Jul 1865	Frontenac, Goodhue, Minnesota, USA
Christened		
Died	16 Nov 1937	Frontenac, Goodhue, Minnesota, USA
Buried	18 Nov 1937	Frontenac, Goodhue, Minnesota, USA
Address	Old Frontenac Cemetery, Frontenac, Minnesota	
Father	Henrich Bernhard Hunecke (1831-1907)	
Mother	Louisa Margaret Henrietta Bremer (1829-1893)	
Marriage	28 Sep 1892	Frontenac, Goodhue, Minnesota, USA

Wife	Catherina (Katie) Poppe	
AKA	Katie	
Born	14 Nov 1865	New York, New York, New York, USA
Christened		
Died	5 Dec 1943	Lake City, Wabasha, Minnesota, USA
Cause of Death	chronic myocarditis	
Buried	7 Dec 1943	Frontenac, Goodhue, Minnesota, USA
Address	Old Frontenac Cemetery, Frontenac, Minnesota	
Father	Nicolaus (Claus) Deidrich Poppe (1822-1871)	
Mother	Rebecca Wilshusen (1834-1914)	

Children		
1	M	Edwin Martin Diedrich Hunecke
Born	19 Jan 1894	Frontenac, Goodhue, Minnesota, USA
Christened	22 Apr 1894	Frontenac Station, Goodhue, Minnesota, USA
Address	St. John's Ev. Lutheran Church, Frontenac Station, Minnesota	
Died	12 Nov 1977	Red Wing, Goodhue, Minnesota, USA
Buried	Nov 1977	Red Wing, Goodhue, Minnesota, USA
Address	St. John's Evangelical Cemetery, Red Wing, Minnesota	
Spouse	Ruth Marie Brenn (1899-1989)	2 Jun 1920 - Frontenac, Goodhue, Minnesota, USA
2	M	Walter Peter Hunecke
Born	26 Apr 1896	Florence Township, Goodhue, Minnesota, USA
Christened	26 Jun 1896	Frontenac Station, Goodhue, Minnesota, USA
Address	St. John's Ev. Lutheran Church, Frontenac Station, Minnesota	
Died	2 Jul 1986	Frontenac, Goodhue, Minnesota, USA
Cause of Death	luekemia	
Buried	5 Jul 1986	Frontenac, Goodhue, Minnesota, USA
Address	Old Frontenac Cemetery, Frontenac, Minnesota	
Spouse	Evelyn Gladys Peniston (1903-1957)	Abt 1929 - , Goodhue, Minnesota, USA
3	M	Arthur Louis Hunecke
Born	15 Feb 1903	Frontenac, Goodhue, Minnesota, USA
Christened	3 Apr 1903	Frontenac Station, Goodhue, Minnesota, USA
Address	St. John's Ev. Lutheran Church, Frontenac Station, Minnesota	
Died	Bef Dec 1903	Frontenac, Goodhue, Minnesota, USA
Cause of Death	pneumonia	
Buried	Bef Dec 1903	Frontenac, Goodhue, Minnesota, USA
Address	Old Frontenac Cemetery, Frontenac, Minnesota	
Spouse		

Children (cont.)			
4	**M**	**Allan Harold Carl Hunecke**	
Born		20 Aug 1907	Frontenac, Goodhue, Minnesota, USA
Christened		22 Sep 1907	Frontenac Station, Goodhue, Minnesota, USA
Address		St. John's Ev. Lutheran Church, Frontenac Station, Minnesota	
Died		13 Oct 1992	Red Wing, Goodhue, Minnesota, USA
Buried		16 Oct 1992	Frontenac, Goodhue, Minnesota, USA
Address		Old Frontenac Cemetery, Frontenac, Minnesota	
Spouse		Did Not Marry	

Family Group Record Edwin Martin Diedrich Hunecke & Ruth Brenn

Husband	Edwin Martin Diedrich Hunecke	
Born	19 Jan 1894	Frontenac, Goodhue, Minnesota, USA
Christened	22 Apr 1894	Frontenac Station, Goodhue, Minnesota, USA
Address	St. John's Ev. Lutheran Church, Frontenac Station, Minnesota	
Died	12 Nov 1977	Red Wing, Goodhue, Minnesota, USA
Buried	Nov 1977	Red Wing, Goodhue, Minnesota, USA
Address	St. John's Evangelical Cemetery, Red Wing, Minnesota	
Father	Edward Frederick Hunecke (1865-1937)	
Mother	Catherina (Katie) Poppe (1865-1943)	
Marriage	2 Jun 1920	Frontenac, Goodhue, Minnesota, USA

Wife	Ruth Marie Brenn	
Born	26 Jun 1899	Red Wing, Goodhue, Minnesota, USA
Christened		
Died	25 Aug 1989	Red Wing, Goodhue, Minnesota, USA
Buried	Aug 1989	Red Wing, Goodhue, Minnesota, USA
Address	St. John's Evangelical Cemetery, Red Wing, Minnesota	
Father	George W. Brenn (1855-1928)	
Mother	Mathelda Christine Bertha Bracher (1865-)	

Children		
1 M	Corp Robert Arthur Hunecke	
Born	27 May 1921	Frontenac, Goodhue, Minnesota, USA
Christened	10 Jul 1921	Frontenac, Goodhue, Minnesota, USA
Address	Christ Episcopal Church, Old Frontenac, Minnesota	
Died	14 May 1945	Bacolod Negros, Philippines
Buried	May 1945	Philippines
Spouse		
2 M	Donald George Hunecke	
Born	24 Apr 1923	Frontenac, Goodhue, Minnesota, USA
Christened	1 Jun 1923	Lake City, Wabasha, Minnesota, USA
Address	St. Mark's Church, Lake City, MN	
Died		
Buried		
Spouse	Charlotte June Weed (1926-2015)	
Marr. Date	24 Jun 1951 - Surrey, Ward, North Dakota, USA	
3 F	Nancy Joy Hunecke	
AKA	Freeman	
Born	6 May 1937	Frontenac, Goodhue, Minnesota, USA
Christened		
Died		
Buried		
Spouse	David Henry Pomroy (1938-2013)	12 Oct 1959 - , Goodhue, Minnesota, USA
Spouse	Donald Freeman (-2005)	11 Jul 1999

Family Group Record Thomas Spencer Huntington & Frances Williamson

Husband	Thomas Spencer Huntington	
AKA	Spencer	
Born	20 Jun 1820	Hartford, Hartford, Connecticut, USA
Died	10 Oct 1896	Cincinnati, Hamilton, Ohio, USA
Buried	Oct 1896	Cincinnati, Hamilton, Ohio, USA
Address	Spring Grove Cemetary, Cincinnati, Ohio	
Father	Eleazer Huntington (-)	
Mother	Maria Hinsdale (-)	
Marriage	Dec 1848	Cincinnati, Hamilton, Ohio, USA

Wife	Frances Eliza Williamson	
Born	7 Dec 1820	Cincinnati, Hamilton, Ohio, USA
Died	12 Apr 1885	Cincinnati, Hamilton, Ohio, USA
Buried	Apr 1885	Cincinnati, Hamilton, Ohio, USA
Address	Spring Grove Cemetary, Cincinnati, Ohio	
Father	Williamson (-)	
Mother	Moriah Williamson (1779-)	

Children		
1	M	George Spencer Huntington
Born	20 Mar 1850	Cincinnati, Hamilton, Ohio, USA
2	F	Maria Frances Huntington
Born	16 Dec 1852	Cynthiana, Harrison, Kentucky, USA
3	F	Sarah Amelia Huntington
Born	20 Dec 1854	Troy, , Ohio, USA
4	F	Fannie Rawlins Huntington
Born	4 Jan 1856	Cincinnati, Hamilton, Ohio, USA
5	M	Spencer Hinsdale Huntington
Born	4 Jul 1858	Cincinnati, Hamilton, Ohio, USA
Died	26 Jun 1867	Batavia, , Ohio, USA

Family Group Record Henry Isensee & Caroline Opperman

Husband	Henry Isensee	
Born	1833	, , Duchy of Brunswick, Prussia
Died	May 1907	, , Minnesota, USA
Marriage	Abt 1851	, , , Prussia

Wife	Caroline Opperman	
Born	1837	, , Duchy of Brunswick, Prussia
Died	Sep 1906	, , Minnesota, USA

Children		
1	F	**Helena Isensee**
Born	27 Feb 1853	Lockport, Niagara, New York, USA
Died	4 Feb 1923	, Wabasha, Minnesota, USA
Buried	Feb 1923	Belvidere Mills, Goodhue, Minnesota, USA
Address	Belvidere Union Cemetery, Belvidere Mills,, MN	
Spouse	Henry M. Burfeind (1850-1901)	Cir 1877 - , Goodhue, Minnesota, USA
2	F	**Caroline F. Isensee**
Born	Dec 1854	Frontenac, Goodhue, Minnesota, USA
Spouse	Perry George (1847-1931)	10 May 1874 - Belvidere, Goodhue, Minnesota, USA
3	F	**Fredericka B. Isensee**
Born	15 Apr 1856	Frontenac, Goodhue, Minnesota, USA
Died	30 Jun 1907	, Wabasha, Minnesota, USA
Buried	Jul 1907	Lake City, Wabasha, Minnesota, USA
Address	Lakewood Cemetery, Lake City, MN	
Spouse	Frederick William Winters (1840-1918)	16 Dec 1873 - Belvidere Mills, Goodhue, Minnesota, USA
4	M	**Henry F. Isensee**
Born	Jul 1858	Frontenac, Goodhue, Minnesota, USA
Died	16 Apr 1902	Florence Township, Goodhue, Minnesota, USA
Spouse	Dora F. Minnie Kohn (1861-1945)	6 Dec 1883 - Red Wing, Goodhue, Minnesota, USA
5	M	**Julius H. Isensee**
Born	14 Aug 1860	Frontenac, Goodhue, Minnesota, USA
Died	27 Dec 1925	Lake City, Wabasha, Minnesota, USA
Spouse	Alvina Meta Kriett (1873-1963)	15 Jun 1893 - , Wabasha, Minnesota, USA
6	F	**Mary Louisa Isensee**
Born	1864	Florence Township, Goodhue, Minnesota, USA
Died	10 Mar 1939	
Spouse	Frederick W. Kohn (1856-1931)	14 Mar 1882 - , Goodhue, Minnesota, USA

Family Group Record Hans Johnson & Gurine Pedersdatter

Husband	Hans Johnson	
Born	16 Jan 1842	Eidsvold Verk, Eidsvoll, Akershus, Norway
Christened		
Died	18 Oct 1908	, Goodhue, Minnesota, USA
Buried	Oct 1908	Red Wing, Goodhue, Minnesota, USA
Address	Oakwood Cemetery, Red Wing, MN	
Father	John Olsson (Abt 1802-1877)	
Mother	Anne Johansdatter (1810-1856)	
Marriage	3 Jan 1867	Eidsvoll, Akershus, Norway

Wife	Gurine Pedersdatter	
AKA	Gerena, Jurene, Curina, Pertersdotter	
Born	20 Dec 1845	Eidsvoll Verk, Akershus, Norway
Christened		
Died	24 Jul 1920	, Goodhue, Minnesota, USA
Buried	Jul 1920	Red Wing, Goodhue, Minnesota, USA
Address	Oakwood Cemetery, Red Wing, MN	
Father	Peder Christopherson Svensplad (-)	
Mother	Margaretha Halvorsdatter (-)	

Children

1	F	Anne Marie Hansdatter Johnson	
AKA		Mary	
Born		18 Oct 1866	Eidsvoll Verk, Akershus, Norway
Christened			
Died		22 Dec 1940	Kenyon, Goodhue, Minnesota, USA
Buried		Dec 1940	Frontenac, Goodhue, Minnesota, USA
Address		Old Frontenac Cemetery, Frontenac, Minnesota	
Spouse		Joseph John Picha (1868-1944)	25 Jun 1891 - Frontenac, Goodhue, Minnesota, USA

2	M	John Johnson	
Born		1869	Frontenac, Goodhue, Minnesota, USA
Christened			
Died		Bef 1909	, Goodhue, Minnesota, USA
Buried			
Spouse			

3	F	Lesa M. Johnson	
AKA		Lizzie	
Born		Mar 1872	Frontenac, Goodhue, Minnesota, USA
Christened			
Died		1942	Red Wing, Goodhue, Minnesota, USA
Buried		1942	Red Wing, Goodhue, Minnesota, USA
Address		Oakwood Cemetery, Red Wing, MN	
Spouse		Christian A. Rasmussen (1868-1946)	30 Apr 1901 - , Goodhue, Minnesota, USA

4	M	George Gerrard Johnson	
Born		1874	Frontenac, Goodhue, Minnesota, USA
Christened			
Died		1918	
Buried			
Spouse		Lucille E. Sullivan (1882-1968)	Abt 1905 - , , Minnesota, USA

Children (cont.)			
5	**M**	**Henry McLean Johnson**	
Born	5 Sep 1877	Frontenac, Goodhue, Minnesota, USA	
Christened	16 Dec 1879	Frontenac, Goodhue, Minnesota, USA	
Address	Christ Episcopal Church, Old Frontenac, Minnesota		
Died	1923	Red Wing, Goodhue, Minnesota, USA	
Buried	1923	Red Wing, Goodhue, Minnesota, USA	
Address	Oakwood Cemetery, Red Wing, MN		
Spouse			
6	**F**	**Maude Louise Johnson**	
Born	22 Feb 1880	Frontenac, Goodhue, Minnesota, USA	
Christened			
Died	23 Feb 1963	, Goodhue, Minnesota, USA	
Buried	26 Feb 1963	Red Wing, Goodhue, Minnesota, USA	
Address	Oakwood Cemetery, Red Wing, MN		
Spouse			
7	**F**	**Elizabeth Johnson**	
Born	Jul 1882	Frontenac, Goodhue, Minnesota, USA	
Christened			
Died			
Buried			
Spouse			
8	**F**	**Linda Edith Johnson**	
Born	26 Jul 1884	Frontenac, Goodhue, Minnesota, USA	
Christened	31 Aug 1884	Frontenac, Goodhue, Minnesota, USA	
Address	Christ Episcopal Church, Old Frontenac, Minnesota		
Died			
Buried			
Spouse			
9	**F**	**Florence Helen Johnson**	
Born	Nov 1889	Burnside, Goodhue, Minnesota, USA	
Christened	25 Dec 1889	Frontenac, Goodhue, Minnesota, USA	
Address	Christ Episcopal Church, Old Frontenac, Minnesota		
Died	4 Mar 1934	, Goodhue, Minnesota, USA	
Buried			
Spouse			

Family Group Record Michel Katzenberger & Dorothea Shale

Husband	Michel Katzenberger	
Born	1806	Mailes, , Königreich Bayern
Christened		
Died	Bef 1856	Cincinnati, Hamilton, Ohio, USA
Buried		
Marriage	Abt 1833	Mailes, , Königreich Bayern

Wife	Dorothea Shale	
AKA	Sarah	
Born	17 Sep 1815	Mailes, , Königreich Bayern
Christened		
Died	18 Mar 1887	Frontenac, Goodhue, Minnesota, USA
Buried	Mar 1887	Frontenac, Goodhue, Minnesota, USA
Address	Old Frontenac Cemetery, Frontenac, Minnesota	
Father	Shale (-)	
Mother		
Other Spouse	Jakob Schneider (1831-1893)	May 1856 - Cincinnati, Hamilton, Ohio, USA

Children			
1	M	Balthasar Katzenberger	
Born		1834	Mailes, , Königreich Bayern
Christened			
Died			
Buried			
Spouse		Sarah (1829-)	
2	M	Johan Adam Katzenberger	
Born		28 Nov 1836	Mailes, , Königreich Bayern
Christened			
Died		8 Jul 1917	Sprinfield, Brown, Minnesota, USA
Buried			
Spouse		Louisa Lembruch (1836-1924)	1867 - , , Indiana, USA
3	M	Johann-Lorenz Katzenberger	
Born		1838	Mailes, , Königreich Bayern
Christened			
Died			
Buried			
Spouse			
4	F	Barbara Katzenberger	
Born		17 Jan 1843	Mailes, , Königreich Bayern
Christened			
Died		17 Jan 1870	Frontenac, Goodhue, Minnesota, USA
Cause of Death		scarlet fever	
Buried		Jan 1870	Frontenac, Goodhue, Minnesota, USA
Address		Old Frontenac Cemetery, Frontenac, Minnesota	
Spouse		Johann Michael Ackerman (1834-1911)	
Marr. Date		13 Jun 1860 - Red Wing, Goodhue, Minnesota, USA	

Family Group Record Michel Katzenberger & Dorothea Shale

Children (cont.)			
5	**F**	**Margaretha Grace Katzenberger**	
Born		21 May 1844	Mailes, , Königreich Bayern
Christened			
Died		29 Dec 1869	Frontenac, Goodhue, Minnesota, USA
Buried		31 Dec 1869	Frontenac, Goodhue, Minnesota, USA
Address		Old Frontenac Cemetery, Frontenac, Minnesota	
Spouse		Engelbert Haller (1832-1890)	4 Nov 1865 - St. Paul, Ramsey, Minnesota, USA
6	**M**	**Johan Katzenberger**	
Born		1846	Mailes, , Königreich Bayern
Christened			
Died			
Buried			
Spouse			
7	**M**	**Michael Katzenberger (Schneider)**	
AKA		Snider	
Born		30 Aug 1851	Cincinnati, Hamilton, Ohio, USA
Christened			
Died		21 Feb 1876	Atlantic Ocean
Cause of Death		consumption	
Buried		21 Feb 1876	Buried at Sea
Spouse		Mary Smith (-)	5 Nov 1871 - , Goodhue, Minnesota, USA
8	**M**	**William Katzenberger (Schneider)**	
Born		Jan 1853	Cincinnati, Hamilton, Ohio, USA
Christened			
Died		18 Jan 1930	St. Paul, Ramsey, Minnesota, USA
Buried			
Spouse		Charlotte Freund (1854-)	1874 - , Goodhue, Minnesota, USA

Family Group Record Michael Katzenberger (Schneider) & Mary Smith

Husband	Michael Katzenberger (Schneider)	
AKA	Snider	
Born	30 Aug 1851	Cincinnati, Hamilton, Ohio, USA
Christened		
Died	21 Feb 1876	Atlantic Ocean
Cause of Death	consumption	
Buried	21 Feb 1876	Buried at Sea
Father	Michel Katzenberger (1806-Bef 1856)	
Mother	Dorothea Shale (1815-1887)	
Marriage	5 Nov 1871	, Goodhue, Minnesota, USA

Wife	Mary Smith	
Born		
Christened		
Died		
Buried		

Children			
1	F	Daughter Katzenberger (Schneider)	
Born		Abt Oct 1875	Lake City, Wabasha, Minnesota, USA
Christened			
Died		23 Apr 1876	Lake City, Wabasha, Minnesota, USA
Buried			
Spouse			

Family Group Record William Katzenberger (Schneider) & Charlotte Freund

Husband	William Katzenberger (Schneider)	
Born	Jan 1853	Cincinnati, Hamilton, Ohio, USA
Christened		
Died	18 Jan 1930	St. Paul, Ramsey, Minnesota, USA
Buried		
Father	Michel Katzenberger (1806-Bef 1856)	
Mother	Dorothea Shale (1815-1887)	
Marriage	1874	, Goodhue, Minnesota, USA

Wife	Charlotte Freund	
Born	Nov 1854	, , , Germany
Christened		
Died		
Buried		

Children		
1	M	Henry C. Schneider
Born	Sep 1877	Frontenac Station, Goodhue, Minnesota, USA
Christened		
Died		
Buried		
Spouse		
2	F	Annie H. Schneider
Born	Jul 1878	Frontenac Station, Goodhue, Minnesota, USA
Christened		
Died		
Buried		
Spouse		
3	F	Carrie F. Schneider
Born	Oct 1881	Frontenac Station, Goodhue, Minnesota, USA
Christened		
Died		
Buried		
Spouse		
4	F	Minnie C. Schneider
Born	Jan 1884	Frontenac Station, Goodhue, Minnesota, USA
Christened		
Died		
Buried		
Spouse		
5	M	Walter J. Schneider
Born	Jul 1888	South St. Paul, Dakota, Minnesota, USA
Christened		
Died		
Buried		
Spouse		

Family Group Record William Katzenberger (Schneider) & Charlotte Freund

6	M	Albert Schneider	
Born	Jul 1890	South St. Paul, Dakota, Minnesota, USA	
Christened			
Died			
Buried			
Spouse			

7	M	William J. Schneider	
Born	Sep 1892	South St. Paul, Dakota, Minnesota, USA	
Christened			
Died			
Buried			
Spouse			

8	M	Clarence Chester Schneider	
Born	14 Jan 1894	South St. Paul, Dakota, Minnesota, USA	
Christened			
Died			
Buried			
Spouse			

Family Group Record James E. Kells & Theresa Schloerstein

Husband	James E. Kells	
Born	1857	, , Wisconsin, USA
Christened		
Died	20 Jul 1918	Minneapolis, Hennepin, Minnesota, USA
Buried	22 Jul 1918	Minneapolis, Hennepin, Minnesota, USA
Address	Lakewood Cemetery, Minneapolis, MN	
Father	Henry Jacob Kells (1833-1916)	
Mother	Naomi Stewart (1834-1917)	
Marriage	10 Sep 1879	Red Wing, Goodhue, Minnesota, USA

Wife	Theresa Schloerstein	
AKA	Tracy Hill	
Born	1857	, , , Austria
Christened		
Died	11 Jul 1929	
Buried	Jul 1929	Minneapolis, Hennepin, Minnesota, USA
Address	Lakewood Cemetery, Minneapolis, MN	
Father	Wolfgang Schloerstein (1814-1897)	
Mother	Mary Barbara (1814-Between 1885/1895)	

Children

1	F	Daisy F. Kells	
	Born	1885	Florence Township, Goodhue, Minnesota, USA
	Christened		
	Died		
	Buried		
	Spouse		

2	F	Edna Kells	
	Born	1886	Florence Township, Goodhue, Minnesota, USA
	Christened		
	Died		
	Buried		
	Spouse	Andrew Dursen (1857-)	

3	M	Alfred Gordon Kells	
	Born	17 May 1889	Florence Township, Goodhue, Minnesota, USA
	Christened		
	Died		
	Buried		
	Spouse		

4	M	Walter J. Kells	
	Born	1896	
	Christened		
	Died	1955	
	Buried		
	Spouse		

Family Group Record Fred R. Kingsley & Jennie Weed

Husband	Fred R. Kingsley	
Born	15 Jun 1863	Waverly, Wright, Minnesota, USA
Christened		
Died	14 Mar 1934	Lake City, Wabasha, Minnesota, USA
Cause of Death	acute peritonitis	
Buried	17 Mar 1934	Frontenac, Goodhue, Minnesota, USA
Address	Old Frontenac Cemetery, Frontenac, Minnesota	
Father	Ammon D. Kingsley (1829-1911)	
Mother	Emerette S. Dusten (1830-1873)	
Marriage	16 May 1905	Red Wing, Goodhue, Minnesota, USA

Wife	Jennie B. Weed	
Born	28 Oct 1867	Central Point Township, Goodhue, Minnesota, USA
Christened		
Died	27 May 1961	Red Wing, Goodhue, Minnesota, USA
Cause of Death	old age	
Buried	31 May 1961	Frontenac, Goodhue, Minnesota, USA
Address	Old Frontenac Cemetery, Frontenac, Minnesota	
Father	David T. Weed (1818-Abt 1886)	
Mother	Mary F. Northfield (1836-Abt 1901)	

Children		

Family Group Record Ignatius Kittle & Margaret Kittle

Husband	Ignatius Kittle	
Born	1831	, , , Switzerland
Marriage	Abt 1857	, , Illinois, USA

Wife	Margaret	
Born	1840	, , , Bavaria

Children			
1	M	Henry Kittle	
Born		1858	, , Illinois, USA
2	M	George Kittle	
Born		1859	, , Illinois, USA
3	F	Marie Kittle	
Born		1863	, Goodhue, Minnesota, USA
4	F	Elizabeth Kittle	
Born		1865	, Goodhue, Minnesota, USA
5	M	William Kittle	
Born		1866	, , Iowa, USA
6	M	Frederick Kittle	
Born		1872	, , Iowa, USA
7	F	Fanny Kittle	
Born		1878	, , Iowa, USA

Family Group Record Franz Karl Koch & Franzsika Dannecker

Husband	Franz Karl Koch	
Born	2 Nov 1803	Ratshausen, Schwarzwald, Wurttemburg
Christened		
Died	25 Mar 1868	Ratshausen, Schwarzwald, Wurttemburg
Buried		
Marriage	Abt 1828	Ratshausen, Schwarzwald, Wurttemburg

Wife	Franzsika Dannecker	
Born	5 Mar 1805	Ratshausen, Schwarzwald, Wurttemburg
Christened		
Died	24 Feb 1849	Ratshausen, Schwarzwald, Wurttemburg
Buried		

Children

1 M Engelbert Koch

Born	1830	Ratshausen, Schwarzwald, Wurttemburg
Christened		
Died	1914	St. Paul, Ramsey, Minnesota, USA
Buried		
Spouse		

2 M Kasper Koch

Born	3 Jan 1832	Ratshausen, Schwarzwald, Wurttemburg
Christened		
Died	20 May 1876	Hay Creek Township, Goodhue, Minnesota, USA
Cause of Death	injuries sustained from colt kicking him in abdomen	
Buried	May 1876	Red Wing, Goodhue, Minnesota, USA
Address	Calvary Cemetery, Red Wing, Minnesota	
Spouse	Margaretha Bahr (1820-1903)	
Marr. Date	28 Nov 1871 - Red Wing, Goodhue, Minnesota, USA	

3 F Maria Koch

Born	4 Sep 1836	Ratshausen, Schwarzwald, Wurttemburg
Christened		
Died	22 Oct 1876	Hay Creek Township, Goodhue, Minnesota, USA
Buried		
Spouse	Sebastian Schmitz (-)	

4 F Victoria Koch

Born	10 Sep 1839	Ratshausen, Schwarzwald, Wurttemburg
Christened		
Died	5 May 1914	Red Wing, Goodhue, Minnesota, USA
Buried	May 1914	Red Wing, Goodhue, Minnesota, USA
Address	Calvary Cemetery, Red Wing, Minnesota	
Spouse	John Staiger (1833-1915)	29 Sep 1868 - Wells Township, Goodhue, Minnesota, USA

5 F Anna Koch

Born	21 Feb 1841	Ratshausen, Schwarzwald, Wurttemburg
Christened		
Died	15 Apr 1927	Red Wing, Goodhue, Minnesota, USA
Buried		
Spouse	Joseph Edward Haustein (1845-1902)	21 Jun 1870 - Red Wing, Goodhue, Minnesota, USA

Children (cont.)			
6	**M**	**Fidelis (Fidel) Koch**	
Born	20 Nov 1846	Ratshausen, , Wurttemburg	
Christened			
Died	27 Feb 1910	Red Wing, Goodhue, Minnesota, USA	
Buried	Feb 1910	Red Wing, Goodhue, Minnesota, USA	
Address	Calvary Cemetery, Red Wing, Minnesota		
Spouse	Mathilda Schaefer (1845-1917)		

Family Group Record Kasper Koch & Margaretha Bahr

Husband	Kasper Koch		
Born	3 Jan 1832	Ratshausen, Schwarzwald, Wurttemburg	
Christened			
Died	20 May 1876	Hay Creek Township, Goodhue, Minnesota, USA	
Cause of Death	injuries sustained from colt kicking him in abdomen		
Buried	May 1876	Red Wing, Goodhue, Minnesota, USA	
Address	Calvary Cemetery, Red Wing, Minnesota		
Father	Franz Karl Koch (1803-1868)		
Mother	Franzsika Dannecker (1805-1849)		
Marriage	28 Nov 1871	Red Wing, Goodhue, Minnesota, USA	

Wife	Margaretha Bahr	
Born	21 Jul 1820	
Christened		
Died	25 Nov 1903	Red Wing, Goodhue, Minnesota, USA
Buried		
Other Spouse	George Bachman (-)	

Children

129

Family Group Record Kohn

Husband	Kohn	
Born		
Christened		
Died		
Buried		
Marriage		

Wife	Sophia Elesa	
AKA	Elesa Kohn	
Born	1815	, , , Mecklenburg-Schwerin
Christened		
Died	1903	, Goodhue, Minnesota, USA
Buried	1903	Frontenac, Goodhue, Minnesota, USA
Address	Old Frontenac Cemetery, Frontenac, Minnesota	

Children			
1	M	Joachim (Joseph) Koehn	
Born		7 Feb 1838	, , , Mecklenburg-Schwerin
Christened			
Died		15 Jan 1927	Florence Township, Goodhue, Minnesota, USA
Buried		19 Jan 1927	Red Wing, Goodhue, Minnesota, USA
Address		Oakwood Cemetery, Red Wing, MN	
Spouse		Louisa Schumacher (1846-1921)	6 Jan 1867 - , Goodhue, Minnesota, USA

Family Group Record Joachim (Joseph) Koehn & Louisa Schumacher

Husband	Joachim (Joseph) Koehn	
Born	7 Feb 1838	, , , Mecklenburg-Schwerin
Christened		
Died	15 Jan 1927	Florence Township, Goodhue, Minnesota, USA
Buried	19 Jan 1927	Red Wing, Goodhue, Minnesota, USA
Address	Oakwood Cemetery, Red Wing, MN	
Father	Kohn (-)	
Mother	Sophia Elesa (1815-1903)	
Marriage	6 Jan 1867	, Goodhue, Minnesota, USA

Wife	Louisa Schumacher	
Born	22 May 1846	, , , Mecklenburg-Schwerin
Christened		
Died	20 Feb 1921	Florence Township, Goodhue, Minnesota, USA
Buried	23 Feb 1921	Red Wing, Goodhue, Minnesota, USA
Address	Oakwood Cemetery, Red Wing, MN	

Children		
1	F	Maria Koehn
Born	Abt 1867	Frontenac, Goodhue, Minnesota, USA
Christened		
Died	Bef 1900	Florence Township, Goodhue, Minnesota, USA
Buried		
Spouse		
2	F	Lena Catherina Koehn
Born	12 Jul 1871	Florence Township, Goodhue, Minnesota, USA
Christened		
Died	4 Jan 1956	Consort, Albert, Canada
Buried		
Spouse	Carl August Radefeldt (-)	17 Sep 1899 - Frontenac, Goodhue, Minnesota, USA
3	F	Louisa Koehn
Born	6 Nov 1873	Florence Township, Goodhue, Minnesota, USA
Christened		
Died	5 Oct 1953	, Wabasha, Minnesota, USA
Buried	10 Oct 1953	Florence Township, Goodhue, Minnesota, USA
Address	Immanuel Lutheran Church Cemeter, aka Cordes, West Florence, MN	
Spouse	John C. Tackmann (1869-1940)	28 May 1896 - Featherston Township, Goodhue, Minnesita, USA
4	F	Elizabeth Marie Koehn
Born	16 Jan 1876	Florence Township, Goodhue, Minnesota, USA
Christened		
Died	10 Jun 1971	, Goodhue, Minnesota, USA
Buried	12 Jun 1971	Red Wing, Goodhue, Minnesota, USA
Address	Oakwood Cemetery, Red Wing, MN	
Spouse	Did Not Marry	

Family Group Record Joachim (Joseph) Koehn & Louisa Schumacher

Children (cont.)			
5	**F**	**Annie Koehn**	
Born	Dec 1878	Florence Township, Goodhue, Minnesota, USA	
Christened			
Died			
Buried			
Spouse			
6	**F**	**Freda Marie Koehn**	
Born	18 Mar 1882	Florence Township, Goodhue, Minnesota, USA	
Christened			
Died	8 Apr 1976	, Goodhue, Minnesota, USA	
Buried	12 Apr 1976	Red Wing, Goodhue, Minnesota, USA	
Address	Oakwood Cemetery, Red Wing, MN		
Spouse	Charles Phillip Schilling (-)	14 Jun 1900 - Red Wing, Goodhue, Minnesota, USA	
7	**F**	**Emma Sophia Koehn**	
Born	11 Oct 1884	Florence Township, Goodhue, Minnesota, USA	
Christened	25 Jan 1885	Frontenac Station, Goodhue, Minnesota, USA	
Address	St. John's Ev. Lutheran Church, Frontenac Station, Minnesota		
Died	25 May 1960	, Goodhue, Minnesota, USA	
Buried	May 1960	Red Wing, Goodhue, Minnesota, USA	
Address	Oakwood Cemetery, Red Wing, MN		
Spouse	Irwin Julius Isensee (1885-1958)	3 Sep 1908 - Frontenac, Goodhue, Minnesota, USA	

Family Group Record Johan Karl Heinrich Koenig & Hanna Friedericka Pringel

Husband	Johan Karl Heinrich Koenig	
AKA	Henry	
Born	19 Jan 1820	Klinkenberg, Prussia
Christened		
Died	12 Jan 1888	Oronoco, Olmsted, Minnesota, USA
Cause of Death	heart disease	
Buried	Jan 1888	Oronoco, Olmsted, Minnesota, USA
Address	Oronoco Cemetery, Oronoco, MN	
Marriage	Abt 1837	, , , Prussia

Wife	Hanna Friedericka Elizabeth Pringel	
Born	9 May 1818	, , , Prussia
Christened		
Died	30 Mar 1902	Oronoco, Olmsted, Minnesota, USA
Cause of Death	gastritis//old age	
Buried	Apr 1902	Oronoco, Olmsted, Minnesota, USA
Address	Oronoco Cemetery, Oronoco, MN	

Children		
1 M	**William Koenig**	
Born	8 Nov 1839	, , , Pommern, Prussia
Christened		
Died	15 Jan 1925	Oronoco, Olmsted, Minnesota, USA
Cause of Death	old age	
Buried	Jan 1925	Oronoco, Olmsted, Minnesota, USA
Address	Oronoco Cemetery, Oronoco, MN	
Spouse	Marie Steffenhagen (1838-1920)	5 Apr 1861 - , Pommern, Prussia
2 M	**John Koenig**	
Born	1 Jan 1841	, , , Prussia
Christened		
Died	27 Jun 1931	Rochester, Olmsted, Minnesota, USA
Cause of Death	cerebral arteriosclerosis//infarction of myocardiam	
Buried	Jun	Oronoco, Olmsted, Minnesota, USA
Address	Oronoco Cemetery, Oronoco, MN	
Spouse	Fredericka Wilhelma Muller (1849-1886)	
3 M	**Christopher Koenig**	
AKA	Christ	
Born	8 Oct 1843	, , , Prussia
Christened		
Died	2 Jul 1919	, Olmsted, Minnesota, USA
Buried	Jul 1919	Oronoco, Olmsted, Minnesota, USA
Address	Oronoco Cemetery, Oronoco, MN	
Spouse	Augusta Amelia Rauch (1847-1922)	

Family Group Record Johan Karl Heinrich Koenig & Hanna Friedericka Pringel

Children (cont.)		
4	**M**	**Fredrick Koenig**
Born	25 Feb 1846	, , , Prussia
Christened		
Died	13 May 1921	Oronoco, Olmsted, Minnesota, USA
Buried	May 1921	Oronoco, Olmsted, Minnesota, USA
Address	Oronoco Cemetery, Oronoco, MN	
Spouse	Anne Marie Magdelene Fadelmann (1857-1950)	
5	**F**	**Friedericka Koenig**
Born	30 Oct 1853	, , , Prussia
Christened		
Died	31 Mar 1918	, Olmsted, Minnesota, USA
Buried	Apr 1918	Oronoco, Olmsted, Minnesota, USA
Address	Oronoco Cemetery, Oronoco, MN	
Spouse	Johann Frederick Rucker (1848-1912)	
6	**F**	**Sophia Koenig**
Born	1855	, , , Prussia
Christened		
Died	Bef 1902	
Buried		
Spouse		

Family Group Record William Koenig & Marie Steffenhagen

Husband	William Koenig	
Born	8 Nov 1839	, , , Pommern, Prussia
Christened		
Died	15 Jan 1925	Oronoco, Olmsted, Minnesota, USA
Cause of Death	old age	
Buried	Jan 1925	Oronoco, Olmsted, Minnesota, USA
Address	Oronoco Cemetery, Oronoco, MN	
Father	Johan Karl Heinrich Koenig (1820-1888)	
Mother	Hanna Friedericka Elizabeth Pringel (1818-1902)	
Marriage	5 Apr 1861	, Pommern, Prussia

Wife	Marie Steffenhagen	
AKA	Stavenhagen (in Germany)	
Born	26 Sep 1838	, , , Pommern, Prussia
Christened		
Died	5 Jun 1920	Oronoco, Olmsted, Minnesota, USA
Cause of Death	excess dilitation of heart	
Buried	Jun 1920	Oronoco, Olmsted, Minnesota, USA
Address	Oronoco Cemetery, Oronoco, MN	
Father	Carl C. Steffenhagen (1803-1877)	
Mother	Sophia Winkelman (Abt 1803-Bef 1842)	

Children		
1	M	William John Koenig
Born	18 Jun 1862	, , , Pommern, Prussia
Christened		
Died	1 Feb 1935	Oronoco Township, Olmsted, Minnesota, USA
Buried	Feb 1935	Oronoco, Olmsted, Minnesota, USA
Address	Oronoco Cemetery, Oronoco, MN	
Spouse	Ida Kurth (1871-1946)	1890 - , Olmsted, Minnesota, USA
2	F	Lena Helena Koenig
Born	Oct 1864	Frontenac, Goodhue, Minnesota, USA
Christened		
Died	27 Sep 1936	Oronoco Township, Olmsted, Minnesota, USA
Buried	Sep 1936	Oronoco, Olmsted, Minnesota, USA
Address	Oronoco Cemetery, Oronoco, MN	
Spouse	Henry Tiedeman (1865-1947)	1888 - , Olmsted, Minnesota, USA
3	M	Frederick William Koenig
Born	Oct 1869	, , Minnesota, USA
Christened		
Died	5 Mar 1936	Oronoco, Olmsted, Minnesota, USA
Buried	Mar 1936	Oronoco, Olmsted, Minnesota, USA
Address	Oronoco Cemetery, Oronoco, MN	
Spouse	Hulda Agusta Nickels (1873-1948)	1893 - , Olmsted, Minnesota, USA

Family Group Record John J. Krelberg & Martha Bartels

Husband	John J. Krelberg	
Born	Sep 1851	, , , Mecklenburg
Christened		
Died	11 Mar 1918	
Buried	Mar 1918	Frontenac, Goodhue, Minnesota, USA
Address	Old Frontenac Cemetery, Frontenac, Minnesota	
Father	Henry Krelberg (1835-)	
Mother	Dora (1840-)	
Marriage	Abt 1878	Kinderhook, Columbia, New York, USA

Wife	Martha Bartels	
Born	May 1857	, , , Hanover
Christened		
Died	1935	
Buried	1935	Frontenac, Goodhue, Minnesota, USA
Address	Old Frontenac Cemetery, Frontenac, Minnesota	
Father	George Bartels Sr. (1827-1898)	
Mother	Katie (1828-Between 1885/1895)	

Children			
1	M	Henry George Krelberg	
Born		Feb 1878	Kinderhook, Columbia, New York, USA
Christened			
Died		19 Aug 1942	Rivanna, Dakota, Minnesota, USA
Buried			
Spouse		Anna (-)	
2	F	Katherine L. Krelberg	
Born		8 Nov 1881	Frontenac, Goodhue, Minnesota, USA
Christened			
Died		8 Oct 1971	Lake City, Wabasha, Minnesota, USA
Buried		Oct 1971	Lake City, Wabasha, Minnesota, USA
Address		Lakewood Cemetery, Lake City, MN	
Spouse		Asa Doughty Clifford (1878-1946)	29 Mar 1898 - Red Wing, Goodhue, Minnesota, USA
Spouse		Charles Martin Scherf (1874-1942)	24 Nov 1903 - Red Wing, Goodhue, Minnesota, USA
3	F	Lillian Krelberg	
Born		18 Dec 1889	Florence Township, Goodhue, Minnesota, USA
Christened			
Died		1977	
Buried		1977	Minnetonka, Hennepin, Minnesota USA
Spouse		Frank J. Sauter (1882-1968)	17 Nov 1906 - Red Wing, Goodhue, Minnesota, USA

Family Group Record Martin L. Larson & Caroline A. Sorenson

Husband	Martin L. Larson	
Born	14 Oct 1833	, , , Norway
Christened		
Died	13 Aug 1900	, Goodhue, Minnesota, USA
Buried	Aug 1900	Frontenac, Goodhue, Minnesota, USA
Address	Old Frontenac Cemetery, Frontenac, Minnesota	
Marriage	Abt 1866	, , , Norway

Wife	Caroline A. Sorenson	
Born	Sep 1842	, , , Norway
Christened		
Died	1927	, Goodhue, Minnesota, USA
Buried	1927	Frontenac, Goodhue, Minnesota, USA
Address	Old Frontenac Cemetery, Frontenac, Minnesota	

Children			
1	F	Mary Larson	
Born		1866	, , , Norway
Christened			
Died			
Buried			
Spouse			
2	M	Ludwig Larson	
Born		16 Aug 1868	, , , Norway
Christened			
Died		20 Mar 1892	Frontenac Station, Goodhue, Minnesota, USA
Buried		Mar 1892	Frontenac, Goodhue, Minnesota, USA
Address		Old Frontenac Cemetery, Frontenac, Minnesota	
Spouse			

3	M	John S. Larson	
Born		1871	Frontenac, Goodhue, Minnesota, USA
Christened			
Died		11 Sep 1922	Appleton Village, Swift, Minnesota USA
Buried		Sep 1922	
Spouse		Bertha Dahl (-)	

Family Group Record Martin L. Larson & Caroline A. Sorenson

Children (cont.)		

4	M	**Christian Larson**	
Born	Sep 1873	Frontenac, Goodhue, Minnesota, USA	
Christened			
Died	1943		
Buried	1943	Frontenac, Goodhue, Minnesota, USA	
Address	Old Frontenac Cemetery, Frontenac, Minnesota		
Spouse			

5	M	**Baby boy Larson**
Born	Cir 1875	Frontenac Station, Goodhue, Minnesota, USA
Christened		
Died	Cir 1875	Frontenac Station, Goodhue, Minnesota, USA
Buried	Cir 1875	Frontenac, Goodhue, Minnesota, USA
Address	Old Frontenac Cemetery, Frontenac, Minnesota	
Spouse		

6	M	**Martin Larson**
Born	1877	Frontenac, Goodhue, Minnesota, USA
Christened		
Died	1953	
Buried	1953	Frontenac, Goodhue, Minnesota, USA
Address	Old Frontenac Cemetery, Frontenac, Minnesota	
Spouse	Johanna Christina Thomsen (1875-1950)	

7	M	**Henry Larson**	
Born	Mar 1880	Frontenac Station, Goodhue, Minnesota, USA	
Christened			
Died	1948		
Buried	1948	Frontenac, Goodhue, Minnesota, USA	
Address	Old Frontenac Cemetery, Frontenac, Minnesota		
Spouse			

8	M	**Carl William Larson**
Born	23 Jun 1883	Frontenac Station, Goodhue, Minnesota, USA
Christened		
Died	1963	
Buried	1963	Pine Island, Goodhue, Minnesota, USA
Spouse		

9	M	**George M. Larson**	
Born	22 Jun 1885	Frontenac Station, Goodhue, Minnesota, USA	
Christened			
Died	22 Nov 1956	, Goodhue, Minnesota, USA	
Buried	Nov 1956	Frontenac, Goodhue, Minnesota, USA	
Address	Old Frontenac Cemetery, Frontenac, Minnesota		
Spouse			

Family Group Record Lars Larson Loken & Johanna Olsdatter

Husband	Lars Larson Loken	
Born	Abt 1799	, Akershus, Norway
Christened		
Died	Bef 1865	, Akershus, Norway
Buried		
Marriage	Abt 1826	, , , Norway

Wife	Johanna Olsdatter	
Born	7 Oct 1799	Ulensaker, Akershus, Norway
Christened	13 Oct 1799	Hovin Sokn, Ullensaker Prestigaard, Akershus County, Norway
Died	Cir 1870	Brownsville, Ontario, Canada
Buried		
Father	Ole Christopherson Algrim (-)	
Mother	Marie Berthe Madsdatter (-)	

Children		
1	F	Berthe Karine Larsdatter Loken
AKA	Carrie, Karine, Corine Finstad	
Born	Jan 1827	Eidsvoll, Akershus, Norway
Christened		
Died	9 Sep 1893	Frontenac, Goodhue, Minnesota, USA
Cause of Death	Rheumatism	
Buried	11 Sep 1893	Frontenac, Goodhue, Minnesota, USA
Address	Old Frontenac Episcopal Church Cemetery, Frontenac, Minnesota	
Spouse	Karl Olson Finstad (1837-1907)	17 Jul 1863 - Eidsvoll prestegaard, Akershus County, Norway
2	M	Ole Christian Larson Loken
Born	13 Mar 1828	Nordlien, Akershus, Norway
Christened	26 Apr 1828	Hurdal, Akershus, Norway
Address	Hurdal Parish Church, Hurdal, Akershus, Norway	
Died	23 Aug 1903	Frontenac, Goodhue, Minnesota, USA
Cause of Death	paralysis	
Buried	26 Aug 1903	Frontenac, Goodhue, Minnesota, USA
Address	Old Frontenac Cemetery, Frontenac, Minnesota	
Spouse	Martha Wilhelmsdatter Allergodt (1840-1915)	
Marr. Date	14 Apr 1859 - Hovind sokn in Ullensaker, Akershus, Norway	
3	F	Marta Marie LARSDATTER Loken
Born	1833	, Akershus fylke, Norway
Christened		
Died		
Buried		
Spouse		

Family Group Record Lars Larson Loken & Johanna Olsdatter

Children (cont.)		

4	F	**Lena Larsdatter Loken**
Born	25 May 1834	Eidsvoll, Akershus, Norway
Christened		
Died	4 Feb 1882	Frontenac, Goodhue, Minnesota, USA
Buried	Feb 1882	Frontenac, Goodhue, Minnesota, USA
Address	Old Frontenac Cemetery, Frontenac, Minnesota	
Spouse	Even Evensen (1833-1892)	Abt 1860 - , , , Norway

5	F	**Kristine Larsdatter Loken**
Born	Abt 1836	Eidsvoll, Akershus, Norway
Christened		
Died		, McHenry, North Dakota, USA
Buried		
Spouse	C. Johnson (-)	

6	F	**Indiana Larsdatter Loken**
Born	1840	, Akershus fylke, Norway
Christened		
Died	1921	
Buried	1921	St. Paul, Ramsey, Minnesota, USA
Address	Roselawn Cemetery, Roseville, Ramsey,, MN	
Spouse	Samuel J. Williams (1841-1913)	

7	M	**Lars Larson Loken**
Born	1845	, Akershus fylke, Norway
Christened		
Died	1911	
Buried	1911	St. Paul, Ramsey, Minnesota, USA
Address	Roselawn Cemetery, Roseville, Ramsey,, MN	
Spouse	Did Not Marry	

Family Group Record Ole Christian Larson Loken & Martha Wilhelmsdatter Allergodt

Husband	Ole Christian Larson Loken	
Born	13 Mar 1828	Nordlien, Akershus, Norway
Christened	26 Apr 1828	Hurdal, Akershus, Norway
Address	Hurdal Parish Church, Hurdal, Akershus, Norway	
Died	23 Aug 1903	Frontenac, Goodhue, Minnesota, USA
Cause of Death	paralysis	
Buried	26 Aug 1903	Frontenac, Goodhue, Minnesota, USA
Address	Old Frontenac Cemetery, Frontenac, Minnesota	
Father	Lars Larson Loken (Abt 1799-Bef 1865)	
Mother	Johanna Olsdatter (1799-Cir 1870)	
Marriage	14 Apr 1859	Hovind sokn in Ullensaker, Akershus, Norway

Wife	Martha Wilhelmsdatter Allergodt	
Born	11 Jul 1840	Hovind sokn, Ullensaker Prestegaard, Akershus County, Norway
Christened	21 Jul 1840	Hovind sokn, Ullensaker Prestegaard, Akershus County, Norway
Died	12 Jan 1915	Red Wing, Goodhue, Minnesota, USA
Cause of Death	apoplexy	
Buried	15 Jan 1915	Frontenac, Goodhue, Minnesota, USA
Address	Old Frontenac Cemetery, Frontenac, Minnesota	
Father	Wilhlem Gunderson (-)	
Mother	Inga Maria Olsdatter (-)	

Children

1	M	Hans Ludwig Olson	
AKA		Larson	
Born		12 Apr 1860	Hardangerfjord, Vestlandet, Hordaland, Norway
Christened			
Died		6 Jan 1910	Frontenac, Goodhue, Minnesota, USA
Cause of Death		heart failure	
Buried		9 Jan 1910	Frontenac, Goodhue, Minnesota, USA
Address		Old Frontenac Cemetery, Frontenac, Minnesota	
Spouse		Annette Gulbrandsdatter (Gilbertson) (1862-1927)	
Marr. Date		30 Aug 1886 - Red Wing, Goodhue, Minnesota, USA	

2	F	Inge Wilhelmine Olsdatter Loken	
AKA		Anna Olson, Loken	
Born		30 Sep 1861	Eidsvoll, Akershus, Norway
Christened		24 Nov 1861	Eidsvoll, Akershus, Norway
Address		Eidsvoll Parish Church, Eidvoll, Akershus,, Norway	
Died		8 Aug 1937	Frontenac, Goodhue, Minnesota, USA
Cause of Death		chronic myocarditis	
Buried		11 Aug 1937	Frontenac, Goodhue, Minnesota, USA
Address		Old Frontenac Episcopal Church Cemetery, Frontenac, Minnesota	
Spouse		James Richard Lester (1856-1914)	1 Jan 1880 - Frontenac, Goodhue, Minnesota, USA

Children (cont.)			
3	**M**	**Ole Herman Olson**	
Born	20 Oct 1863	Eidsvoll, Akershus, Norway	
Christened	27 Dec 1863	Eidsvoll, Akershus, Norway	
Address	Eidsvoll Parish Church, Eidvoll, Akershus,, Norway		
Died	23 Dec 1935	Wannaska, Roseau, Minnesota, USA	
Cause of Death	parkinson's disease.		
Buried	Dec 1935	Wannaska, Roseau, Minnesota, USA	
Address	Mickinock Cemetery, Wannaska, MN		
Spouse	Mary H. Jacobson (1882-1950)	4 Jan 1902 - Ulen, Clay, Minnesota, USA	

4	**F**	**Maria Olsdatter Loken**	
Born	8 Oct 1865	Eidsvoll, Akershus, Norway	
Christened	25 Dec 1865	Eidsvoll, Akershus, Norway	
Address	Eidsvoll Parish Church, Eidvoll, Akershus,, Norway		
Died	1937	Red Wing, Goodhue, Minnesota, USA	
Buried	1937	Red Wing, Goodhue, Minnesota, USA	
Address	Oakwood Cemetery, Red Wing, MN		
Spouse	John B. Anderson (1870-1941)		
Marr. Date	6 Jun 1900 - Red Wing, Goodhue, Minnesota, USA		

5	**M**	**Lars (OLSON) Loken**	
Born	11 Dec 1867	Eidsvoll, Akershus, Norway	
Christened	26 Dec 1867	Eidsvoll, Akershus, Norway	
Died	2 May 1947	Red Wing, Goodhue, Minnesota, USA	
Buried			
Spouse	Sophia Marie Koehn (1873-1955)		
Marr. Date	7 Apr 1896 - Red Wing, Goodhue, Minnesota, USA		

6	**F**	**Jennie Indiana (OLSON) Loken**	
AKA	Indiana J., Jennie I, Katie, Tilda		
Born	Jul 1870	Frontenac, Goodhue, Minnesota, USA	
Christened	16 Dec 1879	Frontenac, Goodhue, Minnesota, USA	
Address	Christ Episcopal Church, Old Frontenac, Minnesota		
Died	12 Jul 1930	Red Wing, Goodhue, Minnesota, USA	
Buried	Jul 1930	Red Wing, Goodhue, Minnesota, USA	
Address	Oakwood Cemetery, Red Wing, MN		
Spouse	Albert George Hartnagel (1873-1961)	26 Jan 1898 - Red Wing, Goodhue, Minnesota, USA	

7	**F**	**Severina Christina (OLSON) Loken**	
AKA	Sarina, Selina		
Born	Jul 1872	Frontenac, Goodhue, Minnesota, USA	
Christened			
Died	22 Apr 1921	Red Wing, Goodhue, Minnesota, USA	
Buried	Apr 1921	Red Wing, Goodhue, Minnesota, USA	
Address	Oakwood Cemetery, Red Wing, MN		
Spouse	Albin Carl Almquist (1871-1955)		
Marr. Date	22 Dec 1897 - Red Wing, Goodhue, Minnesota, USA		

Family Group Record Ole Christian Larson Loken & Martha Wilhelmsdatter Allergodt

Children (cont.)			

8 M Otto (OLSON) Loken

Born	25 Nov 1874	Frontenac, Goodhue, Minnesota, USA
Christened		
Died	26 Mar 1911	Red Wing, Goodhue, Minnesota, USA
Buried		
Spouse	Tena A. Seamann (1875-)	8 Oct 1901 - , Rice County, Minnesota, USA

9 M John (OLSON) Loken

Born	10 Jun 1876	Frontenac, Goodhue, Minnesota, USA
Christened	21 Aug 1876	Frontenac, Goodhue, Minnesota, USA
Address	Christ Episcopal Church, Old Frontenac, Minnesota	
Died	4 Jul 1949	Red Wing, Goodhue, Minnesota, USA
Cause of Death	heart ailment	
Buried	Jul 1949	Red Wing, Goodhue, Minnesota, USA
Address	Oakwood Cemetery, Red Wing, MN	
Spouse	Minnie Lucinda Hahn (1870-1941)	
Marr. Date	14 Jun 1900 - Red Wing, Goodhue, Minnesota, USA	

10 M Henry Christ (OLSON) Loken

Born	1878	Frontenac, Goodhue, Minnesota, USA
Christened	16 Dec 1879	Frontenac, Goodhue, Minnesota, USA
Address	Christ Episcopal Church, Old Frontenac, Minnesota	
Died	13 Oct 1937	, Hennepin, Minnesota, USA
Buried	16 Oct 1937	Minneapolis, Hennepin, Minnesota, USA
Address	Crystal Lake Cemetery, Minneapolis, MN	
Spouse	Hilda L. Paulson (1882-)	22 Sep 1904 - , Hennepin, Minnesota, USA

11 F Martha Loken

Born	Cir 1880	Frontenac, Goodhue, Minnesota, USA
Christened		
Died	Cir 1880	Frontenac, Goodhue, Minnesota, USA
Buried		
Spouse		

12 M George Carl (OLSON) Loken

Born	25 Jan 1881	Frontenac, Goodhue, Minnesota, USA
Christened	13 Jul 1883	Frontenac, Goodhue, Minnesota, USA
Address	Christ Episcopal Church, Old Frontenac, Minnesota	
Died	31 Jul 1946	, Goodhue, Minnesota, USA
Buried	Aug 1946	Frontenac, Goodhue, Minnesota, USA
Address	Old Frontenac Cemetery, Frontenac, Minnesota	
Spouse	Did Not Marry	

143

Family Group Record Ole Christian Larson Loken & Martha Wilhelmsdatter Allergodt

Children (cont.)				
13	**M**	**Hilmer Anton (OLSON) Loken**		
Born		5 May 1883	Frontenac, Goodhue, Minnesota, USA	
Christened		13 Jul 1883	Frontenac, Goodhue, Minnesota, USA	
Address		Christ Episcopal Church, Old Frontenac, Minnesota		
Died		6 May 1952	Lake City, Wabasha, Minnesota, USA	
Buried		May 1952	Frontenac, Goodhue, Minnesota, USA	
Address		Old Frontenac Cemetery, Frontenac, Minnesota		
Spouse		Did Not Marry		
14	**F**	**Tena Golilda Nelson**		
AKA		Larson		
Born		7 Jun 1892	Brazington, Pierce, Wisconsin, USA	
Christened				
Died		1 Mar 1988	Minneapolis, Hennepin, Minnesota, USA	
Cause of Death		heart failure		
Buried		5 Mar 1988	Crystal, , Minnesota	
Spouse		Charles Cleveland Schloer (1892-1966)		
Marr. Date		13 Jun 1913 - Red Wing, Goodhue, Minnesota, USA		

Family Group Record James Richard Lester & Anna (Olson Larson) Loken

Husband	James Richard Lester	
AKA	Lister	
Born	2 Mar 1856	Dubuque, Dubuque, Iowa, USA
Christened		
Died	24 Dec 1914	Frontenac, Goodhue, Minnesota, USA
Cause of Death	consumption	
Buried	29 Dec 1914	Frontenac, Goodhue, Minnesota, USA
Address	Old Frontenac Episcopal Church Cemetery, Frontenac, Minnesota	
Father	Lester (-)	
Mother		
Marriage	1 Jan 1880	Frontenac, Goodhue, Minnesota, USA

Wife	Inge Wilhelmine Olsdatter Loken	
AKA	Anna Olson, Loken	
Born	30 Sep 1861	Eidsvoll, Akershus, Norway
Christened	24 Nov 1861	Eidsvoll, Akershus, Norway
Address	Eidsvoll Parish Church, Eidvoll, Akershus,, Norway	
Died	8 Aug 1937	Frontenac, Goodhue, Minnesota, USA
Cause of Death	chronic myocarditis	
Buried	11 Aug 1937	Frontenac, Goodhue, Minnesota, USA
Address	Old Frontenac Episcopal Church Cemetery, Frontenac, Minnesota	
Father	Ole Christian Larson Loken (1828-1903)	
Mother	Martha Wilhelmsdatter Allergodt (1840-1915)	

Children		
1 F	Natalie J. Lester	
Born	9 Oct 1881	Frontenac, Goodhue, Minnesota, USA
Christened		
Died	30 Jan 1956	Winona, Winona, Minnesota, USA
Buried		
Spouse	Kenneth Truax (-)	
2 M	Richard George Lester	
AKA	George	
Born	Oct 1882	, , Minnesota, USA
Christened		
Died	Abt 1927	
Buried		
Spouse	Anna (1883-1958)	
3 M	Arthur D. Lester	
Born	16 Jan 1885	Frontenac, Goodhue, Minnesota, USA
Christened		
Died	24 Feb 1953	Frontenac, Goodhue, Minnesota, USA
Buried	Feb 1953	Frontenac, Goodhue, Minnesota, USA
Address	Old Frontenac Episcopal Church Cemetery, Frontenac, Minnesota	
Spouse	Did Not Marry	

Family Group Record Henry Lorentzen & Fredericka Shale

Husband	Henry Lorentzen	
Born	Dec 1820	, , , Hamburg
Christened		
Died	27 Jun 1901	So. St. Paul, Ramsey, Minnesota, USA
Buried		
Marriage	Cir 1855	

Wife	Fredericka Shale	
Born	1823	Lindenberg, Lindau, Bavaria
Christened		
Died	Aug 1888	Frontenac Station, Goodhue, Minnesota, USA
Buried		
Father	Shale (-)	
Mother		

Children

Family Group Record August John Lubeck & Fredericka Friedericks

Husband	August John Lubeck	
Born	1827	, , , Mecklenburg
Christened		
Died	Abt 1864	, Goodhue, Minnesota, USA
Buried		
Father	Lubeck (-)	
Mother	Mina (1790-)	
Marriage	Abt 1857	. Goodhue, Minnesota, USA

Wife	Fredericka Lisetta Friedericks	
Born	8 May 1832	, , , Mecklenburg
Christened		
Died	7 Nov 1911	Red Wing, Goodhue, Minnesota, USA
Buried	Nov 1911	Red Wing, Goodhue, Minnesota, USA
Address	St. John's Evangelical Cemetery, Red Wing, Minnesota	
Father	Johann Christian Friedericks (Abt 1805-)	
Mother	Maria Frederica Volkert (Abt 1805-)	
Other Spouse	Johan Hinrich Bohmbach (1822-1917)	18 Feb 1865 - Red Wing, Goodhue, Minnesota, USA

Children		
1 M	Augustus J. Lubeck (Lebach)	
AKA	Leeback	
Born	May 1858	Frontenac, Goodhue, Minnesota, USA
Christened		
Died		
Buried		
Spouse	Susan E. Vaughn (1867-)	Abt 1884 - , Goodhue, Minnesota, USA
2 F	Emilie Lubeck	
Born	1 Sep 1861	Frontenac, Goodhue, Minnesota, USA
Christened		
Died	25 Jul 1872	, , Goodhue, Minnesota, USA
Buried	Jul 1872	Belvidere Mills, Goodhue, Minnesota, USA
Address	Belvidere Union Cemetery, Belvidere Mills,, MN	
Spouse		

3 F	Louisa Lubeck	
AKA	Lizzie	
Born	Jan 1863	Frontenac, Goodhue, Minnesota, USA
Christened		
Died	1932	Tacoma, Pierce, Washington, USA
Buried	1932	Tacoma, Pierce, Washington, USA
Spouse	Ernest L. Martens (1857-1931)	1880 - , Goodhue, Minnesota, USA

Family Group Record John August Friedrich Lubeck & Auguste Dannert

Husband	John August Friedrich Lubeck	
Born	10 Feb 1821	, , , Mecklenburg
Christened		
Died	7 Nov 1911	Frontenac, Goodhue, Minnesota, USA
Buried	11 Nov 1911	Frontenac, Goodhue, Minnesota, USA
Address	Old Frontenac Cemetery, Frontenac, Minnesota	
Father	Lubeck (-)	
Mother	Mina (1790-)	
Marriage	21 Jun 1872	, Goodhue, Minnesota, USA

Wife	Auguste Dannart	
Born	Feb 1851	, , , Mecklenburg
Christened		
Died	12 Apr 1923	Frontenac, Goodhue, Minnesota, USA
Buried	1923	Frontenac, Goodhue, Minnesota, USA
Address	Old Frontenac Cemetery, Frontenac, Minnesota	
Father	Dannart (-)	
Mother		

Children

1 M Fredrick D. Lubeck Bremer

Born	23 Sep 1872	Frontenac, Goodhue, Minnesota, USA
Christened		
Died	8 Nov 1932	
Buried		
Spouse	Ida Steffenhagen (1878-1944)	
Marr. Date	6 Jan 1896 - Red Wing, Goodhue, Minnesota, USA	

2 M William (John) Lubeck

Born	1 Dec 1873	Frontenac, Goodhue, Minnesota, USA
Christened		
Died	10 Sep 1874	Frontenac, Goodhue, Minnesota, USA
Buried	Sep 1874	Frontenac, Goodhue, Minnesota, USA
Spouse		

3 F Dora L. Lubeck Bremer

AKA	Dolly	
Born	10 Jan 1876	Frontenac, Goodhue, Minnesota, USA
Christened	7 May 1913	Frontenac, Goodhue, Minnesota, USA
Address	Christ Episcopal Church, Old Frontenac, Minnesota	
Died	3 Mar 1945	Frontenac, Goodhue, Minnesota, USA
Buried	6 Mar 1945	Frontenac, Goodhue, Minnesota, USA
Address	Old Frontenac Cemetery, Frontenac, Minnesota	
Spouse	Henry Strupe (1874-1952)	10 Dec 1895 - Red Wing, Goodhue, Minnesota, USA

4 F Ida (Edith) Lubeck

AKA	Ada, Edith	
Born	29 Jun 1878	Frontenac, Goodhue, Minnesota, USA
Christened	3 Dec 1879	Frontenac, Goodhue, Minnesota, USA
Died	Oct 1903	Frontenac, Goodhue, Minnesota, USA
Buried	Oct 1903	Frontenac, Goodhue, Minnesota, USA
Address	Old Frontenac Cemetery, Frontenac, Minnesota	

Family Group Record John August Friedrich Lubeck & Auguste Dannert

Children (cont.)			
Spouse			

5	**F**	**Pauline F. Lubeck**	
Born	21 Sep 1880	Frontenac, Goodhue, Minnesota, USA	
Christened			
Died	30 Jun 1963	, Wabasha, Minnesota, USA	
Buried			
Spouse	Roy Ezra Northfield (1877-1923)	3 May 1900 - , Goodhue, Minnesota, USA	

6	**M**	**William Lubeck**	
Born	5 Oct 1882	Frontenac, Goodhue, Minnesota, USA	
Christened			
Died	25 Nov 1971	Wabasha, Wabasha, Minnesota, USA	
Buried	Nov 1971	Frontenac, Goodhue, Minnesota, USA	
Address	Old Frontenac Cemetery, Frontenac, Minnesota		
Spouse	Minnie Steffenhagen (1892-1972)	Abt 1930 - , Goodhue, Minnesota, USA	

7	**F**	**Augusta Lubeck**	
AKA	Gustie		
Born	19 Sep 1884	Frontenac, Goodhue, Minnesota, USA	
Christened			
Died	2 Feb 1962	, Wabasha, Minnesota, USA	
Buried	Feb 1962	Frontenac, Goodhue, Minnesota, USA	
Address	Old Frontenac Cemetery, Frontenac, Minnesota		
Spouse	Did Not Marry		

8	**M**	**John Lubeck**	
Born	20 Sep 1886	Frontenac, Goodhue, Minnesota, USA	
Christened			
Died	5 Jun 1972		
Buried	Jun 1972	Frontenac, Goodhue, Minnesota, USA	
Address	Old Frontenac Cemetery, Frontenac, Minnesota		
Spouse			

9	**F**	**Caroline Margarete Lubeck**	
Born	11 Jun 1889	Frontenac, Goodhue, Minnesota, USA	
Christened	13 Sep 1905	Frontenac Station, Goodhue, Minnesota, USA	
Address	St. John's Ev. Lutheran Church, Frontenac Station, Minnesota		
Died	4 Mar 1962		
Buried			
Spouse			

10	**F**	**Daisy Mae Lubeck**	
Born	26 Dec 1891	Frontenac, Goodhue, Minnesota, USA	
Christened	13 Sep 1905	Frontenac Station, Goodhue, Minnesota, USA	
Address	St. John's Ev. Lutheran Church, Frontenac Station, Minnesota		
Died	19 Mar 1969		
Buried	1969	Frontenac, Goodhue, Minnesota, USA	
Address	Old Frontenac Cemetery, Frontenac, Minnesota		
Spouse	Did Not Marry		

Family Group Record Col Israel Ludlow & Charlotte Chambers

Husband	Col Israel Ludlow	
Born	1765	Littlehead , Morris, New Jersey, USA
Christened		
Died	20 Jan 1804	Ludlow Station, Hamilton, Ohio, USA
Buried		
Father	Cornelius Ludlow (-)	
Mother	Martha Lyon (-)	
Marriage	11 Nov 1796	, , Pennsylvania, USA

Wife	Charlotte Chambers	
Born	13 Nov 1768	Fort Loudon, Franklin, Pennsylvania, USA
Christened		
Died	20 May 1821	Franklin, Howard, Missouri, USA
Buried	May 1821	, Howard, Missouri, USA
Father	General James Chambers (Abt 1740-)	
Mother	Catharine Hamilton (Abt 1740-)	
Other Spouse	Rev. David Riske (-1818)	15 Dec 1808 - , , Ohio, USA

Children		
1	M	James Chambers Ludlow
Born	1797	
Christened		
Died	1841	
Buried		
Spouse		
2	F	Martha Catherine Ludlow
Born	1799	
Christened		
Died	1834	
Buried		
Spouse		
3	F	Sarah Bella Ludlow
Born	1802	Cumminsville, Hamilton, Ohio, USA
Christened		
Died	13 Jan 1882	Cincinnati, Hamilton, Ohio, USA
Cause of Death	cholera morbus//exhaustion	
Buried	15 Jan 1882	Cincinnati, Hamilton, Ohio, USA
Address	Spring Grove Cemetary, Cincinnati, Ohio	
Spouse	Jeptha Dudley Garrard (1802-1837)	25 Jun 1824 - Cincinnati, Hamilton, Ohio, USA
Spouse	Justice John B. McLean (1785-1861)	11 May 1843 - Cincinnati, Hamilton, Ohio, USA
4	M	Israel L. Ludlow
Born	1804	
Christened		
Died	1846	
Buried		
Spouse		

Family Group Record Justice John B. McLean & Rebecca E. Edwards

Husband	Justice John B. McLean	
Born	11 Mar 1785	, Morris, New Jersey, USA
Christened		
Died	4 Apr 1861	Cincinnati, Hamilton, Ohio, USA
Cause of Death	pneumonia contracted after attending Lincoln's inauguration in the rain	
Buried	25 Apr 1861	Cincinnati, Hamilton, Ohio, USA
Address	Spring Grove Cemetary, Cincinnati, Ohio	
Father	Fergus McLean (1746-1837)	
Mother	Sophia Blackford (1753-1839)	
Marriage	29 Mar 1807	Lebanon, Warren, Ohio, USA
Other Spouse	Sarah Bella Ludlow (1802-1882)	11 May 1843 - Cincinnati, Hamilton, Ohio, USA

Wife	Rebecca E. Edwards
Born	11 Mar 1786	Newport, Campbell, Kentucky, USA
Christened		
Died	5 Dec 1841	Cincinnati, Hamilton, Ohio, USA
Buried		Cincinnati, Hamilton, Ohio, USA
Address	Spring Grove Cemetary, Cincinnati, Ohio	

Children		
1	F	Arabella Edwards McLean
Born	Abt 1808	
Christened		
Died		
Buried		
Spouse		
2	F	Evelyn Aurella McLean
Born	Abt 1809	
Christened		
Died	1887	
Buried		
Spouse	Joseph Pannel Taylor (-)	
3	F	Rebecca Eliza McLean
Born	1811	
Christened		
Died	1837	
Buried		
Spouse		
4	F	Sarah Ann McLean
Born	1813	
Christened		
Died	1840	
Buried		
Spouse		

Children (cont.)			
5	**M**	**John B. McLean**	
Born		1815	
Christened			
Died		1872	
Buried			
Spouse		Elizabeth Jane Cissna (-)	30 Mar 1854 - , Fayette, Ohio, USA
6	**M**	**Brigadier General Nathanial Collins McLean**	
Born		2 Feb 1818	Ridgeville, Warren, Ohio, USA
Christened			
Died		4 Jan 1905	Bellport, Suffolk, New York, USA
Buried		Jan 1905	Bellport, Suffolk, New York, USA
Address		Woodland Cemetery, Bellport, New York	
Spouse		Caroline Thew Burnet (1820-1856)	
Marr. Date		5 Sep 1838 - Cincinnati, Hamilton, Ohio, USA	
Spouse		Mary Louise Thompson (1835-1909)	1 Jun 1858 - Louisville, Jefferson , Kentucky, USA
7	**M**	**William Monroe McLean**	
Born		1821	
Christened			
Died		1829	
Buried			
Spouse			

Family Group Record Justice John B. McLean & Sarah Bella Ludlow Garrard

Husband	Justice John B. McLean	
Born	11 Mar 1785	, Morris, New Jersey, USA
Christened		
Died	4 Apr 1861	Cincinnati, Hamilton, Ohio, USA
Cause of Death	pneumonia contracted after attending Lincoln's inauguration in the rain	
Buried	25 Apr 1861	Cincinnati, Hamilton, Ohio, USA
Address	Spring Grove Cemetary, Cincinnati, Ohio	
Father	Fergus McLean (1746-1837)	
Mother	Sophia Blackford (1753-1839)	
Marriage	11 May 1843	Cincinnati, Hamilton, Ohio, USA
Other Spouse	Rebecca E. Edwards (1786-1841)	29 Mar 1807 - Lebanon, Warren, Ohio, USA

Wife	Sarah Bella Ludlow	
Born	1802	Cumminsville, Hamilton, Ohio, USA
Christened		
Died	13 Jan 1882	Cincinnati, Hamilton, Ohio, USA
Cause of Death	cholera morbus//exhaustion	
Buried	15 Jan 1882	Cincinnati, Hamilton, Ohio, USA
Address	Spring Grove Cemetary, Cincinnati, Ohio	
Father	Col Israel Ludlow (1765-1804)	
Mother	Charlotte Chambers (1768-1821)	
Other Spouse	Jeptha Dudley Garrard (1802-1837)	25 Jun 1824 - Cincinnati, Hamilton, Ohio, USA

Children		
1 M	Ludlow McLean	
Born	8 Jan 1846	Cincinnati, Hamilton, Ohio, USA
Christened		
Died	8 Oct 1846	Cincinnati, Hamilton, Ohio, USA
Buried	Oct 1846	Cincinnati, Hamilton, Ohio, USA
Address	Spring Grove Cemetary, Cincinnati, Ohio	
Spouse		

Family Group Record Jacob Burnet McLean & Mary Jane Hazlett

Husband	Jacob Burnet McLean	
Born	10 Aug 1841	Versailles, Yvelines, , France
Christened		
Died	31 May 1926	Lake City, Wabasha, Minnesota, USA
Buried		
Father	Brigadier General Nathanial Collins McLean (1818-1905)	
Mother	Caroline Thew Burnet (1820-1856)	
Marriage	20 Feb 1876	Frontenac, Goodhue, Minnesota, USA

Wife	Mary Jane Hazlett	
Born	31 Dec 1851	, , Ohio, USA
Christened		
Died	11 Jan 1927	Lake City, Wabasha, Minnesota, USA
Buried		
Father	Silas Hazlett (-)	
Mother	Eliza Jane Patton (-)	

Children		
1	F	Eloise McLean
Born	17 Feb 1877	Frontenac, Goodhue, Minnesota, USA
Christened		
Died		
Buried		
Spouse		
2	M	Hazlett McLean
Born	28 May 1879	Frontenac, Goodhue, Minnesota, USA
Christened		
Died	15 Dec 1969	Eston, , Sadkatchewan, Canada
Buried		
Spouse	Grace Violet Chambers (1894-1969)	
Marr. Date	5 Dec 1911 - McTaggart, Saskatchewan, Canada	

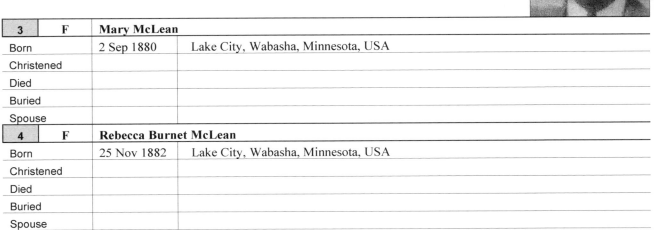

3	F	Mary McLean
Born	2 Sep 1880	Lake City, Wabasha, Minnesota, USA
Christened		
Died		
Buried		
Spouse		
4	F	Rebecca Burnet McLean
Born	25 Nov 1882	Lake City, Wabasha, Minnesota, USA
Christened		
Died		
Buried		
Spouse		

Children (cont.)			
5	**F**	**Frances Louise McLean**	
Born		20 Jul 1886	Lake City, Wabasha, Minnesota, USA
Christened			
Died			
Buried			
Spouse		George Joseph Purcell (-)	
6	**M**	**Burnett McLean**	
Born		13 Sep 1891	Lake City, Wabasha, Minnesota, USA
Christened			
Died			
Buried			
Spouse			
7	**M**	**Nathaniel Collins McLean**	
Born		24 Feb 1894	Lake City, Wabasha, Minnesota, USA
Christened			
Died			
Buried			
Spouse			

Family Group Record Brigadier General Nathanial Collins McLean & Caroline Thew Burnet

Husband	Brigadier General Nathanial Collins McLean	
Born	2 Feb 1818	Ridgeville, Warren, Ohio, USA
Christened		
Died	4 Jan 1905	Bellport, Suffolk, New York, USA
Buried	Jan 1905	Bellport, Suffolk, New York, USA
Address	Woodland Cemetery, Bellport, New York	
Father	Justice John B. McLean (1785-1861)	
Mother	Rebecca E. Edwards (1786-1841)	
Marriage	5 Sep 1838	Cincinnati, Hamilton, Ohio, USA
Other Spouse	Mary Louise Thompson (1835-1909)	1 Jun 1858 - Louisville, Jefferson , Kentucky, USA

Wife	Caroline Thew Burnet	
Born	26 Aug 1820	Cincinnati, Hamilton, Ohio, USA
Christened		
Died	15 Apr 1856	Cincinnati, Hamilton, Ohio, USA
Cause of Death	inflamation of bowels	
Buried	22 Apr 1856	Cincinnati, Hamilton, Ohio, USA
Address	Spring Grove Cemetary, Cincinnati, Ohio	
Father	Jacob Burnet (-)	
Mother	Rebecca (-)	

Children		
1 F	Rebecca Burnet McLean	
Born	28 Jan 1839	Cincinnati, Hamilton, Ohio, USA
Christened		
Died	1850	Cincinnati, Hamilton, Ohio, USA
Buried		
Spouse		
2 M	Jacob Burnet McLean	
Born	10 Aug 1841	Versailles, Yvelines, , France
Christened		
Died	31 May 1926	Lake City, Wabasha, Minnesota, USA
Buried		
Spouse	Mary Jane Hazlett (1851-1927)	20 Feb 1876 - Frontenac, Goodhue, Minnesota, USA
3 F	Caroline Burnett McLean	
Born	14 Jul 1843	Cincinnati, Hamilton, Ohio, USA
Christened		
Died		
Buried		
Spouse	H. A. V. Post (-)	
4 M	Nathaniel Collins McLean Jr.	
Born	15 Oct 1845	Cincinnati, Hamilton, Ohio, USA
Christened		
Died	18 Sep 1846	Cincinnati, Hamilton, Ohio, USA
Cause of Death	consumption	
Buried		
Spouse		

Children (cont.)			
5	F	**Evaline Elizabeth McLean**	
Born	5 Jan 1851	Cincinnati, Hamilton, Ohio, USA	
Christened			
Died			
Buried			
Spouse	Charles Henry Whipple (1850-)	5 Dec 1871 - Cincinnati, Hamilton, Ohio, USA	
6	M	**Dr. John M. McLean**	
Born	23 Jun 1854	Cincinnati, Hamilton, Ohio, USA	
Christened			
Died	2 Apr 1932	Chicago, Cook, Illinois, USA	
Buried	4 Apr 1932	Chicago, Cook, Illinois, USA	
Address	Graceland Cemetery, Chicago, Illinois 60613		
Spouse	Nellie Adele Sheldon (1855-1877)	28 Aug 1876 - Red Wing, Goodhue, Minnesota, USA	
Spouse	Jane Elizabeth Riley (1854-)	1881	

Family Group Record Brigadier General Nathanial Collins McLean & Mary Louise Thompson

Husband	Brigadier General Nathanial Collins McLean	
Born	2 Feb 1818	Ridgeville, Warren, Ohio, USA
Christened		
Died	4 Jan 1905	Bellport, Suffolk, New York, USA
Buried	Jan 1905	Bellport, Suffolk, New York, USA
Address	Woodland Cemetery, Bellport, New York	
Father	Justice John B. McLean (1785-1861)	
Mother	Rebecca E. Edwards (1786-1841)	
Marriage	1 Jun 1858	Louisville, Jefferson , Kentucky, USA
Other Spouse	Caroline Thew Burnet (1820-1856)	5 Sep 1838 - Cincinnati, Hamilton, Ohio, USA

Wife	Mary Louise Thompson	
Born	14 Nov 1835	Louisville, Jefferson , Kentucky, USA
Christened		
Died	13 Aug 1909	Bellport, Suffolk, New York, USA
Buried	Aug 1909	Bellport, Suffolk, New York, USA
Address	Woodland Cemetery, Bellport, New York	
Father	Phillip R. Thompson (-)	
Mother	Elizabeth (-)	

Children			
1	M	Nathaniel Collins McLean	
Born		21 May 1861	Glendale, Columbiana, Ohio, USA
Christened			
Died		22 Jul 1861	Glendale, Columbiana, Ohio, USA
Buried		24 Jul 1861	Cincinnati, Hamilton, Ohio, USA
Spouse			
2	F	Elizabeth Maud McLean	
Born		30 Aug 1862	Glendale, Columbiana, Ohio, USA
Christened			
Died		30 Jan 1943	
Buried			
Spouse		William Hampden Sage (1858-1922)	
3	M	Larz Anderson McLean	
Born		7 Feb 1864	
Christened			
Died		20 May 1876	Frontenac, Goodhue, Minnesota, USA
Cause of Death		drowning	
Buried		May 1876	Frontenac, Goodhue, Minnesota, USA
Spouse			

Family Group Record   Brigadier General Nathanial Collins McLean & Mary Louise Thompson

Children (cont.)				
4	**F**	**Mary Louise McLean**		
Born		9 Jul 1865	, , Ohio, USA	
Christened				
Died		6 Sep 1929		
Buried		Sep 1929	Bellport, Suffolk, New York, USA	
Address		Woodland Cemetery, Bellport, New York		
Spouse		Did Not Marry		

5	**F**	**Nathalie McLean**		
Born		31 Oct 1867	Frontenac, Goodhue, Minnesota, USA	
Christened		31 Oct 1867	Frontenac, Goodhue, Minnesota, USA	
Died		28 Sep 1950		
Buried		Sep 1950	Bellport, Suffolk, New York, USA	
Address		Woodland Cemetery, Bellport, New York		
Spouse		Did Not Marry		
6	**M**	**Marshall McLean**		
Born		1869	, , Ohio, USA	
Christened				
Died		1952		
Buried		1952	Bellport, Suffolk, New York, USA	
Address		Woodland Cemetery, Bellport, New York		
Spouse		Helen Homas (1877-1949)		
7	**F**	**Henrietta Post McLean**		
Born		1872	, , Ohio, USA	
Christened				
Died				
Buried				
Spouse		Arthur Dehon Hill (-)		
Marr. Date		20 Jun 1895 - Bellport, Suffolk, New York, USA		

Husband	John C. Markman	
Born	20 Jun 1840	Lason, Province Pommerania, Kingdom of Prussia
Christened		
Died	29 Nov 1920	Waterville, Pepin, Wisconsin, USA
Buried		
Marriage	Abt 1868	
Other Spouse	Fredricka J. Betcher (1856-After 1920)	1876 - Frontenac, Goodhue, Minnesota, USA

Wife	Sophia Carolina	
Born	1842	, , , Prussia
Christened		
Died	1876	Frontenac, Goodhue, Minnesota, USA
Buried		

Children		
1 **M**	**William H. Markman**	
Born	Oct 1870	Frontenac, Goodhue, Minnesota, USA
Christened		
Died		
Buried		
Spouse		
2 **F**	**Annie Joanna Markman**	
Born	1872	Frontenac, Goodhue, Minnesota, USA
Christened		
Died		
Buried		
Spouse		
3 **M**	**Louis (Lucy) Markman**	
Born	3 Sep 1874	Frontenac, Goodhue, Minnesota, USA
Christened		
Died	Bef 1880	
Buried		
Spouse		
4 **F**	**Sophia Caroline Markman**	
Born	25 Apr 1876	Frontenac, Goodhue, Minnesota, USA
Christened		
Died		
Buried		
Spouse	Wilcome Sylvester Richie (Abt 1875-)	3 Apr 1891 - Frankfort, Pepin, Wisconsin, USA

Family Group Record John C. Markman & Fredricka Betcher

Husband	John C. Markman	
Born	20 Jun 1840	Lason, Province Pommerania, Kingdom of Prussia
Christened		
Died	29 Nov 1920	Waterville, Pepin, Wisconsin, USA
Buried		
Marriage	1876	Frontenac, Goodhue, Minnesota, USA
Other Spouse	Sophia Carolina (1842-1876)	Abt 1868

Wife	Fredricka J. Betcher	
Born	Dec 1856	, , Province of Pommerania, Kingdom of Prussia
Christened		
Died	After 1920	Waterville, Pepin, Wisconsin, USA
Buried		

Children		
1 **M**	**Carl Friedrich Markman**	
Born	3 Jun 1880	Frontenac, Goodhue, Minnesota, USA
Christened	4 Jul 1880	Frontenac Station, Goodhue, Minnesota, USA
Address	St. John's Ev. Lutheran Church, Frontenac Station, Minnesota	
Died	Bef 1900	
Buried		
Spouse		
2 **M**	**Fred C. Markman**	
Born	Mar 1882	Frontenac, Goodhue, Minnesota, USA
Christened		
Died		
Buried		
Spouse		
3 **F**	**Alla D. Markman**	
Born	Jan 1885	Frontenac, Goodhue, Minnesota, USA
Christened		
Died		
Buried		
Spouse		
4 **F**	**Dora A. Markman**	
Born	Feb 1887	, , Wisconsin, USA
Christened		
Died		
Buried		
Spouse		

Family Group Record Frederick Meyer & Minna Meyer

Husband	Frederick Meyer	
Born	Abt 1840	, , , Hanover
Died	Bef 1880	
Marriage	Abt 1859	, , Ohio, USA

Wife	Minna	
Born	1840	, , , Hamburg
Died	1898	
Buried	1898	Frontenac, Goodhue, Minnesota, USA
Address	Old Frontenac Cemetery, Frontenac, Minnesota	

Children

1	M	George Meyer	
Born		1860	, , Ohio, USA

2	M	Frederick Meyer	
Born		1863	, , Illinois, USA
Spouse		Teresa Eisenbrand (1861-)	Abt 1884

3	F	Catherine W. Meyer	
AKA		Katie	
Born		Sep 1865	, , Illinois, USA
Died		1924	, , Minnesota, USA
Buried		1924	Frontenac, Goodhue, Minnesota, USA
Address		Old Frontenac Cemetery, Frontenac, Minnesota	

4	F	Minnie Meyer	
Born		Jul 1869	, , Illinois, USA
Died		21 Apr 1902	Frontenac, Goodhue, Minnesota, USA
Spouse		George E. Bartels Jr. (1862-1919)	
Marr. Date		25 Nov 1890 - Frontenac Station, Goodhue, Minnesota, USA	

5	F	Bertha Meyer	
Born		Feb 1876	, , Illinois, USA
Died		1945	
Buried		1945	Frontenac, Goodhue, Minnesota, USA
Address		Old Frontenac Cemetery, Frontenac, Minnesota	
Spouse		Charles J. Strupe (Strope) (1876-1933)	Abt 1901 - , Goodhue, Minnesota, USA

Family Group Record Elam R. Miller & Lucy Jane Miller

Husband	Elam R. Miller	
Born	1834	, , Mississippi, USA
Christened		
Died	Bef 1895	Minneapolis, Hennepin, Minnesota, USA
Buried		
Marriage	Abt 1861	, , Ohio, USA

Wife	Lucy Jane	
Born	Abt 1839	, , Kentucky, USA
Christened		
Died	After 1900	Minneapolis, Hennepin, Minnesota, USA
Buried		

Children		
1	F	Minnesota (Minnie) Miller
Born	1863	, , Ohio, USA
Christened		
Died		
Buried		
Spouse		
2	F	Mary Brown Miller
Born	1867	Frontenac, Goodhue, Minnesota, USA
Christened		
Died		
Buried		
Spouse		
3	F	Laura Francis Miller
Born	Dec 1869	Frontenac, Goodhue, Minnesota, USA
Christened		
Died		
Buried		
Spouse		
4	F	Florence Miller
Born	2 Apr 1871	Frontenac, Goodhue, Minnesota, USA
Christened		
Died	4 May 1888	Minneapolis, Hennepin, Minnesota, USA
Cause of Death	COD phthisis pulmonary	
Buried	May 1888	Minneapolis, Hennepin, Minnesota, USA
Address	Minnesota Pioneers and Soldiers Memorial Cemetery, Minneapolis, Minnesota	
Spouse		
5	F	Lucy Jane Miller
Born	1873	Frontenac, Goodhue, Minnesota, USA
Christened		
Died	Bef 1885	
Buried		
Spouse		

Family Group Record Elam R. Miller & Lucy Jane Miller

Children (cont.)		
6	**F**	**Alice R. Miller**
Born	1876	Frontenac, Goodhue, Minnesota, USA
Christened		
Died		
Buried		
Spouse		
7	**M**	**Patric F. Miller**
Born	1878	Frontenac, Goodhue, Minnesota, USA
Christened		
Died	Bef 1885	
Buried		
Spouse		
8	**F**	**Jane E. Miller**
Born	1880	Frontenac, Goodhue, Minnesota, USA
Christened		
Died	Bef 1885	
Buried		
Spouse		
9	**M**	**Eli R. Miller**
Born	1883	, , Minnesota, USA
Christened		
Died		
Buried		
Spouse		

Family Group Record John Minges & Mary Ann Ritzert

Husband	John Minges	
Born	1832	, , , Hessen-Nassau
Christened		
Died	24 Sep 1877	Rollingstone, Winona, Minnesota, USA
Buried		
Marriage	25 Feb 1858	Mantorville, Dodge, Minnesota, USA

Wife	Mary Ann Ritzert	
Born	Mar 1834	, , , Hessen-Darmstadt
Christened	31 Mar 1834	Schwanheim, Starkenburg, , Hessen-Darmstadt
Died	2 Jul 1909	Lewiston, Winona, Minnesota, USA
Buried		
Father	Johann Philip Ritzert (Abt 1814-)	
Mother	Elizabeth Hoelzel (1814-)	

Children			
1	M	Frank Minges	
Born		1860	Mantorville, Dodge, Minnesota, USA
Christened			
Died		27 Sep 1872	Rollingstone, Winona, Minnesota, USA
Buried			
Spouse			
2	F	Rose Minges	
Born		1864	Lake City, Wabasha, Minnesota, USA
Christened			
Died			
Buried			
Spouse			
3	M	Edward Minges	
Born		Sep 1866	Lake City, Wabasha, Minnesota, USA
Christened			
Died			
Buried			
Spouse			
4	M	William Minges	
Born		1870	Rollingstone, Winona, Minnesota, USA
Christened			
Died			
Buried			
Spouse			

Family Group Record Augustus Olcott Moore & Harriet Cornelia Green

Husband	Augustus Olcott Moore	
Born	21 Jul 1822	Augusta, Richmond, Georgia, USA
Christened		
Died	29 Apr 1865	Orange, Essex, New Jersey, USA
Buried		
Marriage	Cir 1842	, Morris, New Jersey, USA

Wife	Harriet Cornelia Green	
Born	15 Jun 1827	New York City, New York, New York, USA
Christened		
Died	7 Jul 1910	St. Paul, Ramsey, Minnesota, USA
Buried		

Children

1	M	Hiland Moore	
Born	1843	, , Ohio, USA	
Christened			
Died			
Buried			
Spouse			

2	F	Maria L. Moore	
Born	1845	, , Ohio, USA	
Christened			
Died			
Buried			
Spouse			

3	F	Nina Moore	
Born	1852	, , Ohio, USA	
Christened			
Died	29 Sep 1958	Roseville, Ramsey, Minnesota, USA	
Buried	Oct 1958	Roseville, Ramsey, Minnesota, USA	
Address	Roselawn Cemetery, Roseville, Ramsey,, MN		
Spouse	Francis Buckman Tiffany (1855-1936)	16 Oct 1889 - West Newton, Middlesex, Massachusetts, USA	

4	F	Lillian Moore	
Born	1856	, , New Jersey, USA	
Christened			
Died			
Buried			
Spouse			

5	M	John Lowell Moore	
Born	1860		
Christened			
Died	1939		
Buried			
Spouse	Jane Hancox (-)		

Family Group Record Augustus Olcott Moore & Harriet Cornelia Green

Children (cont.)		
6 **M**	**Elliot Augustus Moore**	
Born	12 Aug 1863	Frontenac, Goodhue, Minnesota, USA
Christened		
Died	29 Jun 1956	Chula Vista, San Diego, CA, USA
Buried		
Spouse	Alice (-)	

Family Group Record Henry Muller & Mary Muller

Husband	Henry Muller	
Born	9 Mar 1818	, , , Mecklenburg
Christened		
Died	29 Jun 1895	
Buried	Jun 1895	Frontenac, Goodhue, Minnesota, USA
Address	Old Frontenac Cemetery, Frontenac, Minnesota	
Marriage		
Other Spouse	Dorothea (1819-)	

Wife	Mary	
Born	1828	, , , Germany
Christened		
Died		
Buried		

Children		

Family Group Record   Gulbrand Olsen & Petroline Larsdatter

Husband	Gulbrand Olsen	
AKA	Gilbert	
Born	21 Oct 1815	Nittedal, Akershus, Norway
Christened	5 Nov 1815	Nittedal, Akershus, Norway
Died	3 Jul 1901	Frontenac, Goodhue, Minnesota, USA
Buried	Jul 1901	Frontenac, Goodhue, Minnesota, USA
Address	Old Frontenac Cemetery, Frontenac, Minnesota	
Father	Ole Pedersen (-)	
Mother	Anne Nielsdatter (-)	
Marriage	14 May 1852	Nittedal, Akershus, Norway

Wife	Petroline Larsdatter	
AKA	Petrine, Tina	
Born	1828	Nittedal, Akershus, Norway
Christened	25 Jan 1829	Nittedal, Akershus, Norway
Died	Cir 1897	Frontenac, Goodhue, Minnesota, USA
Buried	Cir 1897	Frontenac, Goodhue, Minnesota, USA
Father	Lars Jensen Zinober (1798-1884)	
Mother	Kari Pedersdatter Sørskogen (1807-1876)	

Children

1	F	Caroline Gulbrandsdatter	
	Born	5 Oct 1853	Nittedel, Akershus, Norway
	Christened	6 Nov 1853	Nittedal Parish, Akershus, Norway
	Died		, , , Norway
	Buried		
	Spouse		

2	M	Anton Gulbrandsen	
	Born	28 May 1855	Sinober, Nittedel, Akershus, Norway
	Christened	5 Aug 1855	Aker Parish, Akershus, Oslo County, Norway
	Died	13 Dec 1922	Aker sykehus, Oslo, Norway
	Buried	Dec 1922	Grefsen kirkegård, Oslo, Norway
	Spouse	Pauline Pedersdatter (1856-1912)	

3	M	Olous Gulbrandsen	
	Born	23 Dec 1856	Aker, Christiania, Akershus, Norway
	Christened	22 Mar 1857	Aker Parish, Akershus, Oslo County, Norway
	Died		, , , Norway
	Buried		
	Spouse		

Family Group Record Gulbrand Olsen & Petroline Larsdatter

Children (cont.)				
4	**M**	**Hans Petter Gulbrandsen (Gilbertson)**		
AKA		Peter Gilbertson		
Born		23 Jul 1859	Aker, Christiania, Akershus, Norway	
Christened		18 Sep 1859	Vestre Aker Parish, Akershus, Oslo County, Norway	
Died		22 Jul 1910	Chippewa Falls, Chippewa, Wisconsin, USA	
Cause of Death		burns from powder explosion at quarry		
Buried		26 Jul 1910	Frontenac, Goodhue, Minnesota, USA	
Address		Old Frontenac Cemetery, Frontenac, Minnesota		
Spouse		Linas Caroline Nilsdatter (Nielsen) (1860-1929)	22 May 1883 - Red Wing, Goodhue, Minnesota, USA	

5	**F**	**Annette Gulbrandsdatter (Gilbertson)**		
AKA		Annetta, Annie Gilbertson		
Born		14 Jan 1862	Aker, Christiania, Akershus, Norway	
Christened		21 Apr 1862	Ostre Parish, Akershus, Oslo, Norway	
Died		8 Aug 1927	Red Wing, Goodhue, Minnesota, USA	
Cause of Death		high blood pressure		
Buried		11 Aug 1927	Frontenac, Goodhue, Minnesota, USA	
Address		Old Frontenac Cemetery, Frontenac, Minnesota		
Spouse		Hans Ludwig Olson (1860-1910)		
Marr. Date		30 Aug 1886 - Red Wing, Goodhue, Minnesota, USA		

6	**F**	**Josephine Amalia Gulbrandsdatter**		
Born		14 Nov 1864	Aker, Christiania, Akershus, Norway	
Christened		20 Sep 1865	Aker Parish, Akershus, Oslo County, Norway	
Died			, , , Norway	
Buried				
Spouse				

Family Group Record Hans Ludwig Olson & Annette Gilbertson

Husband	Hans Ludwig Olson	
AKA	Larson	
Born	12 Apr 1860	Hardangerfjord, Vestlandet, Hordaland, Norway
Christened		
Died	6 Jan 1910	Frontenac, Goodhue, Minnesota, USA
Cause of Death	heart failure	
Buried	9 Jan 1910	Frontenac, Goodhue, Minnesota, USA
Address	Old Frontenac Cemetery, Frontenac, Minnesota	
Father	Ole Christian Larson Loken (1828-1903)	
Mother	Martha Wilhelmsdatter Allergodt (1840-1915)	
Marriage	30 Aug 1886	Red Wing, Goodhue, Minnesota, USA

Wife	Annette Gulbrandsdatter (Gilbertson)	
AKA	Annetta, Annie Gilbertson	
Born	14 Jan 1862	Aker, Christiania, Akershus, Norway
Christened	21 Apr 1862	Ostre Parish, Akershus, Oslo, Norway
Died	8 Aug 1927	Red Wing, Goodhue, Minnesota, USA
Cause of Death	high blood pressure	
Buried	11 Aug 1927	Frontenac, Goodhue, Minnesota, USA
Address	Old Frontenac Cemetery, Frontenac, Minnesota	
Father	Gulbrand Olsen (1815-1901)	
Mother	Petroline Larsdatter (1828-Cir 1897)	

Children			
1	F	Violet Olson	
Born		7 Dec 1886	Frontenac, Goodhue, Minnesota, USA
Christened			
Died		24 Mar 1968	, Goodhue, Minnesota, USA
Buried		Mar 1968	Frontenac, Goodhue, Minnesota, USA
Address		Old Frontenac Cemetery, Frontenac, Minnesota	
Spouse		Joseph Michael Schloer (1885-1941)	30 Nov 1912 - , Goodhue, Minnesota, USA

2	F	Henrietta Olson	
Born		18 Dec 1888	Frontenac, Goodhue, Minnesota, USA
Christened			
Died		19 Jul 1957	Frontenac, Goodhue, Minnesota, USA
Buried		Jul 1957	Frontenac, Goodhue, Minnesota, USA
Address		Old Frontenac Cemetery, Frontenac, Minnesota	
Spouse		Bernard (Benjamin) Joseph Sauter (1886-1976)	
Marr. Date		24 Nov 1908 - Red Wing, Goodhue, Minnesota, USA	

Family Group Record Hans Ludwig Olson & Annette Gilbertson

Children (cont.)		

3	F	**Clara Olson**
Born	15 Jul 1891	Frontenac, Goodhue, Minnesota, USA
Christened		
Died	13 Oct 1941	, Goodhue, Minnesota, USA
Cause of Death	heart attack	
Buried	Oct 1941	Red Wing, Goodhue, Minnesota, USA
Address	St. John's Evangelical Cemetery, Red Wing, Minnesota	
Spouse	Harrison Herman Scherf (1888-1944)	
Marr. Date	7 Apr 1915 - Frontenac, Goodhue, Minnesota, USA	

4	M	**Harry John Olson**
Born	15 Oct 1893	Frontenac, Goodhue, Minnesota, USA
Christened	17 Jun 1894	Frontenac, Goodhue, Minnesota, USA
Address	Christ Episcopal Church, Old Frontenac, Minnesota	
Died	16 Aug 1937	Red Wing, Goodhue, Minnesota, USA
Cause of Death	heart attack brought on by shock//elbow fractured in a collision between a truck and his car	
Buried	Aug 1937	Red Wing, Goodhue, Minnesota, USA
Address	Oakwood Cemetery, Red Wing, MN	
Spouse	Amy Carlson (1897-1985)	31 Jan 1922 - St. Paul, Ramsey, Minnesota, USA

5	F	**Marie Amanda Olson**
Born	27 May 1896	Frontenac, Goodhue, Minnesota, USA
Christened	6 Jul 1896	Frontenac, Goodhue, Minnesota, USA
Address	Christ Episcopal Church, Old Frontenac, Minnesota	
Died	12 Jul 1896	Frontenac, Goodhue, Minnesota, USA
Buried		
Spouse		

6	M	**Leo Hilmer Olson**
Born	15 Dec 1900	Frontenac, Goodhue, Minnesota, USA
Christened		
Died	15 Jul 1982	Rochester, Olmsted, Minnesota, USA
Buried	18 Jul 1982	Rochester, Olmsted, Minnesota, USA
Address	Calvary Cemetery, Rochester, Minnesota	
Spouse	Frances Ann Miller (1906-1991)	
Marr. Date	16 Aug 1930 - Red Wing, Goodhue, Minnesota, USA	

Family Group Record John Olson & Mary Hawkes

Husband	John Olson	
Born	1815	, , , Norway
Died		
Buried		
Marriage	Abt 1848	, , , Norway

Wife	Mary Hawkes	
Born	1817	, , , Norway
Died		
Buried		

Children			
1	F	Christine Olson	
Born		1849	, , , Norway
Died			
Buried			
Spouse			
2	M	Louis Olson	
Born		1850	, , , Norway
Died			
Buried			
Spouse			
3	F	Emma Olson	
Born		1853	, , , Norway
Died			
Buried			
Spouse			
4	M	Christian Olson	
Born		1854	, , , Norway
Died			
Buried			
Spouse			
5	F	Mary Olson	
Born		1857	, , , Norway
Died			
Buried			
Spouse			
6	M	Arthur W. Olson	
Born		1858	, , , Norway
Died		28 May 1911	Parker Prairie, Otter Tail, Minnesota, USA
Buried			
Spouse			

Family Group Record Ole W. Olson & Anna Vjorningstad Hansdatter

Husband	Ole W. Olson	
AKA	Olous	
Born	8 Dec 1863	Ulensaker, Akershus, Norway
Died	1932	Colfax, Dunn, Wisconsin, USA
Buried	1932	Colfax, Dunn, Wisconsin, USA
Address	Evergreen Cemetery, Colfax, Dunn, WI	
Father	Ole Williamson (-)	
Mother	Dorothy Ericksdatter (-)	
Marriage	28 Dec 1891	Red Wing, Goodhue, Minnesota, USA

Wife	Anna Vjorningstad Hansdatter	
Born	26 Dec 1868	Ulensaker, Akershus, Norway
Died	18 Jun 1954	Eau Claire, Eau Claire, Wisconsin, USA
Buried	1954	Colfax, Dunn, Wisconsin, USA
Address	Evergreen Cemetery, Colfax, Dunn, WI	
Father	Ole Hanson (-)	
Mother	Anna Marie (-)	

Children

1	F	Bertha Helen Olson	
	Born	12 Oct 1892	Frontenac, Goodhue, Minnesota, USA
	Died		
	Buried		
	Spouse	Alvin Hillson (-)	

2	M	Norman Richard Olson	
	Born	13 Jun 1894	Frontenac, Goodhue, Minnesota, USA
	Died	19 Mar 1984	Bedford, Lawrence, Indiana, USA
	Buried		
	Spouse	Myrtle Studlie (-)	

3	F	Elizabeth Mina Olson	
	Born	21 Oct 1895	Frontenac, Goodhue, Minnesota, USA
	Died	1963	Colfax, Dunn, Wisconsin, USA
	Buried	1963	Colfax, Dunn, Wisconsin, USA
	Address	Evergreen Cemetery, Colfax, Dunn, WI	
	Spouse	William Stockland (-)	

4	F	Hulda Marie Olson	
	Born	6 Dec 1896	Frontenac, Goodhue, Minnesota, USA
	Died	1972	
	Buried		
	Spouse	Albert Cardinal (-)	

Children (cont.)			
5	**F**	**Selma Louise Olson**	
Born	5 May 1898	Frontenac, Goodhue, Minnesota, USA	
Died			
Buried			
Spouse	Edward Close (-)		

6	**M**	**Roy Hiram Olson**	
Born	17 Dec 1899	Frontenac, Goodhue, Minnesota, USA	
Died			
Buried			
Spouse			

7	**M**	**Stanley Alexander Olson**	
Born	15 Sep 1901	Frontenac, Goodhue, Minnesota, USA	
Died	1948	Colfax, Dunn, Wisconsin, USA	
Buried	1948	Colfax, Dunn, Wisconsin, USA	
Address	Evergreen Cemetery, Colfax, Dunn, WI		
Spouse			

8	**F**	**Esther May Olson**	
Born	8 Sep 1903	Frontenac, Goodhue, Minnesota, USA	
Died			
Buried			
Spouse			

9	**F**	**Dorothy Margaret Olson**	
Born	30 Mar 1905	Frontenac, Goodhue, Minnesota, USA	
Died			
Buried			
Spouse			

Family Group Record John Peterson & Anna Neilson

Husband	John Peterson	
Born	8 Jun 1851	, , , Sweden
Christened		
Died	2 Jan 1933	Florence Township, Goodhue, Minnesota, USA
Buried	Jan 1933	Frontenac, Goodhue, Minnesota, USA
Address	Old Frontenac Cemetery, Frontenac, Minnesota	
Marriage	1879	, , , Sweden

Wife	Anna Neilson	
Born	2 Jan 1859	, , , Sweden
Christened		
Died	1909	Florence Township, Goodhue, Minnesota, USA
Buried	1909	Frontenac, Goodhue, Minnesota, USA
Address	Old Frontenac Cemetery, Frontenac, Minnesota	

Children		

1	F	Mary A. Peterson
Born	17 Jul 1880	, , , Canada
Christened		
Died	28 Jan 1914	
Buried	Jan 1914	Frontenac, Goodhue, Minnesota, USA
Address	Old Frontenac Cemetery, Frontenac, Minnesota	
Spouse		

2	M	Fred John Peterson
Born	26 Mar 1882	Florence Township, Goodhue, Minnesota, USA
Christened		
Died	30 Jan 1965	Frontenac, Goodhue, Minnesota, USA
Cause of Death	stroke	
Buried	3 Feb 1965	Frontenac, Goodhue, Minnesota, USA
Address	Old Frontenac Cemetery, Frontenac, Minnesota	
Spouse	Mary Martha Sepke (1885-1991)	12 Nov 1907 - Red Wing, Goodhue, Minnesota, USA

3	F	Betsey L. Peterson
AKA	Bessie	
Born	12 Dec 1883	Florence Township, Goodhue, Minnesota, USA
Christened		
Died	22 Nov 1905	
Buried	Nov 1905	Frontenac, Goodhue, Minnesota, USA
Address	Old Frontenac Cemetery, Frontenac, Minnesota	
Spouse		

4	M	William N. Peterson
Born	2 Feb 1886	Florence Township, Goodhue, Minnesota, USA
Christened		
Died	23 Jun 1940	
Buried	Jun 1940	Frontenac, Goodhue, Minnesota, USA
Address	Old Frontenac Cemetery, Frontenac, Minnesota	
Spouse		

Children (cont.)			
5	**F**	**Claire Augusta Peterson**	
Born	12 Sep 1887	Florence Township, Goodhue, Minnesota, USA	
Christened			
Died	3 Apr 1967		
Buried	Apr 1967	Frontenac, Goodhue, Minnesota, USA	
Address	Old Frontenac Cemetery, Frontenac, Minnesota		
Spouse			
6	**F**	**Sadie Molly Peterson**	
Born	4 Aug 1889	Florence Township, Goodhue, Minnesota, USA	
Christened			
Died			
Buried			
Spouse			
7	**M**	**Harry Peterson**	
Born	Oct 1891	Florence Township, Goodhue, Minnesota, USA	
Christened			
Died			
Buried			
Spouse			
8	**M**	**Richard James Peterson**	
Born	15 Sep 1893	Florence Township, Goodhue, Minnesota, USA	
Christened			
Died	26 Sep 1959		
Buried	Sep 1959	Frontenac, Goodhue, Minnesota, USA	
Address	Old Frontenac Cemetery, Frontenac, Minnesota		
Spouse			
9	**F**	**Mabel E. Peterson**	
Born	30 Nov 1894	Florence Township, Goodhue, Minnesota, USA	
Christened			
Died	6 Oct 1971		
Buried	Oct 1971	Frontenac, Goodhue, Minnesota, USA	
Address	Old Frontenac Cemetery, Frontenac, Minnesota		
Spouse			
10	**M**	**Nathanial Peterson**	
Born	Jul 1899	Florence Township, Goodhue, Minnesota, USA	
Christened			
Died			
Buried			
Spouse			
11	**F**	**Corneil Helen Peterson**	
Born	13 Sep 1900	Florence Township, Goodhue, Minnesota, USA	
Christened			
Died	25 Jun 1997		
Buried	Jun 1997	Frontenac, Goodhue, Minnesota, USA	
Address	Old Frontenac Cemetery, Frontenac, Minnesota		
Spouse			

Family Group Record Poppe

Husband	Poppe

Children

1	M	Nicolaus (Claus) Deidrich Poppe	
Born	5 Feb 1822	, , , Hanover	
Died	15 Jul 1871	Frontenac, Goodhue, Minnesota, USA	
Buried	17 Jul 1871	Frontenac, Goodhue, Minnesota, USA	
Address	Old Frontenac Cemetery, Frontenac, Minnesota		
Spouse	Rebecca Wilshusen (1834-1914)		
Marr. Date	Abt 1857 - New York City, New York, New York, USA		

2	M	Dietrich Poppe	
Born	27 Aug 1826	, , , Hanover	
Died	21 Feb 1875	, Goodhue, Minnesota, USA	
Buried	Feb 1875	Frontenac, Goodhue, Minnesota, USA	
Address	Old Frontenac Cemetery, Frontenac, Minnesota		
Spouse	Anna (-)		

3	F	Margaret Poppe	
AKA	Mary Martha		
Born	23 Aug 1827	, , , Hanover	
Died	12 May 1895	Frontenac, Goodhue, Minnesota, USA	
Buried	14 May 1895	Frontenac, Goodhue, Minnesota, USA	
Address	Old Frontenac Cemetery, Frontenac, Minnesota		
Spouse	Johann Michael Ackerman (1834-1911)		
Marr. Date	18 Mar 1876 - Frontenac, Goodhue, Minnesota, USA		

Family Group Record Nicolaus (Claus) Deidrich Poppe & Rebecca Wilshusen

Husband	Nicolaus (Claus) Deidrich Poppe	
Born	5 Feb 1822	, , , Hanover
Christened	1824	, , , Hanover
Died	15 Jul 1871	Frontenac, Goodhue, Minnesota, USA
Buried	17 Jul 1871	Frontenac, Goodhue, Minnesota, USA
Address	Old Frontenac Cemetery, Frontenac, Minnesota	
Father	Poppe (-)	
Mother		
Marriage	Abt 1857	New York City, New York, New York, USA

Wife	Rebecca Wilshusen	
AKA	Relhausen	
Born	Jul 1834	, , , Hanover
Christened		
Died	27 Oct 1914	Frontenac, Goodhue, Minnesota, USA
Buried	Oct 1914	Frontenac, Goodhue, Minnesota, USA
Address	Old Frontenac Cemetery, Frontenac, Minnesota	
Other Spouse	Peter Dammann (1847-1925)	23 Oct 1873 - , Goodhue, Minnesota, USA

Children		
1	U	Poppe
Born	Abt 1860	
Christened		
Died	Abt 1860	
Buried		
Spouse		
2	F	Catherina (Katie) Poppe
AKA	Katie	
Born	14 Nov 1865	New York, New York, New York, USA
Christened		
Died	5 Dec 1943	Lake City, Wabasha, Minnesota, USA
Cause of Death	chronic myocarditis	
Buried	7 Dec 1943	Frontenac, Goodhue, Minnesota, USA
Address	Old Frontenac Cemetery, Frontenac, Minnesota	
Spouse	Edward Frederick Hunecke (1865-1937)	28 Sep 1892 - Frontenac, Goodhue, Minnesota, USA
3	F	Lena Maria (Mary) Poppe
AKA	Mary, Maria	
Born	20 Sep 1867	Boston, Suffolk, Massachusetts, USA
Christened	1 Mar 1868	Boston, Suffolk, Massachusetts, USA
Died	10 May 1929	Frontenac, Goodhue, Minnesota, USA
Buried	May 1929	Frontenac, Goodhue, Minnesota, USA
Address	Old Frontenac Cemetery, Frontenac, Minnesota	
Spouse	Jens Casper Carstenson (Carsten) (1863-1942)	
Marr. Date	29 Dec 1898 - , Goodhue, Minnesota, USA	

Family Group Record John Possehl & Augusta Strom

Husband	John Possehl	
Born	Feb 1850	, , , Mecklenburg
Christened		
Died	31 Jul 1912	Red Wing, Goodhue, Minnesota, USA
Cause of Death	suicide by gun shot	
Buried	Aug 1912	Red Wing, Goodhue, Minnesota, USA
Address	Oakwood Cemetery, Red Wing, MN	
Father	Possehl (-)	
Mother		
Marriage	Abt 1875	, , , Mecklenburg

Wife	Augusta Strom	
Born	12 Jul 1850	, , , Mecklenburg
Christened		
Died	12 May 1932	Red Wing, Goodhue, Minnesota, USA
Buried	May 1932	Red Wing, Goodhue, Minnesota, USA
Address	Oakwood Cemetery, Red Wing, MN	

Children			
1	F	Clara E. Possehl	
Born		25 Feb 1877	, , , Mecklenburg
Christened			
Died		14 Jun 1928	Red Wing, Goodhue, Minnesota, USA
Buried		Jun 1928	Red Wing, Goodhue, Minnesota, USA
Address		Oakwood Cemetery, Red Wing, MN	
Spouse		Did Not Marry	

2	F	Augusta (Gustie) Possehl	
Born		1879	, , , Mecklenburg
Christened			
Died		Btw 1910 and 1915	Red Wing, Goodhue, Minnesota, USA
Buried			
Spouse		Fred Husby (1880-Bef 1910)	Cir 1897 - , , Minnesota, USA

3	M	Paul Frederick Adolph Possehl	
Born		15 Sep 1881	, , , Mecklenburg
Christened			
Died		26 Mar 1963	, Goodhue, Minnesota, USA
Buried		Mar 1963	Red Wing, Goodhue, Minnesota, USA
Address		Oakwood Cemetery, Red Wing, MN	
Spouse		Emily (-)	

Children (cont.)			
4	**M**	**Ludwig Adolph Alfred Possehl**	
AKA	Louis, Lucy		
Born	9 Aug 1884	Frontenac, Goodhue, Minnesota, USA	
Christened	21 Sep 1884	Red Wing, Goodhue, Minnesota, USA	
Died	15 Sep 1946	Red Wing, Goodhue, Minnesota, USA	
Buried	Sep 1946	Red Wing, Goodhue, Minnesota, USA	
Address	Oakwood Cemetery, Red Wing, MN		
Spouse	Adelheite (Adela) Wilhelmina Brunner (1891-1983)		
Marr. Date	9 Oct 1909 - Frontenac, Goodhue, Minnesota, USA		

Family Group Record Johann Philip Ritzert & Elizabeth Hoelzel

Husband	Johann Philip Ritzert	
Born	Abt 1814	, , , Hessen-Darmstadt
Christened		
Died		
Buried		
Marriage	9 Jan 1834	Schwanheim, Starkenburg, , Hessen-Darmstadt

Wife	Elizabeth Hoelzel	
AKA	Heltzel	
Born	1814	, , , Hessen-Darmstadt
Christened		
Died		
Buried	·	

Children			
1	F	Mary Ann Ritzert	
Born		Mar 1834	, , , Hessen-Darmstadt
Christened		31 Mar 1834	Schwanheim, Starkenburg, , Hessen-Darmstadt
Died		2 Jul 1909	Lewiston, Winona, Minnesota, USA
Buried			
Spouse		John Minges (1832-1877)	25 Feb 1858 - Mantorville, Dodge, Minnesota, USA
2	F	Phillippine Elizabeth Ritzert	
Born		6 Aug 1842	, , , Hessen-Darmstadt
Christened		15 Aug 1842	Schwanheim, Starkenburg, , Hessen-Darmstadt
Died		9 Feb 1920	St. Paul, Ramsey, Minnesota, USA
Buried		Feb 1920	St. Paul, Ramsey, Minnesota, USA
Address		Calvary Cemetery, St. Paul, Minnesota	
Spouse		John Sauter (1834-1896)	3 Nov 1861 - Frontenac, Goodhue, Minnesota, USA
3	M	Frank Ritzert	
Born		1861	Tonawanda, Erie, New York, USA
Christened			
Died			
Buried			
Spouse			

Family Group Record Adam Roafe (Raab) & Carolina Shale

Husband	Adam Roafe (Raab)	
Born	1806	, , , Bavaria
Marriage	Cir 1842	, , , Bavaria

Wife	Carolina Shale	
Born	1825	, , , Bavaria
Father	Shale (-)	
Mother		

Children		
1	F	Dorothea Roafe
Born	1844	, , , Bavaria
2	M	George Roafe
Born	1851	, , , Bavaria
3	F	Margaret Roafe
Born	1853	, , , Bavaria
4	M	John Roafe
Born	1855	, , , Bavaria
5	F	Carolina Roafe
Born	1857	, , , Bavaria
6	F	Mina Roafe
Born	1859	, , , Bavaria

Family Group Record August A. Sauter & Agatha Schafer

Husband	August A. Sauter	
Born	Sep 1846	Ratshausen, , Wurttemburg
Died	16 Nov 1914	Red Wing, Goodhue, Minnesota, USA
Buried	Nov 1914	Red Wing, Goodhue, Minnesota, USA
Address	Calvary Cemetery, Red Wing, Minnesota	
Father	Sauter (Abt 1800-)	
Mother		
Marriage	Abt 1874	, , Minnesota, USA

Wife	Agatha Schafer	
AKA	Agatha	
Born	17 Jun 1853	Ratshausen, , Wurttemburg
Died	13 Mar 1892	, Goodhue, Minnesota, USA
Buried	Mar 1892	Red Wing, Goodhue, Minnesota, USA
Address	Calvary Cemetery, Red Wing, Minnesota	

Children		
1	**F**	**Mary Agnes Sauter**
Born	Sep 1875	, , Minnesota, USA
Died		
Buried		
Spouse	John Dammann (1872-)	13 Jun 1899 - Red Wing, Goodhue, Minnesota, USA
2	**M**	**Ferdinand Sauter**
Born	22 Sep 1876	, , Minnesota, USA
Died	20 Dec 1914	, Goodhue, Minnesota, USA
Buried	Dec 1914	Red Wing, Goodhue, Minnesota, USA
Address	Calvary Cemetery, Red Wing, Minnesota	
Spouse	Alvina L. Johnson (1879-1968)	25 Nov 1903 - Red Wing, Goodhue, Minnesota, USA
3	**M**	**Leo Sauter**
Born	1880	Florence Township, Goodhue, Minnesota, USA
Died	1923	
Buried		
Spouse	Anna Wiech (-1956)	14 Nov 1906 - Red Wing, Goodhue, Minnesota, USA
4	**M**	**Frank J. Sauter**
Born	Aug 1882	Florence Township, Goodhue, Minnesota, USA
Died	1968	
Buried	1968	Minnetonka, Hennepin, Minnesota USA
Spouse	Lillian Krelberg (1889-1977)	17 Nov 1906 - Red Wing, Goodhue, Minnesota, USA
5	**M**	**Bernard (Benjamin) Joseph Sauter**
Born	17 Nov 1886	Florence Township, Goodhue, Minnesota, USA
Died	1976	
Buried	1976	Frontenac, Goodhue, Minnesota, USA
Address	Old Frontenac Cemetery, Frontenac, Minnesota	
Spouse	Henrietta Olson (1888-1957)	
Marr. Date	24 Nov 1908 - Red Wing, Goodhue, Minnesota, USA	

Family Group Record John Sauter & Phillippine Elizabeth Ritzert

Husband	John Sauter	
Born	12 Dec 1834	Ratshausen, , Wurttemburg
Christened		
Died	22 Oct 1896	St. Paul, Ramsey, Minnesota, USA
Buried	Oct 1896	St. Paul, Ramsey, Minnesota, USA
Address	Calvary Cemetery, St. Paul, Minnesota	
Father	Sauter (Abt 1800-)	
Mother		
Marriage	3 Nov 1861	Frontenac, Goodhue, Minnesota, USA

Wife	Phillippine Elizabeth Ritzert	
Born	6 Aug 1842	, , , Hessen-Darmstadt
Christened	15 Aug 1842	Schwanheim, Starkenburg, , Hessen-Darmstadt
Died	9 Feb 1920	St. Paul, Ramsey, Minnesota, USA
Buried	Feb 1920	St. Paul, Ramsey, Minnesota, USA
Address	Calvary Cemetery, St. Paul, Minnesota	
Father	Johann Philip Ritzert (Abt 1814-)	
Mother	Elizabeth Hoelzel (1814-)	

Children			
1	F	Florence E. Sauter	
Born		1863	Hay Creek Township, Goodhue, Minnesota, USA
Christened			
Died			
Buried			
Spouse		Charles Henry Bell (1886-1948)	21 Jun 1911 - Minneapolis, Hennepin, Minnesota, USA
2	M	Albert E. Sauter	
Born		Dec 1866	Hay Creek Township, Goodhue, Minnesota, USA
Christened			
Died		10 Mar 1954	, Wilkin, Minnesota, USA
Buried			
Spouse		Ella E. (-)	
3	F	Augusta Sauter	
Born		1868	Frontenac, Goodhue, Minnesota, USA
Christened			
Died			
Buried			
Spouse		Edward Luthge (-)	21 Dec 1885 - Frontenac, Goodhue, Minnesota, USA
4	M	August Sauter	
Born		Abt 1870	Florence Township, Goodhue, Minnesota, USA
Christened			
Died			
Buried			
Spouse			

Family Group Record John Sauter & Phillippine Elizabeth Ritzert

Children (cont.)		

5	F	**Rosa Mary Sauter**
Born	2 Jan 1871	Florence Township, Goodhue, Minnesota, USA
Christened		
Died		
Buried		
Spouse	Ned A. Blaisdell (-)	8 Feb 1899 - St. Paul, Ramsey, Minnesota, USA

6	M	**Frank Casper Sauter**
Born	27 Aug 1873	Florence Township, Goodhue, Minnesota, USA
Christened		
Died		
Buried		
Spouse	Grace M. (-)	

7	M	**George John Sauter**
Born	4 Apr 1876	Florence Township, Goodhue, Minnesota, USA
Christened		
Died		
Buried		
Spouse		

8	F	**Francis H. Sauter**
Born	Nov 1878	Florence Township, Goodhue, Minnesota, USA
Christened		
Died		
Buried		
Spouse	George J. Klein (-)	24 Jan 1906 - St. Paul, Ramsey, Minnesota, USA

9	F	**Isabelle V. Sauter**	
Born	Aug 1881	Florence Township, Goodhue, Minnesota, USA	
Christened			
Died			
Buried			
Spouse	George E. Earley (-)		
Marr. Date	21 Aug 1906 - St. Paul, Ramsey, Minnesota, USA		

10	F	**Elenora Sauter**
Born	Nov 1884	Florence Township, Goodhue, Minnesota, USA
Christened		
Died		
Buried		
Spouse		

Family Group Record John B. Sauter & Mary Francesca Wegrich

Husband	John B. Sauter	
Born	20 Mar 1857	Ratshausen, , Wurttemburg
Christened		
Died	22 Apr 1913	, Goodhue, Minnesota, USA
Cause of Death	accidental drowning in Lake Pepin	
Buried	Apr 1913	Red Wing, Goodhue, Minnesota, USA
Address	Calvary Cemetery, Red Wing, Minnesota	
Father	Ferdinand Sauter (-)	
Mother	Maria Sauter (-)	
Marriage	26 Nov 1878	Red Wing, Goodhue, Minnesota, USA

Wife	Mary Francesca (Frances) Wegrich	
Born	17 Apr 1857	Dayton, Montgomery, Ohio, USA
Christened		
Died	3 Oct 1887	Red Wing, Goodhue, Minnesota, USA
Cause of Death	consumption	
Buried	Oct 1887	Red Wing, Goodhue, Minnesota, USA
Address	Calvary Cemetery, Red Wing, Minnesota	
Father	Severin Wegrich (1830-1884)	
Mother	Victoria Walburga Ewerz (1824-1883)	

Children			
1	F	Mary Victoria Sauter	
Born		29 Dec 1879	Florence Township, Goodhue, Minnesota, USA
Christened			
Died		4 Feb 1947	, , Oregon, USA
Buried		Feb 1947	Lake City, Wabasha, Minnesota, USA
Address		St. Mary's Cemetery, Lake City, MN	
Spouse		Constance F. Koch (1874-1964)	7 Nov 1899 - , Goodhue, Minnesota, USA
2	F	Elizabeth Sauter	
Born		22 Jan 1882	Frontenac, Goodhue, Minnesota, USA
Christened			
Died		28 Nov 1884	Frontenac, Goodhue, Minnesota, USA
Buried			
Spouse			

Family Group Record Joseph William M. Sauter & Maria Caroline (Lena) Hunecke

Husband	Joseph William M. Sauter	
Born	19 Mar 1857	Ratshausen, , Wurttemburg
Christened		
Died	30 Sep 1930	Synnes, Stevens, Minnesota, USA
Buried	Oct 1930	Morris, Stevens, Minnesota, USA
Address	Calvary Cemetery, Morris, Stevens County, Minnesota	
Father	Ferdinand Sauter (-)	
Mother	Maria Sauter (-)	
Marriage	6 Jun 1882	Red Wing, Goodhue, Minnesota, USA

Wife	Maria Caroline (Lena) Hunecke	
AKA	Lena	
Born	19 May 1858	Red Wing, Goodhue, Territory of Minnesota
Christened		
Died	3 Nov 1923	Synnes, Stevens, Minnesota, USA
Buried	Nov 1923	Morris, Stevens, Minnesota, USA
Address	Calvary Cemetery, Morris, Stevens County, Minnesota	
Father	Henrich Bernhard Hunecke (1831-1907)	
Mother	Louisa Margaret Henrietta Bremer (1829-1893)	

Children

1	M	Joseph Sauter	
	Born	3 May 1883	Goodhue Village, Goodhue, Minnesota, USA
	Christened		
	Died	1894	Goodhue Village, Goodhue, Minnesota, USA
	Buried		
	Spouse		
2	F	Louise Mary Sauter	
	Born	4 Jun 1885	Florence Township, Goodhue, Minnesota, USA
	Christened		
	Died	10 Feb 1981	Morris, Stevens, Minnesota, USA
	Buried		
	Spouse	Timothy Mccarthy (-)	
3	M	Wilhelm Joseph Sauter	
	Born	25 Mar 1887	Hay Creek Township, Goodhue, Minnesota, USA
	Christened		
	Died	9 Jun 1959	, Carroll, Iowa, USA
	Buried	Jun 1959	Morris, Stevens, Minnesota, USA
	Address	Calvary Cemetery, Morris, Stevens County, Minnesota	
	Spouse	Catherine Heinen (1895-1986)	
4	F	Bathilda Tilla Sauter	
	Born	16 Feb 1889	Florence Township, Goodhue, Minnesota, USA
	Christened		
	Died	13 Dec 1965	Wabasha, Wabasha, Minnesota, USA
	Buried		
	Spouse	Thomas Foley (1887-1947)	

Family Group Record Joseph William M. Sauter & Maria Caroline (Lena) Hunecke

Children (cont.)			
5	**F**	**Barbara Sauter**	
Born		1893	Florence Township, Goodhue, Minnesota, USA
Christened			
Died		1985	Morris, Stevens, Minnesota, USA
Buried			
Spouse			
6	**F**	**Elizabeth Agnes Sauter**	
Born		1898	Florence Township, Goodhue, Minnesota, USA
Christened			
Died		1990	
Buried			
Spouse			
7	**M**	**Joseph August Sauter**	
Born		28 Apr 1900	Florence Township, Goodhue, Minnesota, USA
Christened			
Died		2 Jun 1971	Fergus Falls, Otter Tail, Minnesota, USA
Buried		Jun 1971	Morris, Stevens, Minnesota, USA
Address		Calvary Cemetery, Morris, Stevens County, Minnesota	
Spouse		Rose Mullen Hover (-)	

Family Group Record Gottfried Schenach & Marianne (Anna) Berktold

Husband	Gottfried Schenach	
Born	6 Mar 1822	Lermoos, , Tyrol, Austria
Christened		
Died	2 Feb 1892	Frontenac, Goodhue, Minnesota, USA
Buried	Feb 1892	Frontenac, Goodhue, Minnesota, USA
Address	Old Frontenac Cemetery, Frontenac, Minnesota	
Father	Joseph Schenach (1794-1874)	
Mother	Maria Theresia Feineler (1798-1854)	
Marriage	Abt 1855	, , Tyrol, Austria

Wife	Marianne (Anna) Berktold	
AKA	Mary, Annie, Nannie, Hannah	
Born	27 Oct 1830	, Landgericht Ehrenberg, Tyrol, Austria
Christened		
Died	12 Feb 1898	Frontenac, Goodhue, Minnesota, USA
Buried	Feb 1898	Frontenac, Goodhue, Minnesota, USA
Address	Old Frontenac Cemetery, Frontenac, Minnesota	
Father	Berktold (-)	
Mother		

Children		
1 F	Elenor (Ariel) (Hellah) Schenach	
AKA	Delarius, Hillarius	
Born	Abt 1857	Lermoos, , Tirol, Austria
Christened		
Died		
Buried		
Spouse		
2 M	Engelbert Schenach	
Born	1864	Frontenac, Goodhue, Minnesota, USA
Christened		
Died	After 1940	St. Paul, Ramsey, Minnesota, USA
Buried		
Spouse	Catherine L. (-)	Abt 1887
3 M	Joseph Schenach	
Born	1865	Frontenac, Goodhue, Minnesota, USA
Christened		
Died	12 Feb 1880	Frontenac, Goodhue, Minnesota, USA
Cause of Death	typhoid fever	
Buried	Feb 1880	Frontenac, Goodhue, Minnesota, USA
Address	Old Frontenac Cemetery, Frontenac, Minnesota	
Spouse	Did Not Marry	

Family Group Record Emmanuel Schenach & Annastasia Schretter

Husband	Emmanuel Schenach	
Born	17 Apr 1824	Lermoos, , Tirol, Austria
Christened		
Died	11 May 1909	Frontenac, Goodhue, Minnesota, USA
Cause of Death	Bronchitis//senility	
Buried	May 1909	Frontenac, Goodhue, Minnesota, USA
Address	Old Frontenac Cemetery, Frontenac, Minnesota	
Father	Joseph Schenach (1794-1874)	
Mother	Maria Theresia Feineler (1798-1854)	
Marriage	1860	...USA

Wife	Annastasia Schretter	
AKA	Anna	
Born	16 Dec 1829	Lermoos, , Tirol, Austria
Christened		
Died	17 Aug 1890	Frontenac, Goodhue, Minnesota, USA
Buried	Aug 1890	Frontenac, Goodhue, Minnesota, USA
Address	Old Frontenac Cemetery, Frontenac, Minnesota	

Children			
1	F	Josephine Schenach	
Born		1861	Frontenac, Goodhue, Minnesota, USA
Christened			
Died		1884	, , Minnesota, USA
Buried			
Spouse		Nicholas Wilson (Wiltgen) (1851-1938)	29 Dec 1879 - Red Wing, Goodhue, Minnesota, USA
2	F	Victoria Schenach	
Born		19 Nov 1863	Frontenac, Goodhue, Minnesota, USA
Christened			
Died		23 May 1911	Rochester, Olmsted, Minnesota, USA
Buried			
Spouse			
3	M	John Schenach	
Born		22 Dec 1864	Frontenac, Goodhue, Minnesota, USA
Christened			
Died		12 Mar 1940	Frontenac, Goodhue, Minnesota, USA
Buried			
Spouse		Mary (1866-Bef 1915)	Abt 1894 - , Goodhue, Minnesota, USA
Spouse		Ellen Mary Furney (1872-1951)	Abt 1915 - , Goodhue, Minnesota, USA

Family Group Record John Schenach & Mary Schenach

Husband	John Schenach	
Born	22 Dec 1864	Frontenac, Goodhue, Minnesota, USA
Christened		
Died	12 Mar 1940	Frontenac, Goodhue, Minnesota, USA
Buried		
Father	Emmanuel Schenach (1824-1909)	
Mother	Annastasia Schretter (1829-1890)	
Marriage	Abt 1894	, Goodhue, Minnesota, USA
Other Spouse	Ellen Mary Furney (1872-1951)	Abt 1915 - , Goodhue, Minnesota, USA

Wife	Mary	
Born	Sep 1866	, , Minnesota, USA
Christened		
Died	Bef 1915	, , Minnesota, USA
Buried		

Children		
1 M	Son Schenach	
Born	28 Apr 1899	Florence Township, Goodhue, Minnesota, USA
Christened		
Died	28 Apr 1899	Florence Township, Goodhue, Minnesota, USA
Buried		
Spouse		

Family Group Record John Schenach & Ellen Furney Hackett

Husband	John Schenach	
Born	22 Dec 1864	Frontenac, Goodhue, Minnesota, USA
Christened		
Died	12 Mar 1940	Frontenac, Goodhue, Minnesota, USA
Buried		
Father	Emmanuel Schenach (1824-1909)	
Mother	Annastasia Schretter (1829-1890)	
Marriage	Abt 1915	, Goodhue, Minnesota, USA
Other Spouse	Mary (1866-Bef 1915)	Abt 1894 - , Goodhue, Minnesota, USA

Wife	Ellen Mary Furney	
Born	Apr 1872	Nininger, Dakota, Minnesota, USA
Christened		
Died	29 Sep 1951	, Goodhue, Minnesota, USA
Buried		
Father	George W. Furney (1832-)	
Mother	Arminte (1839-)	
Other Spouse	James Harold Hackett (1865-1911)	Abt 1893

Children

Family Group Record Engelbert Schenach & Maria Friedericks

Husband	Engelbert Schenach	
Born	15 Feb 1832	Biberwier, Ruetta, Tyrol, Austria
Christened		
Died	15 Apr 1922	Frontenac, Goodhue, Minnesota, USA
Cause of Death	cerebral hemorrhage//senility	
Buried	Apr 1922	Frontenac, Goodhue, Minnesota, USA
Address	Old Frontenac Cemetery, Frontenac, Minnesota	
Father	Joseph Schenach (1794-1874)	
Mother	Maria Theresia Feineler (1798-1854)	
Marriage	Apr 1861	, Goodhue, Minnesota, USA

Wife	Maria (Mary) Sophia Henrietta Friedericks	
AKA	Marg	
Born	27 Feb 1838	Waren, Muritz, Mecklenburg
Christened		
Died	15 Jan 1913	Frontenac, Goodhue, Minnesota, USA
Cause of Death	acute bronchities	
Buried	Jan 1913	Frontenac, Goodhue, Minnesota, USA
Address	Old Frontenac Cemetery, Frontenac, Minnesota	
Father	Johann Christian Friedericks (Abt 1805-)	
Mother	Maria Frederica Volkert (Abt 1805-)	

Children

1	F	Clara Schenach	
Born		1862	Frontenac, Goodhue, Minnesota, USA
Christened			
Died		17 Feb 1943	Tacoma, Pierce, Washington, USA
Buried		Feb 1943	Lakewood, , Washington, USA
Address		Mountain View Memoria Park Cemetery, Lakewood, Washington	
Spouse		John M. Kade (1857-1924)	1891 - Tacoma, Pierce, Washington, USA

2	M	Louis G. Schenach	
Born		4 Jul 1863	Frontenac, Goodhue, Minnesota, USA
Christened			
Died		17 Feb 1936	Frontenac, Goodhue, Minnesota, USA
Cause of Death		bronchial pneumonia	
Buried		Feb 1936	Frontenac, Goodhue, Minnesota, USA
Address		Old Frontenac Cemetery, Frontenac, Minnesota	
Spouse		Did Not Marry	

Family Group Record Engelbert Schenach & Maria Friedericks

Children (cont.)			
3	**M**	**Edmund Martin Schenach**	
Born		19 Mar 1865	Frontenac, Goodhue, Minnesota, USA
Christened			
Died		21 Jan 1962	Red Wing, Goodhue, Minnesota, USA
Buried		23 Jan 1962	Red Wing, Goodhue, Minnesota, USA
Address		Calvary Cemetery, Red Wing, Minnesota	
Spouse		Mary Ann Taggert (1863-1947)	
Marr. Date		15 Oct 1890 - Clayfield Township, Pierce, Wisconsin, USA	
4	**M**	**Francis (Frank) Joseph Schenach**	
Born		13 May 1868	Frontenac, Goodhue, Minnesota, USA
Christened			
Died		1 Jul 1931	Red Wing, Goodhue, Minnesota, USA
Buried		Jul 1931	Red Wing, Goodhue, Minnesota, USA
Address		Calvary Cemetery, Red Wing, Minnesota	
Spouse		Julia Theresa Quigley (1867-1930)	14 Nov 1894 - Wabasha, Wabasha, Minnesota, USA
5	**F**	**Bertha Elizabeth Ruth Schenach**	
AKA		Ruth	
Born		13 Oct 1871	Florence Township, Goodhue, Minnesota, USA
Christened			
Died		29 Sep 1943	Red Wing, Goodhue, Minnesota, USA
Cause of Death		hypertension- heart disease	
Buried		2 Oct 1943	Red Wing, Goodhue, Minnesota, USA
Address		Calvary Cemetery, Red Wing, Minnesota	
Spouse		Albert Schmidt (1860-1934)	20 Jun 1894 - Frontenac, Goodhue, Minnesota, USA
6	**M**	**Frederick Schenach**	
Born		27 Aug 1875	Florence Township, Goodhue, Minnesota, USA
Christened			
Died		22 Jan 1890	Frontenac, Goodhue, Minnesota, USA
Cause of Death		pneumonia	
Buried		Jan 1890	Frontenac, Goodhue, Minnesota, USA
Address		Old Frontenac Cemetery, Frontenac, Minnesota	
Spouse			
7	**F**	**Emily Marie Schenach**	
AKA		Amelia Francis, Emma	
Born		31 Dec 1879	Frontenac, Goodhue, Minnesota, USA
Christened			
Died		22 Jul 1961	, Goodhue, Minnesota, USA
Buried		Jul 1961	Frontenac, Goodhue, Minnesota, USA
Address		Old Frontenac Cemetery, Frontenac, Minnesota	
Spouse		Earl Casmir Kells (1890-1961)	1922 - , Goodhue, Minnesota, USA

Family Group Record Herman Scherf & Carolyn J. Steffenhagen

Husband	Herman Scherf	
AKA	Anton Schurzel	
Born	6 Oct 1842	, , , Saxe Weimer Eisenach
Christened	17 Oct 1842	, , , Saxe Weimer Eisenach
Died	16 Oct 1918	Frontenac, Goodhue, Minnesota, USA
Cause of Death	paralysis	
Buried	19 Oct 1918	Frontenac, Goodhue, Minnesota, USA
Address	Old Frontenac Episcopal Church Cemetery, Frontenac, Minnesota	
Father	Martin Scherf (1799-1880)	
Mother	Christina Schmidt (1804-1887)	
Marriage	12 Nov 1868	Red Wing, Goodhue, Minnesota, USA

Wife	Carolina Johanna Maria Steffenhagen	
AKA	Lena	
Born	9 May 1853	West Grabau, Cummerow, Pommern, Prussia
Died	26 Apr 1927	Florence Township, Goodhue, Minnesota, USA
Cause of Death	Chronic endocarditis (heart attack)	
Buried	28 Apr 1927	Frontenac, Goodhue, Minnesota, USA
Address	Old Frontenac Episcopal Church Cemetery, Frontenac, Minnesota	
Father	Carl C. Steffenhagen (1803-1877)	
Mother	Carolina Pulls (1816-1905)	

Children			
1	F	Carolyn Augusta Scherf	
AKA		Carrie, Caroline	
Born		18 Apr 1870	Cameron, Clinton, Missouri, USA
Christened		7 Apr 1885	Frontenac, Goodhue, Minnesota, USA
Address		Christ Episcopal Church, Old Frontenac, Minnesota	
Died		23 Aug 1953	Red Wing, Goodhue, Minnesota, USA
Cause of Death		stroke	
Buried		25 Aug 1953	Frontenac, Goodhue, Minnesota, USA
Address		Old Frontenac Episcopal Church Cemetery, Frontenac, Minnesota	
Spouse		Ole Ludweg (Louis) Carlson (1863-1935)	14 Jan 1892 - Frontenac, Goodhue, Minnesota, USA
2	F	Emma Emelia Scherf	
AKA		Tootsie	
Born		28 Jun 1872	Cameron, Clinton , Missouri, USA
Christened		7 Apr 1885	Frontenac, Goodhue, Minnesota, USA
Address		Christ Episcopal Church, Old Frontenac, Minnesota	
Died		23 Sep 1937	Lake City, Wabasha, Minnesota, USA
Buried			Lake City, Wabasha, Minnesota, USA
Address		Lakewood Cemetery, Lake City, MN	
Spouse		Charles J. O. Roniek (1873-)	24 Jun 1903 - Frontenac, Goodhue, Minnesota, USA
3	M	Charles Martin Scherf	
Born		25 Jun 1874	Cameron, Clinton , Missouri, USA
Died		9 Apr 1942	Lake City, Wabasha, Minnesota, USA
Buried		Apr 1942	Lake City, Wabasha, Minnesota, USA
Address		Lakewood Cemetery, Lake City, MN	
Spouse		Katherine L. Krelberg (1881-1971)	
Marr. Date		24 Nov 1903 - Red Wing, Goodhue, Minnesota, USA	

Children (cont.)			
4	**M**	**Cortland Herman Scherf**	
Born		13 Apr 1877	Red Wing, Goodhue, Minnesota, USA
Died		9 Nov 1879	, Goodhue, Minnesota, USA
Cause of Death		diptheria	
5	**M**	**William Frederic Scherf**	
Born		30 Apr 1881	Farley Township, Polk, Minnesota, USA
Died		27 Mar 1946	Lake City, Wabasha, Minnesota, USA
Buried		30 Mar 1946	Wacouta, Goodhue, Minnesota, USA
Address		Wacouta Township Cemetery, Wacouta, MN	
Spouse		Alydia Louise Johnson (1882-1967)	29 Jul 1903 - , Goodhue, Minnesota, USA
6	**F**	**Jeannette Hermina Scherf**	
AKA		Nettie	
Born		7 Dec 1885	Frontenac, Goodhue, Minnesota, USA
Christened		4 Apr 1886	Frontenac, Goodhue, Minnesota, USA
Address		Christ Episcopal Church, Old Frontenac, Minnesota	
Died		15 Apr 1955	, Wabasha, Minnesota, USA
Buried		18 Apr 1955	Frontenac, Goodhue, Minnesota, USA
Address		Old Frontenac Episcopal Church Cemetery, Frontenac, Minnesota	
Spouse		Charles Lester Tackaberry (1884-1952)	20 Jul 1914 - , Goodhue, Minnesota, USA
7	**M**	**Harrison Herman Scherf**	
AKA		Harry	
Born		6 Jul 1888	Florence Township, Goodhue, Minnesota, USA
Died		23 Apr 1944	Red Wing, Goodhue, Minnesota, USA
Cause of Death		suicide by hanging//despondant because of wife's death	
Buried		25 Apr 1944	Red Wing, Goodhue, Minnesota, USA
Address		St. John's Evangelical Cemetery, Red Wing, Minnesota	
Spouse		Clara Olson (1891-1941)	7 Apr 1915 - Frontenac, Goodhue, Minnesota, USA
8	**F**	**Etta Mina Scherf**	
AKA		Tootsie	
Born		14 May 1894	Florence Township, Goodhue, Minnesota, USA
Christened		15 Jul 1894	Frontenac, Goodhue, Minnesota, USA
Address		Christ Episcopal Church, Old Frontenac, Minnesota	
Died		1982	Lake City, Wabasha, Minnesota, USA
Buried			Lake City, Wabasha, Minnesota, USA
Address		Lakewood Cemetery, Lake City, MN	
Spouse		Martin Larson (-)	

Family Group Record Wolfgang Schloerstein & Mary Barbara Schloerstein

Husband	Wolfgang Schloerstein		
Born	1814	, , , Austria	
Christened			
Died	19 Sep 1897	Red Wing, Goodhue, Minnesota, USA	
Buried			
Marriage			

Wife	Mary Barbara		
Born	1814	, , , Austria	
Christened			
Died	Between 1885 and 1895	Frontenac, Goodhue, Minnesota, USA	
Buried			

Children			
1	F	Mary Ann (Maria) Schloerstein	
Born	1830-1845	, , , Austria	
Christened			
Died	1 May 1928	, Brown, Minnesota, USA	
Buried	May 1928	New Ulm, Brown, Minnesota, USA	
Address	New Ulm Catholic Cemetery, New Ulm, Minnesota		
Spouse	Joseph Sperl (1832-1867)	Abt 1862 - , , , Austria	
2	F	Theresa Schloerstein	
AKA	Tracy Hill		
Born	1857	, , , Austria	
Christened			
Died	11 Jul 1929		
Buried	Jul 1929	Minneapolis, Hennepin, Minnesota, USA	
Address	Lakewood Cemetery, Minneapolis, MN		
Spouse	James E. Kells (1857-1918)	10 Sep 1879 - Red Wing, Goodhue, Minnesota, USA	

Family Group Record Martin Schlunt & Josephine Schupp

Husband	Martin Schlunt	
Born	11 Sep 1828	, , , Wurttemberg
Christened		
Died	18 May 1906	, Goodhue, Minnesota, USA
Buried	May 1906	Red Wing, Goodhue, Minnesota, USA
Address	Calvary Cemetery, Red Wing, Minnesota	
Marriage	10 Jul 1855	, Hamilton, Ohio, USA

Wife	Josephine Schupp	
Born	18 Oct 1833	, , , Bavaria
Christened		
Died	15 Jul 1909	, Goodhue, Minnesota, USA
Buried	Jul 1909	Red Wing, Goodhue, Minnesota, USA
Address	Calvary Cemetery, Red Wing, Minnesota	

Children

1	M	Casper Schlunt	
AKA		Schlund	
Born		23 May 1858	Westervelt, Goodhue, Minnesota, USA
Christened			
Died		7 Aug 1937	Boise, Ada, Idaho, USA
Buried		10 Aug 1937	Emmett, Gem, Idaho, USA
Address		Riverside Cemetery, Emmett, Idaho	
Spouse		Anna B. Barger (1874-1920)	Abt 1895 - , , Idaho, USA

2	F	Josephine Schlunt	
Born		1860	Frontenac, Goodhue, Minnesota, USA
Christened			
Died			
Buried			
Spouse		Frank Schlund (-)	15 Oct 1887 - Red Wing, Goodhue, Minnesota, USA

3	F	Mary Schlunt	
Born		1861	Florence Township, Goodhue, Minnesota, USA
Christened			
Died			
Buried			
Spouse		George Wehle (-)	21 Jun 1892 - St. Paul, Ramsey, Minnesota, USA

4	F	Anna M. Schlunt	
Born		28 Apr 1863	Florence Township, Goodhue, Minnesota, USA
Christened			
Died		1957	
Buried			
Spouse		Thomas Edward Grant (-)	

5	M	Frank Schlunt	
Born		1865	Florence Township, Goodhue, Minnesota, USA
Christened			
Died		5 Feb 1935	, Wabasha, Minnesota, USA
Buried		Feb 1935	Lake City, Wabasha, Minnesota, USA
Spouse		Ida Rothnick (-)	17 Nov 1897 - Red Wing, Goodhue, Minnesota, USA

Children (cont.)			
6	**F**	**Matilda Schlunt**	
Born		1866	Florence Township, Goodhue, Minnesota, USA
Christened			
Died			
Buried			
Spouse			
7	**F**	**Veronica Schlunt**	
Born		3 Dec 1868	Florence Township, Goodhue, Minnesota, USA
Christened			
Died		15 Feb 1891	, Goodhue, Minnesota, USA
Buried		Feb 1891	Red Wing, Goodhue, Minnesota, USA
Address		Calvary Cemetery, Red Wing, Minnesota	
Spouse			
8	**M**	**Martin Reinhart Schlunt**	
Born		31 Dec 1870	Florence Township, Goodhue, Minnesota, USA
Christened			
Died		10 Nov 1964	Lake City, Wabasha, Minnesota, USA
Buried		Nov 1964	Lake City, Wabasha, Minnesota, USA
Address		St. Mary's Cemetery, Lake City, MN	
Spouse		Ida Agnes Hoffman (1876-1956)	
9	**M**	**Joseph R. Schlunt**	
Born		13 Jun 1873	Florence Township, Goodhue, Minnesota, USA
Christened			
Died		4 Nov 1939	, Goodhue, Minnesota, USA
Buried		Nov 1939	Red Wing, Goodhue, Minnesota, USA
Address		Calvary Cemetery, Red Wing, Minnesota	
Spouse		Josephine Koester (1879-1957)	23 Nov 1898 - Red Wing, Goodhue, Minnesota, USA
10	**F**	**Margaret Schlunt**	
AKA		Maggie	
Born		14 Mar 1875	Florence Township, Goodhue, Minnesota, USA
Christened			
Died			
Buried			
Spouse		John Thorne (-)	19 Aug 1895 - St. Paul, Ramsey, Minnesota, USA

Family Group Record Jakob Schneider & Dorothea Shale Katzenberger

Husband	Jakob Schneider	
AKA	Jakob	
Born	24 Nov 1831	, , Hessen-Darmstadt
Christened		
Died	29 Apr 1893	Frontenac, Goodhue, Minnesota, USA
Buried	Apr 1893	Frontenac, Goodhue, Minnesota, USA
Address	Old Frontenac Cemetery, Frontenac, Minnesota	
Marriage	May 1856	Cincinnati, Hamilton, Ohio, USA
Other Spouse	Mary Barbara Schneider (1838-)	
Date	22 Dec 1887 - Frontenac, Goodhue, Minnesota, USA	

Wife	Dorothea Shale	
AKA	Sarah	
Born	17 Sep 1815	Mailes, , Königreich Bayern
Christened		
Died	18 Mar 1887	Frontenac, Goodhue, Minnesota, USA
Buried	Mar 1887	Frontenac, Goodhue, Minnesota, USA
Address	Old Frontenac Cemetery, Frontenac, Minnesota	
Father	Shale (-)	
Mother		
Other Spouse	Michel Katzenberger (1806-Bef 1856)	Abt 1833 - Mailes, , Königreich Bayern

Children

201

Family Group Record John Seba & Margaret Kahrs

Husband	John Seba	
Born	1829	, , , Hanover
Died	Between 1880 and 1885	Breckenridge, Wilkin, Minnesota, USA
Marriage	30 Jul 1855	Manhattan, New York, New York, USA

Wife	Margaret Kahrs	
Born	1835	, , , Hanover
Died	4 Dec 1907	Breckenridge, Wilkin, Minnesota, USA
Buried	Dec 1907	Breckenridge, Wilkin, Minnesota, USA
Address	Riverside Cemetery, Breckenridge, MN	

Children			
1	M	John Seba	
Born		1857	Tonawanda, Erie, New York, USA
2	M	Herman Seba	
Born		1859	Tonawanda, Erie, New York, USA
3	F	Mary Seba	
Born		1868	, , Massachusets, USA
4	F	Margaret Seba	
Born		1871	Frontenac, Goodhue, Minnesota, USA
5	M	Charlie J. Seba	
Born		2 Feb 1873	Frontenac, Goodhue, Minnesota, USA
Died		8 Mar 1950	Doran, Wilkin, Minnesota, USA
Buried		Mar 1950	Breckenridge, Wilkin, Minnesota, USA
Address		Riverside Cemetery, Breckenridge, MN	
6	M	Heinrich Christian Friedrich Seba	
Born		6 Oct 1875	Frontenac, Goodhue, Minnesota, USA
Christened		12 Dec 1875	Red Wing, Goodhue, Minnesota, USA
Died		31 May 1941	Breckenridge, Wilkin, Minnesota, USA

Family Group Record Carl Frederick Sepke & Fredericka Bietz

Husband	Carl Frederick Sepke	
Born	1847	
Christened		
Died	1889	, Goodhue, Minnesota, USA
Buried	1889	Frontenac, Goodhue, Minnesota, USA
Address	Old Frontenac Cemetery, Frontenac, Minnesota	
Father	George Sepke (Abt 1815-)	
Mother	Louise Rasen (1815-1896)	
Marriage		

Wife	Fredericka Bietz	
Born	5 Apr 1849	, , , Germany
Christened		
Died	10 Mar 1887	Hay Creek Township, Goodhue, Minnesota, USA
Cause of Death	milk fever	
Buried	Mar 1887	Belvidere Mills, Goodhue, Minnesota, USA

Children			
1	F	Wilhelmina D. Sepke	
AKA		Minnie	
Born		Jun 1869	Berlin, , Brandenburg, Prussia
Christened			
Died		1962	, Goodhue, Minnesota, USA
Buried		1962	Frontenac, Goodhue, Minnesota, USA
Address		Old Frontenac Cemetery, Frontenac, Minnesota	
Spouse		Charles F. Gohrke (1863-1939)	15 Apr 1890 - Red Wing, Goodhue, Minnesota, USA
2	M	Herman Sepke	
Born		1875	Berlin, , Brandenburg, Prussia
Christened			
Died		1930	British Columbia, , , Canada
Buried			
Spouse			
3	F	Ella Sepke	
Born		14 Jan 1883	, Goodhue, Minnesota, USA
Christened			
Died		28 Dec 1900	Frontenac, Goodhue, Minnesota, USA
Buried			
Spouse			
4	M	Rudolph Sepke	
Born		29 Mar 1884	Hay Creek Township, Goodhue, Minnesota, USA
Christened			
Died		29 Aug 1884	Hay Creek Township, Goodhue, Minnesota, USA
Buried		Aug 1884	Belvidere Mills, Goodhue, Minnesota, USA
Spouse			

Children (cont.)			
5	**F**	**Mary Martha Sepke**	
Born	5 Sep 1885	Hay Creek Township, Goodhue, Minnesota, USA	
Christened			
Died	1991		
Buried	1991	Frontenac, Goodhue, Minnesota, USA	
Address	Old Frontenac Cemetery, Frontenac, Minnesota		
Spouse	Fred John Peterson (1882-1965)		
Marr. Date	12 Nov 1907 - Red Wing, Goodhue, Minnesota, USA		
6	**M**	**Frederick Sepke**	
Born	20 Feb 1887	, Goodhue, Minnesota, USA	
Christened			
Died	13 Aug 1887	, Goodhue, Minnesota, USA	
Buried	Aug 1887	Belvidere Mills, Goodhue, Minnesota, USA	
Spouse			

Family Group Record Shale

Husband	Shale	
Born		
Christened		
Died		
Buried		
Marriage		

Wife		
Born		
Christened		
Died		
Buried		

Children

1	F	Dorothea Shale	
AKA	Sarah		
Born	17 Sep 1815	Mailes, , Königreich Bayern	
Christened			
Died	18 Mar 1887	Frontenac, Goodhue, Minnesota, USA	
Buried	Mar 1887	Frontenac, Goodhue, Minnesota, USA	
Address	Old Frontenac Cemetery, Frontenac, Minnesota		
Spouse	Michel Katzenberger (1806-Bef 1856)	Abt 1833 - Mailes, , Königreich Bayern	
Spouse	Jakob Schneider (1831-1893)	May 1856 - Cincinnati, Hamilton, Ohio, USA	

2	F	Fredericka Shale	
Born	1823	Lindenberg, Lindau, Bavaria	
Christened			
Died	Aug 1888	Frontenac Station, Goodhue, Minnesota, USA	
Buried			
Spouse	Henry Lorentzen (1820-1901)	Cir 1855	

3	F	Carolina Shale	
Born	1825	, , , Bavaria	
Christened			
Died			
Buried			
Spouse	Adam Roafe (Raab) (1806-)	Cir 1842 - , , , Bavaria	

Family Group Record Joseph Sperl & Mary Ann Schloerstein

Husband	Joseph Sperl	
Born	1832	, , , Austria
Christened		
Died	5 May 1867	At Sea - Atllantic Crossing
Buried	5 May 1867	At Sea - Atllantic Crossing
Marriage	Abt 1862	, , , Austria

Wife	Mary Ann (Maria) Schloerstein	
Born	1830-1845	, , , Austria
Christened		
Died	1 May 1928	, Brown, Minnesota, USA
Buried	May 1928	New Ulm, Brown, Minnesota, USA
Address	New Ulm Catholic Cemetery, New Ulm, Minnesota	
Father	Wolfgang Schloerstein (1814-1897)	
Mother	Mary Barbara (1814-Between 1885/1895)	

Children			
1	M	Joseph Wofel Sperl	
Born		1864	, , , Austria
Christened			
Died		5 Feb 1947	, Brown, Minnesota, USA
Buried		Feb 1947	, , ,
Spouse			
2	M	Georg Sperl	
Born		1866	, , , Austria
Christened			
Died		25 Apr 1867	At Sea - Atllantic Crossing
Buried		25 Apr 1867	At Sea - Atllantic Crossing
Spouse			
3	M	Emmanuel Sperl	
Born		1868	, , Minnesota, USA
Christened			
Died			
Buried			
Spouse			

Family Group Record Carl C. Steffenhagen & Sophia Winkelman

Husband	Carl C. Steffenhagen	
AKA	Stavenhagen (in Germany)	
Born	1803	, , , Pommern, Prussia
Died	1877	Frontenac, Goodhue, Minnesota, USA
Buried	1877	Frontenac, Goodhue, Minnesota, USA
Address	Old Frontenac Cemetery, Frontenac, Minnesota	
Marriage	Abt 1830	, , Pommern, Prussia
Other Spouse	Carolina Pulls (1816-1905)	Abt 1842 - , , , Pommern, Prussia

Wife	Sophia Winkelman	
Born	Abt 1803	, , , Pommern, Prussia
Died	Bef 1842	, , , Prussia

Children

1	M	Carl Steffenhagen Jr	
AKA		Stavenhagen (in Germany)	
Born		11 Jun 1831	, , , Pommern, Prussia
Died		14 Sep 1892	Belvidere Township, Goodhue, Minnesota, USA
Buried		Sep 1892	Belvidere Mills, Goodhue, Minnesota, USA
Address		West Florence Cemetary, Belvidere Mills,, MN	
Spouse		Auguste Wilhelmina Koch (1838-1913)	
Marr. Date		6 May 1861 - , Goodhue, Minnesota, USA	

2	M	John Steffenhagen Sr	
AKA		Stavenhagen (in Germany)	
Born		4 Jul 1834	, , , Pommern, Prussia
Died		9 Jul 1912	Florence Township, Goodhue, Minnesota, USA
Buried		12 Jul 1912	Frontenac, Goodhue, Minnesota, USA
Address		Old Frontenac Cemetery, Frontenac, Minnesota	
Spouse		Hannah (Anna) Koch (1834-1908)	1864 - , Goodhue, Minnesota, USA

3	F	Marie Steffenhagen	
AKA		Stavenhagen (in Germany)	
Born		26 Sep 1838	, , , Pommern, Prussia
Died		5 Jun 1920	Oronoco, Olmsted, Minnesota, USA
Cause of Death		excess dilitation of heart	
Buried		Jun 1920	Oronoco, Olmsted, Minnesota, USA
Address		Oronoco Cemetery, Oronoco, MN	
Spouse		William Koenig (1839-1925)	5 Apr 1861 - , Pommern, Prussia

4	F	Sophia Steffenhagen	
AKA		Stavenhagen (in Germany)	
Born		13 Jun 1840	, , , Pommern, Prussia
Died		28 Sep 1915	, Goodhue, Minnesota, USA
Cause of Death		pneumonia	
Buried		Sep 1915	Belvidere Mills, Goodhue, Minnesota, USA
Address		West Florence Cemetary, Belvidere Mills,, MN	
Spouse		George Wimmer (1830-1902)	Abt 1861 - , Goodhue, Minnesota, USA

Family Group Record Carl C. Steffenhagen & Carolina Pulls

Husband	Carl C. Steffenhagen	
AKA	Stavenhagen (in Germany)	
Born	1803	, , , Pommern, Prussia
Christened		
Died	1877	Frontenac, Goodhue, Minnesota, USA
Buried	1877	Frontenac, Goodhue, Minnesota, USA
Address	Old Frontenac Cemetery, Frontenac, Minnesota	
Marriage	Abt 1842	, , , Pommern, Prussia
Other Spouse	Sophia Winkelman (Abt 1803-Bef 1842)	Abt 1830 - , , Pommern, Prussia

Wife	Carolina Pulls	
AKA	Mina, Lena	
Born	3 Oct 1816	, , , Pommern, Prussia
Christened		
Died	3 Dec 1905	Florence Township, Goodhue, Minnesota, USA
Cause of Death	old age	
Buried	Dec 1905	Frontenac, Goodhue, Minnesota, USA
Address	Old Frontenac Cemetery, Frontenac, Minnesota	
Father	John Pulls (-)	
Mother	Caroline (-)	
Other Spouse	Christoph Johann Steffenhagen (1809-1886)	Abt 1879 - , Goodhue, Minnesota, USA

Children			
1	F	Minna Steffenhagen	
Born		18 Apr 1845	, , , Pommern, Prussia
Christened			
Died		3 Aug 1918	Florence Township, Goodhue, Minnesota, USA
Cause of Death		cancer of the rectum	
Buried		Aug 1918	Frontenac, Goodhue, Minnesota, USA
Address		Old Frontenac Cemetery, Frontenac, Minnesota	
Spouse		Johan Helmuth Heinrich Christian Steffenhagen (1843-1923)	
Marr. Date		1 Jan 1868 - Frontenac, Goodhue, Minnesota, USA	
2	F	Carolina Johanna Maria Steffenhagen	
AKA		Lena	
Born		9 May 1853	West Grabau, Cummerow, Pommern, Prussia
Christened			
Died		26 Apr 1927	Florence Township, Goodhue, Minnesota, USA
Cause of Death		Chronic endocarditis (heart attack)	
Buried		28 Apr 1927	Frontenac, Goodhue, Minnesota, USA
Address		Old Frontenac Episcopal Church Cemetery, Frontenac, Minnesota	
Spouse		Herman Scherf (1842-1918)	12 Nov 1868 - Red Wing, Goodhue, Minnesota, USA

Family Group Record Gustav Friedr. Steffenhagen & Cath Maria Jonas

Husband	Gustav Friedr. Steffenhagen	
Born	1761	Ivenack, , , Mecklenburg
Christened		
Died	1842	Ivenack, , , Mecklenburg
Buried		
Marriage		

Wife	Cath. Maria Jonas	
Born	1789	Stavenhagen, , Mecklenburg
Christened		
Died	1837	., , Mecklenburg
Buried		

Children			
1	M	Christoph Johann Steffenhagen	
AKA		Christopher Stavenhagen (in Germany)	
Born		3 Jan 1809	Ivenack, , , Mecklenburg
Christened		8 Jan 1809	Ivenack, , , Mecklenburg
Died		18 Nov 1886	Frontenac, Goodhue, Minnesota, USA
Buried		Nov 1886	Frontenac, Goodhue, Minnesota, USA
Address		Old Frontenac Cemetery, Frontenac, Minnesota	
Spouse		Hanne Sophie Wilhelmine Hornburg (1811-1878)	19 Jun 1834 - Ivenack, , , Mecklenburg
Spouse		Carolina Pulls (1816-1905)	Abt 1879 - , Goodhue, Minnesota, USA

Family Group Record Christoph Johann Steffenhagen & Hanne (Anna) Hornburg

Husband	Christoph Johann Steffenhagen	
AKA	Christopher Stavenhagen (in Germany)	
Born	3 Jan 1809	Ivenack, , , Mecklenburg
Christened	8 Jan 1809	Ivenack, , , Mecklenburg
Died	18 Nov 1886	Frontenac, Goodhue, Minnesota, USA
Buried	Nov 1886	Frontenac, Goodhue, Minnesota, USA
Address	Old Frontenac Cemetery, Frontenac, Minnesota	
Father	Gustav Friedr. Steffenhagen (1761-1842)	
Mother	Cath. Maria Jonas (1789-1837)	
Marriage	19 Jun 1834	Ivenack, , , Mecklenburg
Other Spouse	Carolina Pulls (1816-1905)	Abt 1879 - , Goodhue, Minnesota, USA

Wife	Hanne Sophie Wilhelmine Hornburg	
AKA	Annie, Anna	
Born	1811	Ivenack, , , Mecklenburg
Christened		
Died	1878	Frontenac, Goodhue, Minnesota, USA
Buried	1878	Frontenac, Goodhue, Minnesota, USA
Address	Old Frontenac Cemetery, Frontenac, Minnesota	
Father	Jochim Hornburg (Cir 1780-)	
Mother		

Children		
1	M	Johan Friedrich Jochim Christoph Steffenhagen
AKA	John	
Born	11 Jun 1834	Ivenack, , , Mecklenburg
Christened	19 Jun 1834	Ivenack, , , Mecklenburg
Died	9 Oct 1916	Forest Park, Cook, Illinois, USA
Buried	Oct 1916	Forest Park, Cook, Illinois, USA
Address	Concordia Cemetery, Forest Park, Ill	
Spouse	Maria Caroline Henrietta Sophie Ahlgrim (1833-1898)	
Marr. Date	7 May 1863 - Ivenack, , , Mecklenburg	
2	F	Marie Friedrike Johanne Christiane Steffenhagen
Born	11Jul 1836	Ivenack, , , Mecklenburg
Christened	17 Jul 1836	Ivenack, , , Mecklenburg
Died	19 Apr 1837	Ivenack, , , Mecklenburg
Buried	21 Apr 1837	Ivenack, , , Mecklenburg
Spouse		
3	F	Marie Sophie Friedrike Christine Steffenhagen
AKA	Fredericka	
Born	30 Mar 1838	Ivenack, , , Mecklenburg
Christened	8 Apr 1838	Ivenack, , , Mecklenburg
Died	29 Mar 1913	
Buried	2 Apr 1913	Malchin, , , Mecklenburg
Spouse	Helmuth (Herman) Gohrke (Abt 1830-)	Abt 1858 - , , , Mecklenburg

Children (cont.)		
4	**M**	**Johan Karl Ernst Friedrich Steffenhagen**
AKA	Karl	
Born	1 Aug 1840	Ivenack, , , Mecklenburg
Christened	16 Aug 1840	Ivenack, , , Mecklenburg
Died		, , , Mecklenburg
Buried		
Spouse		

5	**M**	**Johan Helmuth Heinrich Christian Steffenhagen**	
AKA	Herman Stavenhagen		
Born	11 Mar 1843	Ivenack, , , Mecklenburg	
Christened	26 Mar 1843	Ivenack, , , Mecklenburg	
Died	10 Aug 1923	Florence Township, Goodhue, Minnesota, USA	
Cause of Death	acute kidney disease//senile		
Buried	Aug 1923	Frontenac, Goodhue, Minnesota, USA	
Address	Old Frontenac Cemetery, Frontenac, Minnesota		
Spouse	Minna Steffenhagen (1845-1918)	1 Jan 1868 - Frontenac, Goodhue, Minnesota, USA	

6	**M**	**Johann Friedrich August Steffenhagen**	
AKA	Fred, Fritz Stavenhagen		
Born	14 Jul 1845	Ivenack, , , Mecklenburg	
Christened	3 Aug 1845	Ivenack, , , Mecklenburg	
Died	5 May 1930	Florence Township, Goodhue, Minnesota, USA	
Cause of Death	chronic myseantilis		
Buried	May 1930	Frontenac, Goodhue, Minnesota, USA	
Address	Old Frontenac Cemetery, Frontenac, Minnesota		
Spouse	Friedrike Sophie Caroline Hacker (1847-1883)	28 Oct 1870 - Ivenack, , , Mecklenburg	
Spouse	Marie Sepke (1850-1930)	2 Aug 1883 - Frontenac Station, Goodhue, Minnesota, USA	

7	**M**	**Johann Friedrich Theodor Steffenhagen Senior**	
AKA	Ted, Sr. Stavenhagen		
Born	31 Aug 1847	Borgfeld u Stavenhagen, , Mecklenburg	
Christened	12 Sep 1847	Borgfeld u Stavenhagen, , Mecklenburg	
Died	4 Apr 1923	Florence Township, Goodhue, Minnesota, USA	
Cause of Death	senility//cerebral hemorrhage		
Buried	7 Apr 1923	Frontenac, Goodhue, Minnesota, USA	
Address	Old Frontenac Cemetery, Frontenac, Minnesota		
Spouse	Margaret Weyerhauser (1860-1945)	25 Oct 1879 - Red Wing, Goodhue, Minnesota, USA	

8	**F**	**Wilhelmina Sophia Friederica Steffenhagen**
AKA	Wilhelmine	
Born	28 Feb 1850	Borgfeld u Stavenhagen, , Mecklenburg
Christened	24 Mar 1850	Borgfeld u Stavenhagen, , Mecklenburg
Died	30 Aug 1927	Forest Park, Cook, Illinois, USA
Buried	Sep 1927	Forest Park, Cook, Illinois, USA
Spouse	William Koch (1849-1917)	10 Dec 1876 - , Cook, Illinois, USA

Children (cont.)		
9 **M**	**Joachim Wilhelm Friedrich Christoph Steffenhagen I**	

AKA	William, Stavenhagen (in Germany)	
Born	26 Dec 1852	Borgfeld u Stavenhagen, , Mecklenburg
Christened	16 Jan 1853	Borgfeld u Stavenhagen, , Mecklenburg
Died	19 Oct 1909	Florence Township, Goodhue, Minnesota, USA
Cause of Death	hemorrhage of the bowels	
Buried	22 Oct 1909	Frontenac, Goodhue, Minnesota, USA
Address	Old Frontenac Cemetery, Frontenac, Minnesota	
Spouse	Alice Thimijan (1862-1882)	
Marr. Date	6 Jul 1878 - Florence Township, Goodhue, Minnesota, USA	
Spouse	Katherine Caroline Merkins (1859-1927)	25 Jul 1883 - Florence Township, Goodhue, Minnesota, USA

Family Group Record Johann Friedrich August Steffenhagen & Caroline Hacker

Husband	Johann Friedrich August Steffenhagen	
AKA	Fred, Fritz Stavenhagen	
Born	14 Jul 1845	Ivenack, , , Mecklenburg
Christened	3 Aug 1845	Ivenack, , , Mecklenburg
Died	5 May 1930	Florence Township, Goodhue, Minnesota, USA
Cause of Death	chronic myseantilis	
Buried	May 1930	Frontenac, Goodhue, Minnesota, USA
Address	Old Frontenac Cemetery, Frontenac, Minnesota	
Father	Christoph Johann Steffenhagen (1809-1886)	
Mother	Hanne Sophie Wilhelmine Hornburg (1811-1878)	
Marriage	28 Oct 1870	Ivenack, , , Mecklenburg
Other Spouse	Marie Sepke (1850-1930)	2 Aug 1883 - Frontenac Station, Goodhue, Minnesota, USA

Wife	Friedrike Sophie Caroline Hacker	
AKA	Lena, Caroline, Harker, Hack	
Born	30 Aug 1847	, , , Mecklenburg
Christened	5 Sep 1847	Ivenack, , , Mecklenburg
Died	20 Jan 1883	Frontenac, Goodhue, Minnesota, USA
Cause of Death	tumor	
Buried	Jan 1883	Frontenac, Goodhue, Minnesota, USA
Address	Old Frontenac Cemetery, Frontenac, Minnesota	
Father	Johann Friedrich Theodor Hacker (-)	
Mother	Johanne Sophie Magdalene Schumacher (-)	

Children		
1 U	Luise Johanne Friedrike Wilhelmine Steffenhagen	
Born	29 Jul 1871	Ivenack, , , Mecklenburg
Christened	20 Aug 1871	Ivenack, , , Mecklenburg
Died	Cir Jul 1872	At Sea - Atllantic Crossing
Buried		
Spouse		
2 U	Baby Steffenhagen	
Born	Cir Sep 1872	Chicago, Cook, Illinois, USA
Christened		
Died	Cir Sep 1872	Chicago, Cook, Illinois, USA
Buried		
Spouse		
3 M	Baby boy Steffenhagen	
Born	21 May 1875	Frontenac, Goodhue, Minnesota, USA
Christened		
Died	21 May 1875	Frontenac, Goodhue, Minnesota, USA
Buried		
Spouse		

Family Group Record Johann Friedrich August Steffenhagen & Caroline Hacker

Children (cont.)			
4	**F**	**Minnie Steffenhagen**	
Born	1876	Frontenac, Goodhue, Minnesota, USA	
Christened			
Died	1948	British Columbia, , , Canada	
Buried	1948	British Columbia, , , Canada	
Spouse	Herman Sepke (1875-1930)		

5	**F**	**Ida Steffenhagen**	
AKA	Etta		
Born	14 Aug 1878	Frontenac, Goodhue, Minnesota, USA	
Christened			
Died	14 Jun 1944	Red Wing, Goodhue, Minnesota, USA	
Cause of Death	actue cardiac dilation, myocarditis & nephritis//acute arthritis		
Buried	Jun 1944	Red Wing, Goodhue, Minnesota, USA	
Address	Oakwood Cemetery, Red Wing, MN		
Spouse	Fredrick D. Lubeck Bremer (1872-1932)	6 Jan 1896 - Red Wing, Goodhue, Minnesota, USA	
Spouse	Charles J. F. Kepke (1876-1961)	7 Dec 1899 - Frontenac, Goodhue, Minnesota, USA	

6	**M**	**Ludwig (Louis) Wilhelm Steffenhagen**	
Born	3 Aug 1880	Florence Township, Goodhue, Minnesota, USA	
Christened	12 Sep 1880	Frontenac Station, Goodhue, Minnesota, USA	
Address	St. John's Ev. Lutheran Church, Frontenac Station, Minnesota		
Died	1946	North Battleford, Saskatchewan , , Canada	
Buried	1946	Saskachewan, , , Canada	
Spouse	Mathilda Pipke (1891-1959)		

7	**F**	**Maria Johanna Steffenhagen**	
Born	10 Dec 1881	Frontenac, Goodhue, Minnesota, USA	
Christened	2 Oct 1882	Frontenac Station, Goodhue, Minnesota, USA	
Died	16 Oct 1882	Frontenac, Goodhue, Minnesota, USA	
Cause of Death	teething		
Buried			
Spouse			

8	**M**	**Frederick Steffenhagen**	
Born	18 Jan 1883	Frontenac, Goodhue, Minnesota, USA	
Christened			
Died	20 Jan 1883	Frontenac, Goodhue, Minnesota, USA	
Buried	Jan 1883	Frontenac, Goodhue, Minnesota, USA	
Address	Old Frontenac Cemetery, Frontenac, Minnesota		
Spouse			

Family Group Record Johann Friedrich August Steffenhagen & Marie Sepke

Husband	Johann Friedrich August Steffenhagen	
AKA	Fred, Fritz Stavenhagen	
Born	14 Jul 1845	Ivenack, , , Mecklenburg
Christened	3 Aug 1845	Ivenack, , , Mecklenburg
Died	5 May 1930	Florence Township, Goodhue, Minnesota, USA
Cause of Death	chronic myseantilis	
Buried	May 1930	Frontenac, Goodhue, Minnesota, USA
Address	Old Frontenac Cemetery, Frontenac, Minnesota	
Father	Christoph Johann Steffenhagen (1809-1886)	
Mother	Hanne Sophie Wilhelmine Hornburg (1811-1878)	
Marriage	2 Aug 1883	Frontenac Station, Goodhue, Minnesota, USA
Other Spouse	Friedrike Sophie Caroline Hacker (1847-1883)	28 Oct 1870 - Ivenack, , , Mecklenburg

Wife	Marie Sepke	
Born	9 Feb 1850	, , , Germany
Christened		
Died	6 Oct 1930	Frontenac, Goodhue, Minnesota, USA
Cause of Death	cardis renal disease	
Buried	10 Oct 1930	Frontenac, Goodhue, Minnesota, USA
Address	Old Frontenac Cemetery, Frontenac, Minnesota	
Father	George Sepke (Abt 1815-)	
Mother	Louise Rasen (1815-1896)	

Children		
1 F	Anna Louisa Margaretha Steffenhagen	
AKA	Lizzy, Louisa, Elizabeth	
Born	14 May 1885	Frontenac, Goodhue, Minnesota, USA
Christened	21 Jun 1885	Frontenac Station, Goodhue, Minnesota, USA
Address	St. John's Ev. Lutheran Church, Frontenac Station, Minnesota	
Died	15 Sep 1953	Red Wing, Goodhue, Minnesota, USA
Buried	Sep 1953	Frontenac, Goodhue, Minnesota, USA
Address	Old Frontenac Cemetery, Frontenac, Minnesota	
Spouse	George Bernard Santleman Sr (1880-1944)	3 Apr 1912 - Frontenac, Goodhue, Minnesota, USA
2 M	Charles Friedrich Marcus Steffenhagen	
Born	25 Oct 1887	Florence Township, Goodhue, Minnesota, USA
Christened		
Died		
Buried		
Spouse	Marie Hauschildt (1903-)	
3 M	Herman Wilhelm Steffenhagen	
Born	20 Mar 1891	Florence Township, Goodhue, Minnesota, USA
Christened		
Died	1952	
Buried	1952	Red Wing, Goodhue, Minnesota, USA
Spouse	Anna Hauschildt (1906-1984)	

Family Group Record Johann Friedrich Theodor Steffenhagen Senior & Margaret Weyerhauser

Husband	Johann Friedrich Theodor Steffenhagen Senior	
AKA	Ted, Sr. Stavenhagen	
Born	31 Aug 1847	Borgfeld u Stavenhagen, , Mecklenburg
Christened	12 Sep 1847	Borgfeld u Stavenhagen, , Mecklenburg
Died	4 Apr 1923	Florence Township, Goodhue, Minnesota, USA
Cause of Death	senility//cerebral hemorrhage	
Buried	7 Apr 1923	Frontenac, Goodhue, Minnesota, USA
Address	Old Frontenac Cemetery, Frontenac, Minnesota	
Father	Christoph Johann Steffenhagen (1809-1886)	
Mother	Hanne Sophie Wilhelmine Hornburg (1811-1878)	
Marriage	25 Oct 1879	Red Wing, Goodhue, Minnesota, USA

Wife	Margaret Weyerhauser	
Born	23 Sep 1860	, , , Hessen
Christened		
Died	22 Mar 1945	Frontenac Station, Goodhue, Minnesota, USA
Cause of Death	injuries from being drawn into a moving train in Frontenac Station	
Buried	26 Mar 1945	Frontenac, Goodhue, Minnesota, USA
Address	Old Frontenac Cemetery, Frontenac, Minnesota	

Children		
1 M	**Franz (Frank) Theodore Steffenhagen**	
Born	7 Oct 1880	Florence Township, Goodhue, Minnesota, USA
Christened	12 Dec 1880	Frontenac Station, Goodhue, Minnesota, USA
Address	St. John's Ev. Lutheran Church, Frontenac Station, Minnesota	
Died	1967	
Buried		
Spouse	Dora Rieck (1886-1932)	
2 F	**Anna Steffenhagen**	
Born	3 Oct 1882	Florence Township, Goodhue, Minnesota, USA
Christened	19 Oct 1882	Frontenac Station, Goodhue, Minnesota, USA
Address	St. John's Ev. Lutheran Church, Frontenac Station, Minnesota	
Died	1925	
Buried		
Spouse	Edward Schmidt (1882-1938)	
3 M	**William Steffenhagen**	
Born	Jun 1886	
Christened		
Died	1958	
Buried		
Spouse	Henrietta Isensee (1891-)	

Children (cont.)		

4	M	**Theodore Ludwig Johan Steffenhagen**
AKA	Ted, Jr.	
Born	20 Jan 1890	Florence Township, Goodhue, Minnesota, USA
Christened	11 Mar 1890	Frontenac Station, Goodhue, Minnesota, USA
Address	St. John's Ev. Lutheran Church, Frontenac Station, Minnesota	
Died	6 May 1982	Lake City, Wabasha, Minnesota, USA
Buried	May 1982	Red Wing, Goodhue, Minnesota, USA
Address	Burnside Cemetery, Red Wing, MN	
Spouse	Harriet Blanche Westervelt (1891-1976)	12 Oct 1910 - Red Wing, Goodhue, Minnesota, USA
Spouse	Hazel Ann Hattemer (1899-1985)	7 Oct 1922 - , Goodhue, Minnesota, USA

5	M	**Albert Herman Steffenhagen**
Born	24 Sep 1893	Florence Township, Goodhue, Minnesota, USA
Christened		
Died		
Buried		
Spouse		

6	F	**Emma Wilhelmina Steffenhagen**
Born	22 Apr 1899	Florence Township, Goodhue, Minnesota, USA
Christened		
Died		
Buried		
Spouse	Emil Wohlers (-)	

Family Group Record Theodore Ludwig Johan Steffenhagen & Harriet Blanche Westervelt

Husband	Theodore Ludwig Johan Steffenhagen	
AKA	Ted, Jr.	
Born	20 Jan 1890	Florence Township, Goodhue, Minnesota, USA
Christened	11 Mar 1890	Frontenac Station, Goodhue, Minnesota, USA
Address	St. John's Ev. Lutheran Church, Frontenac Station, Minnesota	
Died	6 May 1982	Lake City, Wabasha, Minnesota, USA
Buried	May 1982	Red Wing, Goodhue, Minnesota, USA
Address	Burnside Cemetery, Red Wing, MN	
Father	Johann Friedrich Theodor Steffenhagen Senior (1847-1923)	
Mother	Margaret Weyerhauser (1860-1945)	
Marriage	12 Oct 1910	Red Wing, Goodhue, Minnesota, USA
Other Spouse	Hazel Ann Hattemer (1899-1985)	7 Oct 1922 - , Goodhue, Minnesota, USA

Wife	Harriet Blanche Westervelt	
AKA	Blanche, Harriet Prescott	
Born	9 Feb 1891	Frontenac, Goodhue, Minnesota, USA
Christened		
Died	15 Jun 1976	Minneapolis, Hennepin, Minnesota, USA
Cause of Death	murder from stab wounds	
Buried	19 Jun 1976	Minneapolis, Hennepin, Minnesota, USA
Address	Dawn Valley Memorial Park, Minneapolis, Minnesota	
Father	Edward Everett Westervelt (1853-1937)	
Mother	Ragna Caroline Karlsdatter (1870-1959)	

Children		
1 F	Mary Jeanette Steffenhagen	
Born	28 Jan 1911	, Goodhue, Minnesota, USA
Christened		
Died	1979	Pocatello, Bannock, Idaho, USA
Buried		
Spouse	Parker (-)	
Spouse	Schumacher (-)	
2 M	Everett James Steffenhagen	
AKA	Jamie	
Born	31 Oct 1912	Frontenac, Goodhue, Minnesota, USA
Christened		
Died	1 Jan 1988	Frontenac, Goodhue, Minnesota, USA
Buried	7 Jan 1988	Minneapolis, Hennepin, Minnesota, USA
Address	Fort Snelling Cemetery, Minneapolis, MN	
Spouse	Did Not Marry	

Family Group Record Theodore Ludwig Johan Steffenhagen & Hazel A. Hattemer

Husband	Theodore Ludwig Johan Steffenhagen	
AKA	Ted, Jr.	
Born	20 Jan 1890	Florence Township, Goodhue, Minnesota, USA
Christened	11 Mar 1890	Frontenac Station, Goodhue, Minnesota, USA
Address	St. John's Ev. Lutheran Church, Frontenac Station, Minnesota	
Died	6 May 1982	Lake City, Wabasha, Minnesota, USA
Buried	May 1982	Red Wing, Goodhue, Minnesota, USA
Address	Burnside Cemetery, Red Wing, MN	
Father	Johann Friedrich Theodor Steffenhagen Senior (1847-1923)	
Mother	Margaret Weyerhauser (1860-1945)	
Marriage	7 Oct 1922	, Goodhue, Minnesota, USA
Other Spouse	Harriet Blanche Westervelt (1891-1976)	12 Oct 1910 - Red Wing, Goodhue, Minnesota, USA

Wife	Hazel Ann Hattemer	
Born	8 Oct 1899	Florence Township, Goodhue, Minnesota, USA
Christened		
Died	11 Oct 1985	
Buried	Oct 1985	Red Wing, Goodhue, Minnesota, USA
Address	Burnside Cemetery, Red Wing, MN	

Children			
1	M	Donald Frank Steffenhagen	
	Born	25 Feb 1923	Frontenac, Goodhue, Minnesota, USA
	Christened		
	Died	1997	
	Buried	1997	Frontenac, Goodhue, Minnesota, USA
	Address	Old Frontenac Cemetery, Frontenac, Minnesota	
	Spouse	Virginia Louise Shepard (-)	Abt 1945
2	M	Lloyd V. Steffenhagen	
	Born	5 May 1929	Frontenac, Goodhue, Minnesota, USA
	Christened		
	Died	16 Jun 1962	, , Wisconsin, USA
	Buried	Jun 1962	Burnside, Goodhue, Minnesota, USA
	Spouse	Norma Welty (-)	Abt 1952 - Frontenac, Goodhue, Minnesota, USA
3	F	Darlene Mae Steffenhagen	
	Born	10 Nov 1932	Red Wing, Goodhue, Minnesota, USA
	Christened	4 Jun 1933	Frontenac, Goodhue, Minnesota, USA
	Died		
	Buried		
	Spouse	Ralph Leon Oden (1931-2012)	6 Sep 1952

Family Group Record Carl Strupe & Sophia Martines

Husband	Carl Strupe	
AKA	Strupp, Struppe	
Born	20 Apr 1832	, , , Mecklenburg-Schwerin
Christened		
Died	22 Feb 1907	Frontenac, Goodhue, Minnesota, USA
Cause of Death	lung fever	
Buried	24 Feb 1907	Frontenac, Goodhue, Minnesota, USA
Address	Old Frontenac Cemetery, Frontenac, Minnesota	
Father	Strupe (-)	
Mother		
Marriage	Abt 1865	, , , Mecklenburg-Schwerin

Wife	Sophia Martines	
Born	Jan 1840	, , , Mecklenburg-Schwerin
Christened		
Died	26 Jul 1922	Frontenac, Goodhue, Minnesota, USA
Buried	Jul 1922	Frontenac, Goodhue, Minnesota, USA
Address	Old Frontenac Cemetery, Frontenac, Minnesota	

Children		
1	M	Fred Strupe
Born	Abt 1866	, , , Mecklenburg-Schwerin
Christened		
Died	Bef 1900	, , , Canada
Buried		
Spouse		
2	M	John Strupe
Born	Abt 1867	, , , Mecklenburg-Schwerin
Christened		
Died	Bef 1900	Tonawanda, Erie, New York, USA
Buried		
Spouse		
3	M	William Strupe
Born	Jan 1868	, , , Mecklenburg-Schwerin
Christened		
Died	After 1900	, , Minnesota, USA
Buried		
Spouse		
4	M	Henry Strupe
Born	10 Mar 1874	, , , Mecklenburg-Schwerin
Christened		
Died	29 Apr 1952	, Goodhue, Minnesota, USA
Buried	May 1952	Frontenac, Goodhue, Minnesota, USA
Address	Old Frontenac Cemetery, Frontenac, Minnesota	
Spouse	Dora L. Lubeck Bremer (1876-1945)	
Marr. Date	10 Dec 1895 - Red Wing, Goodhue, Minnesota, USA	

Family Group Record Carl Strupe & Sophia Martines

Children (cont.)		
5 **M**	**Charles J. Strupe (Strope)**	
Born	Dec 1876	, , , Mecklenburg-Schwerin
Christened		
Died	7 Jan 1933	
Buried	Jan 1933	Frontenac, Goodhue, Minnesota, USA
Address	Old Frontenac Cemetery, Frontenac, Minnesota	
Spouse	Bertha Meyer (1876-1945)	Abt 1901 - , Goodhue, Minnesota, USA
6 **M**	**August Strupe**	
AKA	Gustie	
Born	1877	, , , Mecklenburg-Schwerin
Christened		
Died	Abt 1886	, Goodhue, Minnesota, USA
Buried	Abt 1886	Frontenac, Goodhue, Minnesota, USA
Address	Old Frontenac Cemetery, Frontenac, Minnesota	
Spouse		
7 **M**	**Frank Strupe**	
Born	1880	, , , Mecklenburg-Schwerin
Christened		
Died	Bef 1895	Frontenac, Goodhue, Minnesota, USA
Buried		
Spouse		
8 **M**	**Albert M. Strupe**	
Born	26 Feb 1883	, , , Mecklenburg-Schwerin
Christened		
Died	26 Feb 1962	Minneapolis, Hennepin, Minnesota, USA
Buried		
Spouse	Francis Bonnie Hacker (-Cir 1965)	Cir 1945 - Minneapolis, Hennepin, Minnesota, USA

Family Group Record Henry Strupe & Dora L. Lubeck Bremer

Husband	Henry Strupe	
Born	10 Mar 1874	, , , Mecklenburg-Schwerin
Christened		
Died	29 Apr 1952	, Goodhue, Minnesota, USA
Buried	May 1952	Frontenac, Goodhue, Minnesota, USA
Address	Old Frontenac Cemetery, Frontenac, Minnesota	
Father	Carl Strupe (1832-1907)	
Mother	Sophia Martines (1840-1922)	
Marriage	10 Dec 1895	Red Wing, Goodhue, Minnesota, USA

Wife	Dora L. Lubeck Bremer	
AKA	Dolly	
Born	10 Jan 1876	Frontenac, Goodhue, Minnesota, USA
Christened	7 May 1913	Frontenac, Goodhue, Minnesota, USA
Address	Christ Episcopal Church, Old Frontenac, Minnesota	
Died	3 Mar 1945	Frontenac, Goodhue, Minnesota, USA
Buried	6 Mar 1945	Frontenac, Goodhue, Minnesota, USA
Address	Old Frontenac Cemetery, Frontenac, Minnesota	
Father	John August Friedrich Lubeck (1821-1911)	
Mother	Auguste Dannart (1851-1923)	

Children		
1	**M**	**George Strupe**
Born	Jul 1896	Frontenac, Goodhue, Minnesota, USA
Christened		
Died		
Buried		
Spouse	Rena Mackey Klein (1892-)	Abt 1925 - Chicago, Cook, Illinois, USA

2	**F**	**Laura Anna Strupe**
Born	11 Oct 1898	Frontenac, Goodhue, Minnesota, USA
Christened	2 Aug 1903	Frontenac Station, Goodhue, Minnesota, USA
Address	St. John's Ev. Lutheran Church, Frontenac Station, Minnesota	
Died	21 Jan 1959	, Wabasha, Minnesota, USA
Cause of Death	stroke	
Buried	24 Jan 1959	Frontenac, Goodhue, Minnesota, USA
Address	Old Frontenac Episcopal Church Cemetery, Frontenac, Minnesota	
Spouse	Did Not Marry	

Children (cont.)			
3	**M**	**Benjamin Franklin Strupe**	
Born	30 Oct 1899	Frontenac, Goodhue, Minnesota, USA	
Christened	2 Aug 1903	Frontenac Station, Goodhue, Minnesota, USA	
Address	St. John's Ev. Lutheran Church, Frontenac Station, Minnesota		
Died	20 Dec 1971		
Cause of Death	heart		
Buried	Dec 1971	Frontenac, Goodhue, Minnesota, USA	
Address	Old Frontenac Episcopal Church Cemetery, Frontenac, Minnesota		
Spouse	Florence Irene Danielson (1900-1995)	13 Feb 1925 - Frontenac, Goodhue, Minnesota, USA	
4	**F**	**Ethel Marie Strupe**	
Born	28 Nov 1901	Frontenac, Goodhue, Minnesota, USA	
Christened	2 Aug 1903	Frontenac Station, Goodhue, Minnesota, USA	
Address	St. John's Ev. Lutheran Church, Frontenac Station, Minnesota		
Died	27 Nov 1993	, , Minnesota, USA	
Buried	30 Nov 1993	Frontenac, Goodhue, Minnesota, USA	
Address	Old Frontenac Episcopal Church Cemetery, Frontenac, Minnesota		
Spouse	Wilmar Franklin Fritze (1898-1986)	2 Jan 1961 - Frontenac, Goodhue, Minnesota, USA	
5	**F**	**Mildred Rebecca Strupe**	
Born	6 Jun 1903	Frontenac, Goodhue, Minnesota, USA	
Christened	2 Aug 1903	Frontenac Station, Goodhue, Minnesota, USA	
Address	St. John's Ev. Lutheran Church, Frontenac Station, Minnesota		
Died	1904	Frontenac, Goodhue, Minnesota, USA	
Buried	1904	Frontenac, Goodhue, Minnesota, USA	
Address	Old Frontenac Cemetery, Frontenac, Minnesota		
Spouse			

Family Group Record Carsten Stuhr & Elisabeth Racker

Husband	Carsten Stuhr	
Born	1837	, , , Hanover
Died	1923	, Polk, Minnesota, USA
Buried	1923	, Polk, Minnesota, USA
Address	Prairie View Cemetery, Polk County, Minnesota	
Marriage	Abt 1862	, , , Hanover

Wife	Elizabeth (Elsie) Racker	
AKA	Rogga	
Born	1840	, , , Hanover
Died	1928	, Polk, Minnesota, USA
Buried	1928	, Polk, Minnesota, USA
Address	Prairie View Cemetery, Polk County, Minnesota	

Children		
1	F	Annie Stuhr
Born	1864	, , , Hanover
2	M	Peter Stuhr
Born	1866	, , , Hanover
Died	1953	, Polk, Minnesota, USA
Buried	1953	, Polk, Minnesota, USA
Address	Prairie View Cemetery, Polk County, Minnesota	
3	F	Katherine Rebecka Stuhr
Born	5 Dec 1868	, , Minnesota, USA
Christened	16 May 1869	Frontenac Station, Goodhue, Minnesota, USA
Address	St. John's Ev. Lutheran Church, Frontenac Station, Minnesota	
4	F	Mary Stuhr
Born	1871	
5	M	Henry Stuhr
Born	1874	

Family Group Record John Hull Underwood & Mary Ann Kemp

Husband	John Hull Underwood	
Born	Mar 1829	, , , England
Christened		
Died	21 Apr 1902	Wabasha, Wabasha, Minnesota, USA
Buried		
Marriage	May 1856	Barton Upon Irwell, Lancashire, England

Wife	Mary Ann Kemp	
Born	2 May 1850	Manchester, Lancashire, England
Christened		
Died	1876	Chorlton, Lancashire, England
Buried		

Children		
1	F	Emily Katte Underwood
Born	29 Oct 1857	Manchester, Lancashire, England
Christened		
Died		
Buried		
Spouse		
2	M	Thomas Henry Underwood
Born	12 May 1859	
Christened	12 Jun 1859	Eccles, Lancashire, England
Died		
Buried		
Spouse		
3	M	Phillip Augustus Hull Underwood
Born	18 Feb 1861	, Lancashire, England
Christened	13 Jun 1861	Eccles, Lancashire, England
Died		
Buried		
Spouse		
4	M	Charles Albert Underwood
Born	4 May 1863	Manchester, Lancashire, England
Christened		
Died		
Buried		
Spouse		

Family Group Record Dr. Jacob Von Eschen & Margaret Flury

Husband	Dr. Jacob Von Eschen	
Born	2 Sep 1830	, , , Switzerland
Christened		
Died	23 Apr 1898	Hamilton, Fillmore, Minnesota, USA
Buried	Apr 1898	Odessa, Lac qui Parle, Minnesota, USA
Address	Yellow Bank Emmanuel Evangelical Cemetery, Odessa, Minnesota	
Marriage	Abt 1857	

Wife	Margaret Flury	
Born	6 Jul 1834	, , , Switzerland
Christened		
Died	1 Mar 1912	
Buried	Mar 1912	Odessa, Lac qui Parle, Minnesota, USA
Address	Yellow Bank Emmanuel Evangelical Cemetery, Odessa, Minnesota	

Children		
1 F	**Christine Von Eschen**	
Born	1859	, , Wisconsin, USA
Christened		
Died	29 Aug 1944	Minneapolis, Hennepin, Minnesota, USA
Buried		
Spouse	Ferdinand Zummach (-)	
2 M	**George Von Eschen**	
Born	1864	, , Minnesota, USA
Christened		
Died		
Buried		
Spouse		
3 F	**Cecilia Josephine Von Eschen**	
Born	7 Oct 1866	, , Minnesota, USA
Christened		
Died	4 Mar 1953	
Buried	Mar 1953	Faribault, Rice, Minnesota, USA
Spouse	Jacob John Miller (1864-1932)	
4 M	**John I. Von Eschen**	
Born	Jul 1869	, , Minnesota, USA
Christened		
Died		
Buried		
Spouse		

Children (cont.)		
5 **M**	**Leonard Floiron Von Eschen**	
Born	30 Nov 1871	Sharon, Le Sueur, Minnesota, USA
Christened		
Died	24 Apr 1954	Faribault, Rice, Minnesota, USA
Buried		
Spouse		
6 **F**	**Emma Flora Von Eschen**	
Born	16 Apr 1874	Dunbar, Faribault, Minnesota, USA
Christened		
Died	22 Dec 1954	Faribault, Rice, Minnesota, USA
Buried		
Spouse	Aaron E. Miller (-)	
7 **M**	**Walter P. Von Eschen**	
Born	Jan 1880	Yellow Bank, Lac qui Parle, Minnesota, USA
Christened		
Died		
Buried		
Spouse		

Family Group Record William Byron Webster Sr. & Anna Whitman

Husband	William Byron Webster Sr.	
Born	Nov 1863	, , Illinois, USA
Christened		
Died	2 Apr 1915	St. Paul, Ramsey, Minnesota, USA
Buried	4 Apr 1915	Cabot, Washington, Vermont, USA
Father	Byron Webster (Abt 1830-)	
Mother	Abbie Bugbee (1835-)	
Marriage	1891	

Wife	Anna Whitman	
Born	4 Jul 1864	Hastings, Dakota, Minnesota, USA
Christened		
Died	1 Feb 1960	, Wabasha, Minnesota, USA
Buried	Feb 1960	Frontenac, Goodhue, Minnesota, USA
Address	Old Frontenac Cemetery, Frontenac, Minnesota	
Father	G. S. Whitman (1812-)	
Mother	Margarette (1820-)	

Children		
1	F	Margaret Bugbee Webster
Born	30 Jun 1892	St. Paul, Ramsey, Minnesota, USA
Christened		
Died	2 Dec 1986	Lake City, Wabasha, Minnesota, USA
Buried	Dec 1986	Frontenac, Goodhue, Minnesota, USA
Address	Old Frontenac Cemetery, Frontenac, Minnesota	
Spouse		
2	M	Byron Gordon Webster
Born	1 Nov 1894	St. Paul, Ramsey, Minnesota, USA
Christened		
Died	13 Jun 1971	Delray Beach, Palm Beach, Florida, USA
Buried		
Spouse	Eleanor Eastman (-)	Cir 1922
Spouse	Flo (-)	Cir 1942
3	M	William Byron Webster II
Born	7 Aug 1896	St. Paul, Ramsey, Minnesota, USA
Christened		
Died	9 Jun 1978	, Goodhue, Minnesota, USA
Buried	Jun 1978	Frontenac, Goodhue, Minnesota, USA
Address	Old Frontenac Cemetery, Frontenac, Minnesota	
Spouse	Josephine D. Devereaux (1901-1977)	Abt 1922

Family Group Record William Byron Webster II & Josephine Devereaux

Husband	William Byron Webster II	
Born	7 Aug 1896	St. Paul, Ramsey, Minnesota, USA
Christened		
Died	9 Jun 1978	, Goodhue, Minnesota, USA
Buried	Jun 1978	Frontenac, Goodhue, Minnesota, USA
Address	Old Frontenac Cemetery, Frontenac, Minnesota	
Father	William Byron Webster Sr. (1863-1915)	
Mother	Anna Whitman (1864-1960)	
Marriage	Abt 1922	

Wife	Josephine D. Devereaux	
Born	9 Sep 1901	Minneapolis, Hennepin, Minnesota, USA
Christened		
Died	15 Jan 1977	, Wabasha, Minnesota, USA
Buried	Jan 1977	Frontenac, Goodhue, Minnesota, USA
Address	Old Frontenac Cemetery, Frontenac, Minnesota	
Father	William P. Devereaux (-)	
Mother	Annette King (-)	

Children		
1 M	Devereaux D. Webster	
Born	17 Oct 1924	, Ramsey, Minnesota, USA
Christened		
Died	9 Sep 2002	, Hennepin, Minnesota, USA
Buried	Sep 2002	Frontenac, Goodhue, Minnesota, USA
Address	Old Frontenac Cemetery, Frontenac, Minnesota	
Spouse	Edna Mae LaFountain (-)	1957 - Denver, Denver, Colorado, USA

2 M	William Byron Webster III	
Born	30 Sep 1925	St. Paul, Ramsey, Minnesota, USA
Christened		
Died	12 Apr 2015	Frontenac, Goodhue, Minnesota, USA
Buried	17 Apr 2015	Frontenac, Goodhue, Minnesota, USA
Address	Old Frontenac Cemetery, Frontenac, Minnesota	
Spouse	Elizabeth Jean Reding (1933-2011)	
Marr. Date	20 Sep 1952 - Lake City, Wabasha, Minnesota, USA	

3 M	Peter McQuade Webster	
Born	1927	St. Paul, Ramsey, Minnesota, USA
Christened		
Died	10 Jul 2017	Lake City, Wabasha, Minnesota, USA
Buried	Jul 2017	Frontenac, Goodhue, Minnesota, USA
Address	Old Frontenac Cemetery, Frontenac, Minnesota	
Spouse	Barbara Wilwer Heck (1929-2007)	
Marr. Date	23 Feb 1952 - St. Paul, Ramsey, Minnesota, USA	

Children (cont.)			
4	**M**	**Byron Gordon Webster II**	
Born		4 Dec 1936	St. Paul, Ramsey, Minnesota, USA
Christened			
Died			
Buried			
Spouse		Karen Louise Swendson (1940-)	
Marr. Date		29 Jan 1966 - St. Paul, Ramsey, Minnesota, USA	

Family Group Record Joseph Weich & Crescent Weich

Husband	Joseph Weich	
Born	1804	, , , Baden
Christened		
Died	27 Sep 1876	Frontenac, Goodhue, Minnesota, USA
Buried	Sep 1876	Frontenac, Goodhue, Minnesota, USA
Marriage	Bef 1860	

Wife	Crescent	
Born	1835	, , , Wurttemberg
Christened		
Died		
Buried		

Children	

Family Group Record James (Bully) Wells & Jane Graham

Husband	James (Bully) Wells	
Born	1806	Gloucester, , New Jersey, USA
Christened		
Died	18 Aug 1864	Floyd River, , Iowa, USA
Buried	19 Aug 1864	Floyd River, , Iowa, USA
Marriage	12 Sep 1836	Fort Snelling, , Louisiana Purchase

Wife	Jane Graham	
Born	Cir 1817	Prairie du Chien, Mississippi River, Louisiana Purchase
Christened		
Died	1881	Fort Snelling, , Minnesota, USA
Buried		
Father	Captain Duncan Graham (1772-1847)	
Mother	Susanne 'Istag Iwin Hazahotawin' Pennishon (Abt 1784-1848)	

Children			
1	**F**	**Sarah Craft Wells**	
Born		9 Sep 1837	Waconia, Lake Pepin, Louisiana Purchase
Christened			
Died		16 Nov 1909	Stephen, Kingsbury, South Dakota, USA
Buried			
Spouse		Joseph LaCroix (Abt 1834-)	20 Jan 1868 - Fort Snellling, Hennepin, Minnesota, USA
2	**M**	**Henry Alfred Wells**	
Born		1838	Waconia, Lake Pepin, Louisiana Purchase
Christened			
Died		1863	Gettysburg, Adams, Pennsylvania, USA
Buried			
Spouse			
3	**M**	**Orman Graham Wells**	
Born		5 Apr 1841	Waconia, Lake Pepin, Louisiana Purchase
Christened			
Died		13 Apr 1928	Hardisty, Alberta, Canada
Buried		16 Apr 1928	Hardisty, Alberta, Canada
Spouse		Louisa Samantha Devore (1855-1923)	7 Dec 1874 - , Sumner, Kansas, USA
4	**M**	**Mark Wells**	
Born		24 Nov 1842	Waconia, Lake Pepin, Louisiana Purchase
Christened			
Died		1 Jun 1913	Chamberlain, Brule, South Dakota, USA
Buried			
Spouse		Down Hears-The-Wind (-1891)	Abt 1864

Children (cont.)		

5	F	**Elizabeth F. Wells**	
Born	20 Dec 1844	Waconia, Lake Pepin, Louisiana Purchase	
Christened			
Died	Abt 1927	Chicago, Cook, Illinois, USA	
Buried			
Spouse	Nicolas LaCroix (-)	Abt 1872	
Spouse	Antonio Carrier (-)	Abt 1881	

6	M	**William Wallace Wells**	
Born	19 Sep 1846	Fond du Lac, Territory of Wisconsin	
Christened			
Died	17 Apr 1920	Chamberlain, Brule, South Dakota, USA	
Buried			
Spouse	Catherine Louisa Boohr (1855-1883)	Abt 1873 - , Rice County, Minnesota, USA	
Spouse	Emma Oleana Johnson (1863-1927)	12 Nov 1884	

7	F	**Lucy Ann Wells**	
Born	15 Nov 1849	Waconia, Wabashaw County, Territory of Minnesota	
Christened			
Died	11 May 1940	Faribault, Rice, Minnesota, USA	
Buried			
Spouse	Leon Leandre Dulac (1855-1931)	4 Mar 1878 - Faribault, Rice, Minnesota, USA	

8	M	**Phillip Faribault Wells**	
Born	5 Dec 1850	Waconia, Wabashaw County, Territory of Minnesota	
Christened			
Died	2 Jan 1947	White River, Black Hills, South Dakota, USA	
Buried			
Spouse	Mary T. Mcmanus (Abt 1866-1937)	18 Jan 1885	

9	M	**Aaron Charles Wells**	
Born	6 Mar 1852	Waconia, Wabashaw County, Territory of Minnesota	
Christened			
Died	11 Oct 1932	Fort Yates, , North Dakota, USA	
Buried			
Spouse	Josephine St. George (1859-1955)	14 Mar 1877 - Faribault, Rice, Minnesota, USA	

10	F	**Agnes Bernadette Wells**	
Born	6 Oct 1859	Wells Township, Rice, Minnesota, USA	
Christened			
Died	15 Oct 1949	Seattle, King, Washington, USA	
Buried			
Spouse	James Thomas Reedy (1849-1930)	Abt 1879 - Fort Totten, , North Dakota, USA	

Family Group Record Evert V. Westervelt & Dicey Smelly

Husband	Evert V. Westervelt	
Born	1 Mar 1813	Poughkeepsie, Dutchess, New York, USA
Christened	22 Mar 1813	Pleasant Valley, Dutchess, New York, USA
Address	Presbyterian Church, Pleasant Valley, New York	
Died	7 Mar 1888	Frontenac, Goodhue, Minnesota, USA
Cause of Death	heart disease	
Buried	10 Mar 1888	Frontenac, Goodhue, Minnesota, USA
Address	Old Frontenac Episcopal Church Cemetery, Frontenac, Minnesota	
Father	Abraham Westervelt (1783-1841)	
Mother	Catherine Van Blarcum (1786-1859)	
Marriage	14 Nov 1838	Fayette, Greene, Illinois, USA
Other Spouse	Juliann (Julia A.) Bullard (1812-1901)	7 Jun 1845 - Boston, Suffolk, Massachusetts, USA

Wife	Dicey W. Smelly	
Born	Abt 1813	
Christened		
Died	Abt 1843	, , Iowa, Northwest Territory
Buried		

Children		
1 F	Eleanor Caroline Westervelt	
Born	28 Oct 1843	, , Iowa, Northwest Territory
Christened		
Died	1915	, , Minnesota, USA
Buried		
Spouse	Thomas Jefferson Cates (1833-1898)	
Marr. Date	4 Nov 1860 - Frontenac, Goodhue, Minnesota, USA	

Family Group Record Evert V. Westervelt & Juliann Bullard

Husband	Evert V. Westervelt	
Born	1 Mar 1813	Poughkeepsie, Dutchess, New York, USA
Christened	22 Mar 1813	Pleasant Valley, Dutchess, New York, USA
Address	Presbyterian Church, Pleasant Valley, New York	
Died	7 Mar 1888	Frontenac, Goodhue, Minnesota, USA
Cause of Death	heart disease	
Buried	10 Mar 1888	Frontenac, Goodhue, Minnesota, USA
Address	Old Frontenac Episcopal Church Cemetery, Frontenac, Minnesota	
Father	Abraham Westervelt (1783-1841)	
Mother	Catherine Van Blarcum (1786-1859)	
Marriage	7 Jun 1845	Boston, Suffolk, Massachusetts, USA
Other Spouse	Dicey W. Smelly (Abt 1813-Abt 1843)	14 Nov 1838 - Fayette, Greene, Illinois, USA

Wife	Juliann (Julia A.) Bullard	
AKA	Julia Ann	
Born	23 Jul 1812	Holliston, Middlesex, Massachusetts, USA
Christened		
Died	11 Apr 1901	Frontenac, Goodhue, Minnesota, USA
Cause of Death	old age	
Buried	13 Apr 1901	Frontenac, Goodhue, Minnesota, USA
Address	Old Frontenac Episcopal Church Cemetery, Frontenac, Minnesota	
Father	Jonathan Bullard (1781-1842)	
Mother	Polly Whiting (1784-1844)	

Children		
1 M	Everett E. Westervelt	
Born	24 Mar 1846	Hopkinton, Middlesex, Massachusetts, USA
Christened		
Died	23 Jul 1846	Hopkinton, Middlesex, Massachusetts, USA
Buried	Jul 1846	Hopkinton, Middlesex, Massachusetts, USA
Spouse		
2 F	Mary Catherine Westervelt	
Born	21 Sep 1847	Hopkinton, Middlesex, Massachusetts, USA
Christened		
Died	27 Mar 1935	Frontenac, Goodhue, Minnesota, USA
Cause of Death	chronic myocarditis	
Buried	30 Mar 1935	Frontenac, Goodhue, Minnesota, USA
Address	Christ Episcopal Church, Old Frontenac, Minnesota	
Spouse	Did Not Marry	
3 F	Harriet Julia Westervelt	
Born	18 Jan 1850	Hopkinton, Middlesex, Massachusetts, USA
Christened		
Died	1 Nov 1850	Hopkinton, Middlesex, Massachusetts, USA
Buried	Nov 1850	Hopkinton, Middlesex, Massachusetts, USA
Spouse		

Children (cont.)		
4	**F**	**Harriet Jane (Jeannie) Westervelt**
AKA	Jeannie, Jane	
Born	14 May 1851	Hopkinton, Middlesex, Massachusetts, USA
Christened		
Died	11 Feb 1932	, Hennepin, Minnesota, USA
Buried		
Spouse	George Hooper Dodge (1850-1924)	
Marr. Date	1 Oct 1875 - Frontenac, Goodhue, Minnesota, USA	
5	**M**	**Edward Everett Westervelt**
Born	25 Jan 1853	, Wabashaw County, Territory of Minnesota
Christened		
Died	26 Feb 1937	Frontenac, Goodhue, Minnesota, USA
Cause of Death	old age, heart disease//senility	
Buried	1 Mar 1937	Frontenac, Goodhue, Minnesota, USA
Address	Old Frontenac Episcopal Church Cemetery, Frontenac, Minnesota	
Spouse	Ragna Caroline Karlsdatter (1870-1959)	28 May 1890 - Stockholm, Pepin, Wisconsin, USA

Family Group Record Edward Everett Westervelt & Ragna Olson Karlsdatter

Husband	Edward Everett Westervelt	
Born	25 Jan 1853	, Wabashaw County, Territory of Minnesota
Christened		
Died	26 Feb 1937	Frontenac, Goodhue, Minnesota, USA
Cause of Death	old age, heart disease//senility	
Buried	1 Mar 1937	Frontenac, Goodhue, Minnesota, USA
Address	Old Frontenac Episcopal Church Cemetery, Frontenac, Minnesota	
Father	Evert V. Westervelt (1813-1888)	
Mother	Juliann (Julia A.) Bullard (1812-1901)	
Marriage	28 May 1890	Stockholm, Pepin, Wisconsin, USA

Wife	Ragna Caroline Karlsdatter	
AKA	Carlson, Finstad	
Born	11 Aug 1870	Frontenac, Goodhue, Minnesota, USA
Christened		
Died	10 Nov 1959	Frontenac, Goodhue, Minnesota, USA
Cause of Death	old age//heart disease	
Buried	12 Nov 1959	Frontenac, Goodhue, Minnesota, USA
Address	Old Frontenac Episcopal Church Cemetery, Frontenac, Minnesota	
Father	Karl Olson Finstad (1837-1907)	
Mother	Berthe Karine Larsdatter Loken (1827-1893)	

Children		
1 F	Harriet Blanche Westervelt	
AKA	Blanche, Harriet Prescott	
Born	9 Feb 1891	Frontenac, Goodhue, Minnesota, USA
Christened		
Died	15 Jun 1976	Minneapolis, Hennepin, Minnesota, USA
Cause of Death	murder from stab wounds	
Buried	19 Jun 1976	Minneapolis, Hennepin, Minnesota, USA
Address	Dawn Valley Memorial Park, Minneapolis, Minnesota	
Spouse	Theodore Ludwig Johan Steffenhagen (1890-1982)	
Marr. Date	12 Oct 1910 - Red Wing, Goodhue, Minnesota, USA	
2 M	George Everett Westervelt	
Born	12 Jun 1893	Frontenac, Goodhue, Minnesota, USA
Christened	8 Oct 1893	Frontenac, Goodhue, Minnesota, USA
Address	Christ Episcopal Church, Old Frontenac, Minnesota	
Died	21 Apr 1950	St. Paul, Ramsey, Minnesota, USA
Cause of Death	stomach cancer	
Buried	24 Apr 1950	Frontenac, Goodhue, Minnesota, USA
Address	Old Frontenac Episcopal Church Cemetery, Frontenac, Minnesota	
Spouse	Selma E. Harder (1896-1976)	Abt 1915

Family Group Record Edward Everett Westervelt & Ragna Olson Karlsdatter

Children (cont.)			

3	M	Leo Edwin Westervelt Sr.	
Born	31 Jan 1896	Frontenac, Goodhue, Minnesota, USA	
Christened	14 Jun 1896	Frontenac, Goodhue, Minnesota, USA	
Address	Christ Episcopal Church, Old Frontenac, Minnesota		
Died	7 Nov 1982	La Crosse, La Crosse, Wisconsin, USA	
Buried	Nov 1982	Frontenac, Goodhue, Minnesota, USA	
Address	Old Frontenac Episcopal Church Cemetery, Frontenac, Minnesota		
Spouse	Violet L. Hansen (1903-1971)	Abt 1928	

4	M	James Philip Westervelt	
AKA	Jamie		
Born	22 Aug 1900	Frontenac, Goodhue, Minnesota, USA	
Christened	26 Dec 1900	Frontenac, Goodhue, Minnesota, USA	
Address	Christ Episcopal Church, Old Frontenac, Minnesota		
Died	26 Nov 1975	Frontenac, Goodhue, Minnesota, USA	
Cause of Death	heart attack		
Buried	29 Nov 1975	Frontenac, Goodhue, Minnesota, USA	
Address	Old Frontenac Episcopal Church Cemetery, Frontenac, Minnesota		
Spouse	Did Not Marry		

5	M	Lawrence Daniel Westervelt	
AKA	Danny		
Born	7 Sep 1904	Frontenac, Goodhue, Minnesota, USA	
Christened	31 Dec 1904	Frontenac, Goodhue, Minnesota, USA	
Address	Christ Episcopal Church, Old Frontenac, Minnesota		
Died	24 Apr 1951	Red Wing, Goodhue, Minnesota, USA	
Cause of Death	heart attack		
Buried	Apr 1951	Red Wing, Goodhue, Minnesota, USA	
Address	St. John's Evangelical Cemetery, Red Wing, Minnesota		
Spouse	Hattie Anna Louise Jaquith (1901-1988)	Cir 1931 - , Goodhue, Minnesota, USA	

Family Group Record Paul Carlton Wilson & Anna Knapp Garrard

Husband	Paul Carlton Wilson	
AKA		
Born	15 Feb 1869	Reads Landing, Wabasha, Minnesota, USA
Christened		
Died	14 Nov 1950	Red Wing, Goodhue, Minnesota, USA
Buried	Nov 1950	Menomonie, Dunn, Wisconsin, USA
Address	Evergreen Cemetery, Menomonie, Wisconsin	
Father	Thomas Blair Wilson (1832-1898)	
Mother	Julia F. Epley (1836-1911)	
Marriage	26 Feb 1902	Cincinnati, Hamilton, Ohio, USA

Wife	Anna Knapp Garrard	
AKA		
Born	13 Jun 1874	Lake City, Wabasha, Minnesota, USA
Christened		
Died	31 Aug 1954	Frontenac, Goodhue, Minnesota, USA
Buried	Sep 1954	Menomonie, Dunn, Wisconsin, USA
Address	Evergreen Cemetery, Menomonie, Wisconsin	
Father	Dr. Lewis Hector Garrard (1829-1887)	
Mother	Florence Minerva Van Vliet (1844-1897)	

Children			
1	M	Thomas Blair Wilson III	
Born		28 Feb 1903	Red Cedar, Dunn, Wisconsin, USA
Christened			
Died		Aug 1975	Anderson, Shasta, California, USA
Buried			
Spouse		Edith Oliver Cane (1915-1993)	
2	F	Edith Garrard Wilson	
Born		28 Mar 1904	Red Cedar, Dunn, Wisconsin, USA
Christened			
Died		Mar 1904	Alexandria, , Virginia, USA
Buried			
Spouse		Chaplain Newell Dwight Lindner (1908-1961)	

3	M	Lewis Garrard Wilson	
AKA		Gary	
Born		26 May 1905	Red Cedar, Dunn, Wisconsin, USA
Christened			
Died		1987	
Buried			
Spouse		Wilhelmina Lauther Foote (-)	
4	F	Julia Frances Wilson	
AKA		Judy	
Born		1911	Menomonie, Dunn, Wisconsin, USA
Christened			
Died		1995	Oakmont, Allegheny, Pennsylvania, USA
Buried			

Children (cont.)			
Spouse			
5	**F**	**Mary Blair Wilson**	
Born		1915	Menomonie, Dunn, Wisconsin, USA
Christened			
Died		2005	Oakmont, Allegheny, Pennsylvania, USA
Buried			
Spouse		Ralph Sisson Albertson (-1978)	

Husband	Thomas Blair Wilson Jr.	
AKA		
Born	1864	, Dunn, Wisconsin, USA
Christened		
Died	4 Oct 1936	Menomonie, Dunn, Wisconsin, USA
Buried	Oct 1936	Menomonie, Dunn, Wisconsin, USA
Address	Evergreen Cemetery, Menomonie, Wisconsin	
Father	Thomas Blair Wilson (1832-1898)	
Mother	Julia F. Epley (1836-1911)	
Marriage	7 Jun 1906	Menomonie, Dunn, Wisconsin, USA

Wife	Edith Garrard	
AKA	Auny, Onie	
Born	7 Jun 1867	Frontenac, Goodhue, Minnesota, USA
Christened		
Died	12 Sep 1953	Old Fort, McDowell, North Carolina, USA
Buried	15 Sep 1953	Menomonie, Dunn, Wisconsin, USA
Address	Evergreen Cemetery, Menomonie, Wisconsin	
Father	Dr. Lewis Hector Garrard (1829-1887)	
Mother	Florence Minerva Van Vliet (1844-1897)	

Children		
1	M	Baby Boy Wilson
Born	9 Dec 1907	Menomonie, Dunn, Wisconsin, USA
Christened		
Died	10 Dec 1907	Menomonie, Dunn, Wisconsin, USA
Buried		
Spouse		
2	F	Florence Garrard Wilson
Born	10 Oct 1909	
Christened		
Died	21 Dec 1978	
Buried	Dec 1978	Arlington, Arlington, Virginia, USA
Spouse	Col. Robert Gardner Baker (1910-1979)	1937

Family Group Record George Wimmer & Sophia Steffenhagen

Husband	George Wimmer	
AKA	Weimer	
Born	8 Jan 1830	, , , Bavaria
Christened		
Died	21 Oct 1902	, Goodhue, Minnesota, USA
Buried	Oct 1902	Belvidere Mills, Goodhue, Minnesota, USA
Address	West Florence Cementary, Belvidere Mills,, MN	
Marriage	Abt 1861	, Goodhue, Minnesota, USA

Wife	Sophia Steffenhagen	
AKA	Stavenhagen (in Germany)	
Born	13 Jun 1840	, , , Pommern, Prussia
Christened		
Died	28 Sep 1915	, Goodhue, Minnesota, USA
Cause of Death	pneumonia	
Buried	Sep 1915	Belvidere Mills, Goodhue, Minnesota, USA
Address	West Florence Cementary, Belvidere Mills,, MN	
Father	Carl C. Steffenhagen (1803-1877)	
Mother	Sophia Winkelman (Abt 1803-Bef 1842)	

Children		
1	**M**	**J. George Wimmer**
Born	15 Feb 1862	Frontenac, Goodhue, Minnesota, USA
Christened		
Died	11 Mar 1916	Dubuque, Dubuque, Iowa, USA
Buried	Mar 1916	Dubuque, Dubuque, Iowa, USA
Address	Linwood Cemetery, Dubuque, Iowa	
Spouse	Margaretha Von Helmst (1862-1936)	24 Sep 1884 - Red Wing, Goodhue, Minnesota, USA
2	**F**	**Catherine W. Wimmer**
Born	10 May 1864	Frontenac, Goodhue, Minnesota, USA
Christened		
Died	19 Nov 1947	Lake City, Wabasha, Minnesota, USA
Buried	Nov 1947	Belvidere Mills, Goodhue, Minnesota, USA
Address	St. Peter's German Lutheran Cemetery, Belvidere Mills, Goodhue County, Minnesota	
Spouse	Johann Brunkhorst (1861-1946)	26 Nov 1885 - West Florence, , Minnesota, USA
3	**M**	**Max C. Wimmer**
Born	24 Jul 1866	Frontenac, Goodhue, Minnesota, USA
Christened		
Died	23 Jun 1902	Lake City, Wabasha, Minnesota, USA
Buried	Jun 1902	, Wabasha, Minnesota, USA
Address	Trinity Lutheran Cemetery - Lincoln, RR, Wabasha County, MN	
Spouse	Margaret Meyer (1867-1924)	17 Jan 1890 - Gillford, Wabasha, Minnesota, USA
4	**M**	**John Herman Wimmer**
Born	26 Sep 1868	Mt Pleasant Township, Wabasha, Minnesota, USA
Christened		
Died	22 May 1918	Florence Township, Goodhue, Minnesota, USA
Buried	25 May 1918	Belvidere Mills, Goodhue, Minnesota, USA
Address	West Florence Cementary, Belvidere Mills,, MN	
Spouse	Mary K. Witt (1872-1949)	4 Oct 1894 - West Florence, Goodhue, Minnesota, USA

Family Group Record George Wimmer & Sophia Steffenhagen

Children (cont.)

5	F	**Julia Marie Wimmer**	
Born	8 May 1871	Mt Pleasant Township, Wabasha, Minnesota, USA	
Christened			
Died	26 Nov 1936	, Goodhue, Minnesota, USA	
Buried		Goodhue Village, Goodhue, Minnesota, USA	
Address	Grace Lutheran Cemetery, Goodhue Village, MN		
Spouse	Frank Raasch (1870-1924)	1894	

6	M	**Louis Wimmer**	
Born	May 1873	Mt Pleasant Township, Wabasha, Minnesota, USA	
Christened			
Died	28 Apr 1914	Red Wing, Goodhue, Minnesota, USA	
Cause of Death	saw mill accident		
Buried	May 1914	Belvidere Mills, Goodhue, Minnesota, USA	
Address	West Florence Cementary, Belvidere Mills,, MN		
Spouse	Mary Lilie Luth (1877-1964)	3 Sep 1896 - West Florence, Goodhue, Minnesota, USA	

7	F	**Anna Elizabeth Wimmer**	
Born	Jul 1876	Mt Pleasant Township, Wabasha, Minnesota, USA	
Christened			
Died	11 Feb 1952	Lake City, Wabasha, Minnesota, USA	
Buried	Feb 1952	Belvidere Mills, Goodhue, Minnesota, USA	
Address	St. Peter's German Lutheran Cemetery, Belvidere Mills, MN		
Spouse	Diedrich Roschen (1873-1942)	7 Oct 1897 - Mt Pleasant Township, Wabasha, Minnesota, USA	

8	F	**Emma Wilhelmina Wimmer**	
Born	21 Jun 1880	Mt Pleasant Township, Wabasha, Minnesota, USA	
Christened	23 Oct 1880	Frontenac Station, Goodhue, Minnesota, USA	
Address	St. John's Ev. Lutheran Church, Frontenac Station, Minnesota		
Died	29 Jul 1943	Lake City, Wabasha, Minnesota, USA	
Buried	Aug 1943	Lake City, Wabasha, Minnesota, USA	
Address	Bethany Lutheran Cemetery, Lake City, MN		
Spouse	William Frederick Tackmann (1879-1957)	2 Nov 1902 - West Florence, Goodhue, Minnesota, USA	

9	M	**Fred Henry Wimmer**	
Born	25 Feb 1885	Mt Pleasant Township, Wabasha, Minnesota, USA	
Christened			
Died	17 Jul 1950	Red Wing, Goodhue, Minnesota, USA	
Buried	19 Jul 1950	Red Wing, Goodhue, Minnesota, USA	
Address	Oakwood Cemetery, Red Wing,, Minnesota		
Spouse	Clara Lorena Mehrkens (1897-1966)	Abt 1921	

Census Records

~~~~~

19th Century
Frontenac, Minnesota

19th Century Frontenac, Minnesota, Census Records

The 19th century transcribed census records are on the following pages. An attempt was made to determine and include those residents living in the area now known as Frontenac, Minnesota.

The Minnesota State Census was taken every ten years in the years ending in five, from 1865 to 1905. This state census was often just a count of people.

The Federal Census was compiled every ten years with years ending in zero. Unfortunately, the 1890 census doesn't exist because a fire destroyed the records. The Federal census changed questions with each year. The transcribed records included here do not include all information that was compiled. Actual proper names are recorded and not as the census taker interpreted them.

The following compiled lists of Frontenac residents are the best estimate of who lived in the village. It was very challenging to follow the census taker, difficult to determine who was residing in the village as opposed to which families who lived in the rural area. Therefore, the counts below may not be entirely accurate.

Recap of the census records and the growth of Frontenac, Minnesota.

Year	Census	Houses	Residents	Boarding Houses	Frontenac Hotel	Lakeside Hotel
1850	Wabashaw County Territorial	2	12			
1857	Minnesota Territorial	2	10			
1860	Federal	16	99	2		
1865	Minnesota State	26	130	2	x	
1870	Federal	42	187	2	x	x
1875	Minnesota State	35	166	1		x
1880	Federal	41	168			x
1885	Minnesota State	36	154			x
1895	Minnesota State	36	135			x
1900	Federal	37	147			x

1850 Census Wabashaw County, Territory of Minnesota, District #1
July 10, 1850, Alex Baily

#	Last Name	First Name	Age	Born	Birth Place	Occupation	
	Waconia Settlement						
43	Bullard	N.	33	1817	New York	Trader	
		Levina	33	1817	Ohio		
44	Wells	James	46	1804	New Jersey	Trader	
		Jane	29	1821	Minnisota		
		Sarah C.	13	1837	Minnisota		
		Alfred	11	1839	Minnisota		
		Orman	9	1841	Minnisota		
		Mark	7	1843	Minnisota		
		Elizabeth	5	1845	Minnisota		
		Wallace	4	1846	Minnisota		
		Lucy Ann	3	1847	Minnisota		
	Kelly	James	45	1805	Vermont	Laborer	
	Wabashaw Settlement						
45	Bunnell	Willard	36	1814	New York	Trader	
	Residents in Waconia - would become Frontenac:					2	houses
						12	residents

1850 Census Wabashaw County, Territory of Minnesota, District #1
July 10, 1850, Alex Baily

#	Last Name	First Name	Age	Born	Birth Place	Occupation	
	Additional people in the census to give a perspective of 1850 residents in the area.						
	Dominant occupations were trader, voyageur, hunter, farmer, and missionary.						
	Lapamboise	Joseph	46	1804	Michigan	Trader	
		Joseph, Jr.	22	1828		Trader	
	Latour	Joseph	46	1804	Canada East	Voyageur	
	Hoptions	Robert	34	1816	Ohio	Missionary	
	Huggins	Alexander	48	1802	North Carolina	Farmer	
	Provencalle	Joseph	35	1815	Minnisota Territory	Hunter & farmer	
		Margaret	30	1820	Minnisota Territory		
		George	25	1825	Minnisota Territory	Hunter & farmer	
		Angelique	25	1825	Minnisota Territory		
	Graham	Alexander	28	1822	Minnisota Territory	Indian Trader	
		Blossom	25	1825	Minnisota Territory		
	Belland	Henry	35	1815	Canada East	Trader	
	Leblane	Thomas	36	1814	Minnisota Territory	Voyageur	
	Yarton	IAT	48	1802	Canada East	Trader	
		Susan	36	1814	Minnisota Territory		
	Faribault	Oliver	36	1814	Prairie du Chen, Wis	Trader	
	Montrelle, Jr	Joseph, Jr	46	1804	Prairie du Chen, Wis	Hunter	
	Moores	John	30	1820	Blue Fountain	Indian Farmer	
	Pond	L.	30	1820	Ohio	Missionary	
	Baily	Alexis	52	1798	Michigan	Trader	

1857 Minnesota Territorial Census,
Township 112N, Range 13 W, Goodhue County,
H. C. Hoffman, Assistant Marshall, September 21, 1857

Last Name	First Name	Age	Born	Birth Place	Occupation	
Westervelt	Evert	43	1814	New York		
	Julia A.	43	1814	Massachusetts		
	Elinor	14	1843	Iowa		
	Mary	10	1847	Massachusetts		
	Jane	8	1849	Massachusetts		
	Everet	4	1853	Minnesota		
Schlunt	Martin	28	1829	Germany	Laborer	
	Josephine	25	1832	Germany		
Hassemer	Nicholas	22	1835	Germany	Laborer	
	John	25	1832	Germany	Laborer	
Census taken same month and year as the Village of Westervelt plat map is recorded						
1857 Westervelt		Homes	2			
		Residents	10			

1860 Federal Census for Township 112N, Range 13W
Goodhue County, State of Minnesota

Enumerated by me on the 4th of July,1860.

Norris Neobart, Asst Marshall, Post Office: Wacouta

	Last Name	First Name	Race	Age	Born	Birth Place	Occupation	Real Estate	Personal Property
	Schneider	Jacob	w	28	1832	Hessen-Darmstadt	Laborer		30
		Dorothea	w	40	1820	Bavaria	Housekeeper		
		Michael	w	9	1851	Ohio			
		William	w	7	1853	Ohio			
	Roafe	Adam	w	54	1806	Bavaria	Farmer		30
		Caroline	w	35	1825	Bavaria	Housekeeper		
		Dorothea	w	16	1844	Bavaria			
		Geo	w	9	1851	Bavaria			
		Margaret	w	7	1853	Bavaria			
		John	w	5	1855	Bavaria			
		Carolina	w	3	1857	Bavaria			
		Mina	w	1	1859	Bavaria			
BH	Miller	John W.	w	29	1831	Wurttemberg	Carpenter	900	200
BH		Josephine Mary	w	28	1832	Wurttemberg	Housekeeper		
BH		Wilhelmina Katie	w	3	1857	Minn			
BH		Josephine Mary	w	1/12	1860	Minn			
BH	Miller	Elam	m	24	1836	Miss	Plasterer	250	50
BH	Hassemer	Nicholas	w	25	1835	Hessen-Darmstadt	Laborer	250	100
BH	Schenach	Engelbert	w	26	1834	Tyrol	Baker		50
BH	Bartseh	Francis	w	35	1825	Prussia	Mason		300
BH	Sandstrom	Bity	w	26	1834	Sweden	Laborer	500	40
BH		Oliver	w	28	1832	Sweden		600	200
BH	Adams	Adams, Elizabeth	w	34	1826	Penn	Housekeeper	150	75
	Garrard	Lewis H.	w	31	1829	Ohio	Farmer	20,000	10,000
		Israel	w	34	1826	Kentucky	Attorney		
	Owens	J. A.	w	21	1839	Kentucky	Clerk		
	Lambrecht	Louisa	w	22	1838	Prussia	Domestic		
	Westervelt	Evert	w	49	1811	NY	Farmer	6,000	765
		Julia	w	47	1813	Mass	Housekeeper		
		Elanor C.	w	16	1844	Iowa			
		Mary C.	w	12	1848	Mass			
		Harriet F.	w	9	1851	Mass			
		Evert E.	w	6	1854	Minn			
	Oleson	Chas	w	29	1831	Sweden	farm hand	320	30
	Johnson	Andrew	w	30	1830	Sweden	farm hand	640	20

Race: W-White, M-Mulatto, B-Black

1860 Federal Census for Township 112N, Range 13W
Goodhue County, State of Minnesota
Enumerated by me on the 4th of July, 1860.
Norris Neobart, Asst Marshall, Post Office: Wacouta

	Last Name	First Name	Race	Age	Born	Birth Place	Occupation	Real Estate	Personal Property
	Huntington	T.S.	w	40	1820	Connecticut	Civil Engineer	1,000	2,000
		Francis E.	w	39	1821	Ohio	Housekeeper		
		George S.	w	10	1850	Ohio			
		Marie	w	8	1852	Kentucky			
		Sally	w	6	1854	Ohio			
		Fanny	w	4	1856	Ohio			
		Spencer	w	2	1858	Ohio			
		Jane E.	w	30	1830	Connecticut	Housekeeper		
BH	Schlunt	Martin	w	31	1829	Wurttemberg	Boarding	550	900
BH		Josephine	w	27	1833	Bavaria	Housekeeper		
BH		Casper	w	2	1858	Maine			
BH		Josephine	w	9/12	1860	Maine			
BH	Koch	Casper	w	28	1832	Wurttemberg	Gardner	530	100
BH	Sauter	John	w	25	1835	Wurttemberg	farmer	350	200
BH	Haller	Engelbert	w	27	1833	Wurttemberg	Carpenter	350	600
BH	Meyer	Chas	w	21	1839	Bavaria	Blacksmith		50
BH		Frank	w	30	1830	Bavaria	farmer		100
BH		Christine	w	22	1838	Iowa	Housekeeper		
	Herder	Chas	w	27	1833	Prussia	Laborer		50
		Mary S.	w	29	1831	Prussia	Housekeepr		
		Emma	w	2	1858	Illinois			
		Louis	w	6/12	1860	Minnesota			
	Schenach	Gottfried	w	37	1823	Austria	Blacksmith		50
		Mary	w	27	1833	Austria	Housekeeper		
		Elenor	w	3	1857	Austria			
	Friedericks	John	w	28	1832	Wurttmburg	Laborer		200
		Elizabeth	w	27	1833	Hessen	Housekeeper		
		Elizabeth	w	6	1854	Minnesota			
		John	w	3	1857	Minnesota			
		Helen	w	1	1859	Minnesota			
	Hofmeister	Wm	w	32	1828	Mecklenburg	Carpenter		220
		Amelia	w	26	1834	Saxony	Housekeeper		
		Caroline	w	5	1855	Wisconsin			
		Wm	w	1	1859	Minnesota			

Race: W-White, M-Mulatto, B-Black

1860 Federal Census for Township 112N, Range 13W
Goodhue County, State of Minnesota
Enumerated by me on the 4th of July,1860.
Norris Neobart, Asst Marshall, Post Office: Wacouta

Last Name	First Name	Race	Age	Born	Birth Place	Occupation	Real Estate	Personal Property
Lubeck	August	w	33	1827	Mecklenburg	Stone Cutter		250
	Fredricka	w	29	1831	Mecklenburg	Housekeeper		
	Augustus	w	2	1858	Minnesota			
	Louisa	w	6/12	1860	Minnesota			
	Mina	w	70	1790	Mecklenburg	Housekeeping		
Friedericks	John	w	20	1840	Mecklenburg	Laborer		
Weich	Joseph	w	56	1804	Bavaria	Laborer	250	850
	Cresent	w	25	1835	Wurttemburg	housekeeping		
Hunecke	Henry	w	28	1832	Prussia	Carpenter		600
	Louisa	w	29	1831	Mecklenburg	housekeeping		
	Lena	w	2	1858	Minnesota			
	Elizabeth	w	9/12	1859	Minnesota			
Wimmer	George	w	28	1832	Prussia	Carpenter		600
Berktold	Engelbert	w	15	1845	Tyrol, Austria	Laborer		
Hager	John	w	28	1832	Bavaria	Laborer		
	Wolf	w	25	1835	Bavaria	Laborer		
	Elizabeth	w	17	1843	Bavaria	Housekeeper		
Ackerman	Michael	w	25	1835	Bavaria	Carpenter		425
	Barbara	w	17	1843	Bavaria	Housekeeper		
Isensee	Henry	w	37	1823	Prussia	Stone Cutter	800	225
	Caroline	w	34	1826	Prussia	Housekeeper		
	Helene	w	7	1853	New York			
	Caroline	w	5	1855	Minn			
	Fredricka	w	4	1856	Minn			
	Henry	w	2	1858	Minn			
Hunecke	John	w	27	1833	Prussia	Tailor	100	75
	Caroline	w	26	1834	Mecklenburg	Housekeeper		
Creagh	J. F.	w	32	1828	Ireland	Miller		850
	Emily	w	35	1825	Ohio	Housekeeper		
Williamson	Moriah	w	81	1779	England	Housekeeper		10,000
	Frontenac Homes		16					
	Boarding Houses		2					
	Frontenac Residents		99					

Race: W-White, M-Mulatto, B-Black

1860 Census
Page 3 of 3

1865 Minnesota State Census, as of June 1, 1865
Township of Florence in the County of Goodhue, State of Minnesota,
as enumerated by me according to law: E. F. K. Munger, Assessor

Last Name	First Name		
Lorentzen	Henry		
	Fredericke		
Garrard	Lewis H.		
	Florence V.		
	Winfred		
McLean	S.B. McLean		
Sandstrom	Caroline		
Dannielson	Augusta		
Sandstrom	Bingt		
	Annie		
	Theodore		
	Olfot		
Weich	Joseph		
	Crescent		
Ludow	Georgia		
Miller	William		
	Wilhelmina		
	Wilhelmina		
Wimmer	George		
	Sophia		
	George		
	Catherine		
Lubeck	Fredericka		
Koenig	Henry		
	Freidericka		
	John		
	Christopher		
	Sophia		
	Freidricka		
Koenig	William		
	Mary		
	Wm.		
	Lena		
	Freiderick		
Hunecke	John		
	Caroline		

1865 Minnesota State Census, as of June 1, 1865
Township of Florence in the County of Goodhue, State of Minnesota,
as enumerated by me according to law: E. F. K. Munger, Assessor

	Last Name	First Name		
	Hunecke	Henry		
		Louisa		
		Elizabeth		
		Louisa		
	Schneider	Jacob		
		Dorothea		
	Katzenberger	John		
		Margaret		
		Michael		
		Win		
	Ackerman	Michael		
		Barbara		
		Annie		
		Edward		
	Muller	Henry		
		Leisetta		
		Joseph		
	Schenach	Emmanuel		
		Anna		
		Josephine		
		Victoria		
		John		
	Schenach	Gottfried		
		Hannah		
		Hilliarus		
		Engelbret		
		Joseph		
	Schenach	Engelbret		
		Marg		
		Clare		
		Lewis		
		Gottfried		

1865 Minnesota State Census, as of June 1, 1865
Township of Florence in the County of Goodhue, State of Minnesota,
as enumerated by me according to law: E. F. K. Munger, Assessor

	Last Name	First Name		
	Herder	Charles		
		Mary		
		Emma		
		Caroline		
		Lewis		
		Wilhelm		
	Owens	James		
		Mary		
		Lewis		
		Kate		
	Friedericks	Fritz		
		Lisetta		
	Henry	John		
Boarding House	Hassemer	Nicholas		
Boarding House		Annie		
Boarding House		Kate		
Boarding House		Annie		
Boarding House		Maggie		
Boarding House	Schlunt	Martin		
Boarding House		Josephine		
Boarding House		Casper		
Boarding House		Josephine		
Boarding House		Marg		
Boarding House		Anna		
Boarding House		Frank		
Boarding House	Campbell	Dugall		
Boarding House		Marg		
Boarding House		Herbert		
Boarding House	Bullard	Charles		
	Westervelt	Evert		
		Julia		
		Marg		
		Jane		
		Everett		

1865 Minnesota State Census, as of June 1, 1865
Township of Florence in the County of Goodhue, State of Minnesota,
as enumerated by me according to law: E. F. K. Munger, Assessor

	Last Name	First Name		
	Beals	Susan		
		James		
		Mary		
		Samuel		
		Carrie		
	Roafe	Adam		
		Caroline		
		Dorothea		
		George		
		John		
		Kina		
		Carrie		
Frontenac Hotel	Loomis	Marg E.		
Frontenac Hotel		Julia A.		
Frontenac Hotel	Cates	Eleanor		
Frontenac Hotel		D. D.		
Frontenac Hotel	Haller	Engelbret		
Frontenac Hotel	Koch	Kasper		
	Garrard	Jeptha		
		Annie R.		
	Isensee	Henry		
		Caroline		
		Helene		
		Caroline		
		Fredricka		
		Henry		
		Julius		
		Leorisa		
	1865 Frontenac Village			
	Houses	26		
	Residents	130		
	Boarding Houses	2		
	Frontenac Hotel	x		

1870 Federal Census: Inhabitants in the Town of Florence
County of Goodhue, State of Minnesota

Enumerated by me on the 29th of August 1870, Orrin Densmore, Ass't Marshal, Post Office: Red Wing

	Last Name	First Name	Race	Age	Born	Birth Place	Occupation	Real Estate	Personal Property
	Sauter	John	w	35	1835	Wurttemberg	Laborer		200
		Phillippine	w	28	1842	Hesse-Darmstad	Keeping House		
		Flora	w	7	1863	Minnesota			
		Albert	w	5	1865	Minnesota			
		Augusta	w	2	1868	Minnesota			
		August	w	24	1846	Wurttemberg	Laborer		
	Ritzert	Frank	w	9	1861	New York			
		Elizabeth	w	56	1814	Hesse-Darmstadt			
	Miller	Elam	m	34	1836	Mississippi	Plasterer	1,000	100
		Lucy	m	31	1839	Kentucky	Keeping House		
		Minnie	m	7	1863	Ohio			
		Mary	m	3	1867	Minnesota			
		Laura	m	1	1869	Minnesota			
LS	Burleigh	Charles	w	35	1835	New Hampshire	Clerk in Hotel		
	Batchelder	Josiah	w	37	1833	Maine	Boat Building	700	200
		Lizzie	w	28	1842	Indiana	Keeping House		
		Jessie	w	7	1863	Wisconsin			
		Edwin J.	w	4	1866	Wisconsin			
		Harry	w	1	1869	Minnesota			
	Lorentzen	Henry	w	49	1821	Hamburg	Postmaster	3,000	500
		Fredericka	w	47	1823	Hanover	Keeping House		
	Hager	John	w	37	1833	Bavaria	laborer	500	200
		Ursula	w	39	1831	Bavaria	Keeping House		
		Justina	w	8	1862	Minnesota			
		Engebert	w	2	1868	Minnesota			
BH	Schneider	Jacob	w	38	1832	Hesse-Darmstad	Hotel Keeper	3,000	500
BH		Dorothy	w	55	1815	Bavaria	Keeping House		
BH		William	w	18	1852	Ohio			
	Ackerman	Michael	w	35	1835	Bavaria	Carpenter	1,000	300
		Anna	w	10	1860	Minnesota			
		Edward	w	7	1863	Minnesota			
		William	w	4	1866	Minnesota			
	Hunecke	Henry	w	36	1834	Prussia	Carpenter	1,200	300
		Louisa	w	39	1831	Mecklenburg	Keeping House		
		Lena	w	12	1858	Minnesota			
		Louisa	w	7	1863	Minnesota			
		Edward	w	5	1865	Minnesota			

BH: Boarding House, **LS:** Lakeside Hotel
Race: W-White, M-Mulatto, B-Black

1870 Federal Census: Inhabitants in the Town of Florence County of Goodhue, State of Minnesota

Enumerated by me on the 29th of August 1870, Orrin Densmore, Ass't Marshal, Post Office: Red Wing

Last Name	First Name	Race	Age	Born	Birth Place	Occupation	Real Estate	Personal Property
Herder	Charles F.	w	37	1833	Prussia	laborer	1,000	300
	Maria	w	39	1831	Prussia	keeps house		
	Emma	w	13	1857	Illinois			
	Louis	w	11	1859	Minnesota			
	Carrie	w	8	1862	Minnesota			
	William	w	6	1864	Minnesota			
	Edward	w	3	1867	Minnesota			
	Emily	w	1	1869	Minnesota			
Bremer	Joachim	w	39	1831	Mecklenburg	Laborer		
	Dora	w	29	1841	Mecklenburg	Keeping House		
Poppe	Claus	w	46	1824	Hanover	Laborer	600	200
	Rebecca	w	34	1836	Hanover	Keeping House		
	Katie	w	5	1865	New York			
	Maria	w	3	1867	Massachusetts			
Christenson	Christ	w	36	1834	Norway	Laborer		
	Sara	w	21	1849	Mecklenburg	Keeping House		
Gerken	John	w	44	1826	Hanover	Laborer	800	200
	Margaretta	w	37	1833	Hanover	Keeping House		
	John (Joseph)	w	7	1863	Hanover			
Hunecke	John	w	38	1832	Prussia	Tailor	800	300
	Caroline	w	37	1833	Mecklenburg	Keeping House		
Larson	Ole	w	42	1828	Norway	Laborer		
aka Loken	Martha	w	32	1838	Norway	Keeping House		
	Hans	w	10	1860	Norway			
	Inga (Ann)	w	9	1861	Norway			
	Herman (Ole)	w	7	1863	Norway			
	Maria	w	5	1865	Norway			
	Lars	w	3	1867	Norway			
Schenach	Engelbert	w	38	1832	Tyrol, Austira	Laborer	500	400
	Maria	w	32	1838	Mecklenburg	Keeping House		
	Clara	w	8	1862	Minnesota			
	Lewis	w	7	1863	Minnesota			
	Edmund	w	5	1865	Minnesota			
	Frank	w	2	1868	Minnesota			

BH: Boarding House, **LS**: Lakeside Hotel
Race: W-White, M-Mulatto, B-Black

1870 Federal Census: Inhabitants in the Town of Florence
County of Goodhue, State of Minnesota
Enumerated by me on the 29th of August 1870, Orrin Densmore, Ass't Marshal, Post Office: Red Wing

	Last Name	First Name	Race	Age	Born	Birth Place	Occupation	Real Estate	Personal Property
	Haller	Engelbert	w	37	1833	Wurttemberg	Carpenter	1,500	200
		Sarah	w	3	1867	Minnesota			
		Alfred E.	w	2	1868	Minnesota			
	Garrard	Israel	w	44	1826	Kentucky	Farmer	100,000	10,000
		George	w	7	1863	New York			
	Johnson	Haus	w	28	1842	Norway	Laborer		
		Karena	w	25	1845	Norway	Keeping House		
	Loindson	Anna	w	19	1851	Norway	Servant		
	Weich	Joseph	w	66	1804	Baden	Laborer	800	150
	Vierengel	John	w	28	1842	Bavaria	Musician		
		Babette	w	32	1838	Bavaria	Keeping House		
	Markham	John	w	29	1841	Prussia	Laborer		
		Sophia	w	28	1842	Prussia	Keeping House		
	VanEschew	Jacob	w	42	1828	Switzerland	Clergyman		
		Margaret	w	37	1833	Switzerland	Keeps house		
		Christine	w	11	1859	Wisconsin			
		George	w	6	1864	Minnesota			
		Cecilia	w	4	1866	Minnesota			
		John	w	1	1869	Minnesota			
BH	Hauschild	Nicholas	w	37	1833	Hanover	Laborer		
BH		Margaretta	w	38	1832	Hanover	Keeping House		
BH		Metta	w	10	1860	Hanover			
BH		Katie	w	7	1863	Hanover			
BH		Margaret	w	4	1866	Hanover			
BH	Brinkman	Christ	w	38	1832	Hanover	Laborer		
BH		Anna	w	26	1844	Hanover	Keeping House		
BH		Maria	w	3	1867	Hanover			
	Friedericks	John	w	30	1840	Mecklenburg	Laborer	600	150
		Rebecca	w	26	1844	Hanover	Keeping House		
		John	w	4	1866	Hanover			
		Frederick	w	2	1868	Minnesota			
	Gerken	Johnnes	w	46	1824	Hanover	Laborer		

1870 Federal Census: Inhabitants in the Town of Florence County of Goodhue, State of Minnesota

Enumerated by me on the 29th of August 1870, Orrin Densmore, Ass't Marshal, Post Office: Red Wing

Last Name	First Name	Race	Age	Born	Birth Place	Occupation	Real Estate	Personal Property
Seba	John	w	41	1829	Hanover	Laborer	500	100
	Margaret	w	35	1835	Hanover	Keeping House		
	John	w	13	1857	New York			
	Herman	w	11	1859	New York			
	Mary	w	2	1868	Massachusetts			
Olson	John	w	55	1815	Norway	Boot & shoe maker		
	Mary	w	53	1817	Norway	Keeping House		
	Louis	w	19	1851	Norway			
	Christine	w	21	1849	Norway			
	Christian	w	16	1854	Norway			
	Mary	w	13	1857	Norway			
	Arthur	w	12	1858	Norway			
	Emma	w	7	1863	Norway			
Stuhr	Karsten	w	33	1837	Hanover	Laborer	400	100
	Elizabeth	w	30	1840	Hanover	Keeping House		
	Peter	w	4	1866	Hanover			
	Katie	w	2	1868	Minnesota			
Friedericks	Christian	w	43	1827	Mecklenburg	Laborer	400	150
	Sophia	w	41	1829	Mecklenburg	Keeping House		
	Lena	w	12	1858	Mecklenburg			
	Herman	w	6	1864	Mecklenburg			
Schmidt	Doris	w	67	1803	Mecklenburg			
Koehn	John	w	32	1838	Mecklenburg	Laborer	400	100
	Louisa	w	24	1846	Mecklenburg	Keeping House		
	Maria	w	4	1866	Minnesota			
	Sophia	w	55	1815	Mecklenburg			
Bahr	John	w	59	1811	Hanover	Wood Turner	600	150
	Juliana	w	55	1815		Keeping House		
	Frederick	w	21	1849	Prussia	Laborer		
	Pluto	w	14	1856	Wisconsin	Laborer		
Muller	Henry	w	55	1815	Mecklenburg	laborer	600	200
	Dorothea	w	51	1819	Mecklenburg			

1870 Federal Census: Inhabitants in the Town of Florence
County of Goodhue, State of Minnesota

Enumerated by me on the 29th of August 1870, Orrin Densmore, Ass't Marshal, Post Office: Red Wing

	Last Name	First Name	Race	Age	Born	Birth Place	Occupation	Real Estate	Personal Property
	Schenach	Emmanuel	w	45	1825	Tyrol, Austria	Wagon Maker	500	150
		Starel	w	44	1826	Tyrol, Austria	Keeping House		
		Jose	w	9	1861	Minnesota			
		Victoria	w	8	1862	Minnesota			
		John	w	6	1864	Minnesota			
	Schloerstein	Wolf	w	54	1816	Bavaria	Laborer	300	
		Barbara	w	56	1814	Bavaria	Keeping House		
		Theresa	w	13	1857	Bavaria			
	Schenach	Gottfried	w	45	1825	Tyrol, Austria	Blacksmith	800	200
		Nannie	w	36	1834	Tyrol, Austria	Keeping House		
		Ariel	w	14	1856	Tyrol, Austria			
		Englebret	w	6	1864	Minnesota			
		Joseph	w	4	1866	Minnesota			
	Johnson	Christina	w	46	1824	Norway	Keeping House		
		Haus	w	25	1845	Norway	Laborer		
		Ola	w	23	1847	Norway	Laborer		
		Ellena	w	20	1850	Norway			
		Matilda	w	18	1852	Norway			
	Burmeister	George	w	31	1839	Prussia	Miller		
		Amelia	w	29	1841	Prussia	Keeping House		
		Hulda	w	9	1861	Prussia			
BH	Janis	Octarius A.	w	31	1839	Ohio	Cooper		100
BH		Floritta B.	w	35	1835	Maine	Keeping House		
BH		Jennie M.	w	3	1867	Wisconsin			
BH		Paul	w	5/12	1870	Minnesota			
BH	Chapman	Hattie	w	17	1853	Maine			
BH		Ralph H.	w	11	1859	Wisconsin			
BH	Landt	William R.	w	31	1839	New Jersey	Teaming		600
BH		Martha A.	w	33	1837	Pennsylvania	Keeping House		
BH		Laura E.	w	4	1866	Minnesota			
BH		Jay B.	w	2	1868	Minnesota			
BH		Kellam	w	1/12	1870	Minnesota			
	Westervelt	Evert	w	57	1813	New York	Farmer (1st y	6,200	1,500

BH: Boarding House, **LS:** Lakeside Hotel
Race: W-White, M-Mulatto, B-Black

1870 Federal Census: Inhabitants in the Town of Florence
County of Goodhue, State of Minnesota

Enumerated by me on the 29th of August 1870, Orrin Densmore, Ass't Marshal, Post Office: Red Wing

	Last Name	First Name	Race	Age	Born	Birth Place	Occupation	Real Estate	Personal Property
	Westervelt	Evert	w	57	1813	New York	Farmer (1st y	6,200	1,500
		Julia	w	56	1814	Massachusetts	Keeping House		
		Mary	w	20	1850	Massachusetts			
		Janice	w	18	1852	Massachusetts			
		Edward E.	w	16	1854	Minnesota			
	Davidson	James	w	39	1831	Pennsylvania	Lumberman		
		Almira	w	34	1836	New York	Keeping House		
		Alice	w	10	1860	Pennsylvania			
		William M.	w	6	1864	Pennsylvania			
		Purmilla	w	3	1867	Minnesota			
	Christ	Nicholas	w	27	1843	Prussia	Laborer		
		Dora	w	19	1851	Tyrol, Austria	Keeping House		
		Harry	w	2	1868	Minnesota			
		Nicholas	w	1	1869	Minnesota			
LS	Gleason	Patrick	w	26	1844	Ireland	Laborer		1,000
LS		Catharine	w	26	1844	Ireland	Keeping house		
LS		Catharine	w	3	1867	Minnesota			
LS		Edward	w	1	1869	Minnesota			
LS	Wilder	Arthur	w	29	1841	Ohio	Farmer	16,000	730
LS	Beveridge	Robert	w	40	1830	Scotland	Merchant	4,000	8,000
		1870 Frontenac			42	Houses			
					187	Residents			
					2	Boarding Houses			
					x	Frontenac Hotel			
					x	Lakeside Hotel			

	Last Name	First Name	Race	Age	Born	Birth Place	
	Hunecke	Henry	w	42	1833	Prussia	
		Louisa	w	40	1835	Prussia	
		Lena	w	14	1861	Minn	
		Louisa	w	13	1862	Minn	
		Eddie	w	10	1865	Minn	
	Koehn	Joseph	w	35	1840	Mecklenburg-Schwerin	
		Louisa	w	29	1846	Mecklenburg-Schwerin	
		Mary	w	8	1867	Minnesota	
		Lena	w	3	1872	Minnesota	
		Louisa	w	1	1874	Minnesota	
		Sophia	w	58	1817	Mecklenburg-Schwerin	
	Lemke	Chas	w	36	1839	Prussia	
	Johnson	Hans	w	37	1838	Norway	
		Gurina	w	30	1845	Norway	
		Mary	w	9	1866	Norway	
		Johnny	w	6	1869	Minn	
		Eliza	w	3	1872	Minn	
		May	w	18	1857	Minn	
	Olson	Carl	w	46	1829	Norway	
		Corina	w	42	1833	Norway	
		Ole (aka Louis Carlson)	w	12	1863	Norway	
		Annie	w	9	1866	Norway	
		Ragna	w	6	1869	Minn	
	Larson	Annie	w	44	1831	Norway	
		Lewis	w	25	1850	Norway	
	Kelly	Henry	w	25	1850	Mich	
BH	Garrard	Pirach	w	49	1826	Ohio	
BH	Cowels	B. R.	w	34	1841	Ohio	
BH		Luey G.	w	34	1841	Ohio	
BH		H. L.	w	7	1868	Iowa	
BH		Laurie R.	w	5	1870	Iowa	
BH		B. R.	w	1	1874	Wisc	
BH	Buckingham	Kalla	w	14	1861	Iowa	
BH		Harry C.	w	15	1860	Iowa	
	Schloerstein	Wolf	w	60	1815	Bohemia	
		Mary	w	60	1815	Bohemia	

BH: Boarding House
Race: W-White, M-Mulatto, B-Black

Last Name	First Name	Race	Age	Born	Birth Place	
Sperl	Mary	w	30	1845	Bohemia	
	Wofel	w	9	1866	Austria	
	Emmanuel	w	4	1871	Austria	
Kells	Teresa	w	18	1857	Bohemia	
Halverson	Christ	w	38	1837	Norway	
	Laurie	w	33	1842	Norway	
	Katie	w	1	1874	Minn	
Miller	Elam	m	39	1836	Miss	
	Lucy Jane	m	36	1839	Ky	
	Minnie	m	10	1865	Ohio	
	Mary Brown	m	8	1867	Minn	
	Laurie F.	m	6	1869	Minn	
	Florence	m	4	1871	Minn	
	Lucy Jane	m	2	1873	Minn	
Dammann	Peter	w	29	1846	Hanover	
	Rebecka	w	37	1838	Hanover	
Poppe	Katy	w	9	1866	N.Y.	
	Mary	w	8	1867	Mass	
	Margaret	w	48	1827	Hanover	
Hunecke	John	w	43	1832	Westphalen	
	Caroline	w	44	1831	Germany	
	Mary	w	13	1862	Germany	
Steffenhagen	Christoph	w	66	1809	Germany	
	Minnie	w	63	1812	Germany	
	Theodore	w	26	1849	Germany	
Gerken	John	w	46	1829	Hanover	
	Margaret E.	w	41	1834	Hanover	
	John (Joseph)	w	10	1865	Hanover	
Steffenhagen	Carl	w	72	1803	Prussia	
	Carolina	w	62	1813	Germany	
Lubeck	John	w	50	1825	Germany	
	Augusta	w	23	1852	Germany	
	Frea	w	2	1873	Minn	
	Mina	w	89	1786	Reuss	
Ackerman	Michael	w	39	1836	Germany	
	Annie	w	14	1861	Minn	
	Eddie	w	12	1863	Minn	
	Willie	w	9	1866	Minn	

1875 Minnesota State Census as of May 1, 1875

	Last Name	First Name	Race	Age	Born	Birth Place
	Weich	Joseph	w	71	1804	Germany
	Roepke	Wm	w	38	1837	Germany
		Lena	w	35	1840	Prussia
		Sophia	w	10	1865	Prussia
		Minnie	w	6	1869	Prussia
	Schenach	Godfried	w	54	1821	Tyrol
		Annie	w	44	1831	Tyrol
		Kellah	w	18	1857	Tyrol
		Engelbert	w	12	1863	Minn
		Joseph	w	10	1865	Minn
	Steffenhagen	Fritz	w	25	1850	Germany
		Lena	w	24	1851	Germany
	Larson	Martin	w	44	1831	Norway
		Lena	w	34	1841	Norway
		Mary	w	9	1866	Norway
		Ludwig	w	4	1871	Norway
		Johnny	w	3	1872	Minnesota
		Christ	w	1	1874	Minnesota
	Friedericks	John	w	35	1840	Germany
		Betty	w	30	1845	Germany
		John	w	8	1867	Germany
		Fredrika	w	6	1869	Minn
		Henry	w	4	1871	Minn
	Markham	John	w	32	1843	Germany
		Carolina	w	30	1845	Germany
		Wm	w	4	1871	Minn
		Annie	w	3	1872	Minn
		Lucy	w	1	1874	Minn
BH	Brinkman	Christian	w	40	1835	Hanover
BH		Annie	w	31	1844	Hanover
BH		Mary	w	7	1868	Hanover
BH		Annie	w	5	1870	Minn
BH		Billy	w	1	1874	Minn
	Friedericks	Christian	w	45	1830	Germany
		Sophie	w	44	1831	Germany
		Herman	w	10	1865	Germany

BH: Boarding House
Race: W-White, M-Mulatto, B-Black

1875 Minnesota State Census as of May 1, 1875

Last Name	First Name	Race	Age	Born	Birth Place
Olson	Wm	w	30	1845	Norway
	Malen	w	28	1847	Norway
	Aleson	w	3	1872	Minn
Peterson	Mary	w	60	1815	Norway
Bahr	Bahr	w	63	1812	Saxoney
	Julia	w	59	1816	Saxoney
Muller	Henry	w	59	1816	Prussia
	Daisy	w	56	1819	Prussia
	Henry	w	26	1849	Prussia
Schenach	Emmanuel	w	52	1823	Tyrol
	Annie	w	45	1830	Tyrol
	Josephine	w	14	1861	Minn
	Vectora	w	12	1863	Minn
	John	w	10	1865	Minn
Herder	Chas	w	42	1833	Prussia
	Mary	w	43	1832	Prussia
	Emma	w	17	1858	Prussia
	Louis	w	15	1860	Minn
	Carry	w	13	1862	Minn
	Willie	w	11	1864	Minn
	Eddie	w	9	1866	Minn
	Amelia	w	6	1869	Minn
	Herman	w	0	1875	Minn
Bremer	Joseph	w	41	1834	Mecklenburg
	Dora	w	34	1841	Mecklenburg
Westervelt	Evert	w	63	1812	N.Y.
	Julia	w	62	1813	Mass
	Mary C.	w	27	1848	Mass
	Jennie	w	24	1851	Mass
	E. E.	w	21	1854	Minn
Larson	Ole	w	48	1827	Norway
aka Loken	Martha	w	37	1838	Norway

Last Name	First Name	Race	Age	Born	Birth Place
Olson	Hans	w	15	1860	Norway
	Anna	w	12	1863	Norway
	Ole	w	10	1865	Norway
	Mary	w	8	1867	Norway
	Lars	w	6	1869	Norway
	Tilda	w	4	1871	Minn
	Sarina	w	2	1873	Minn
	Otto	w	1	1874	Minn
Haller	Engelbert	w	42	1833	Wurttemburg
	Carrie	w	8	1867	Minnesota
	Alfred	w	6	1869	Minnesota
McLean	Nathaniel C.	w	57	1818	Ohio
	Mary	w	38	1837	Kentucky
	John	w	20	1855	Ohio
	Elizabeth	w	13	1862	Ohio
	Lars A.	w	11	1864	Ohio
	Mary	w	9	1866	Ohio
	Matilda	w	7	1868	Minnesota
	Marshall	w	5	1870	Ohio
	Henrietta	w	3	1872	Ohio
Tomforde	Kate	w	21	1854	Germany
Lawtor	Joseph	w	18	1857	Germany
Thompson	Ann	w	45	1830	Kentucky
	Lucinda	w	32	1843	Kentucky
	1875 Frontenac			35	Houses
				166	Residents
				x	Boarding House
				x	Lakeside Hotel

1880 Federal Census for Florence Township, Goodhue County, State of Minnesota

Taken June 9 and 11th, 1880 by O. P. Francisco

	Last Name	First Name	Race	Age	Born	Birth Place	Occupation
	Russell	William	w	58	1822	Scotland	Miller
		Jane G	w	53	1827	Scotland	Keeping House
		James W.	w	19	1861	Iowa	Grist Mill Work
	Miller	Elam. R.	m	44	1836	Mississippi	Mason
		Lucy Jane	m	41	1839	Kentucky	Keeping House
		Mary B.	m	13	1867	Minnesota	
		Laurie F.	m	11	1869	Minnesota	
		Florence	m	10	1870	Minnesota	
		Alice R.	m	4	1876	Minnesota	
		Patrick F.	m	2	1878	Minnesota	
		Jane E.	m	5/12	1880	Minnesota	
	Westervelt	Evert	w	67	1813	New York	Farmer
		Julia A.	w	66	1814	Massachusetts	Keeping House
		Mary C.	w	28	1852	Massachusetts	
		Edward E.	w	26	1854	Minnesota	Laborer
	Johnson	John	w	22	1858	Sweden	Laborer
	Olson	Carl	w	42	1838	Norway	Laborer
		Corine	w	50	1830	Norway	Keeping House
		Louis	w	17	1863	Norway	Laborer
		Annie	w	15	1865	Norway	
		Ragna	w	11	1869	Minnesota	
	Carsten	Ole	w	52	1828	Norway	Farmer
		Olena	w	52	1828	Norway	Keeping House
		Carolina	w	23	1857	Norway	Servant
		Mina	w	14	1866	Norway	Servant
		Tarvel	w	12	1868	Norway	
		John	w	8	1872	Wisconsin	
	Garrard	Israel	w	54	1826	Kentucky	Farmer
LS	Fahey	Joseph C.	w	25	1855	Canada	Hotel Manager
LS	Cobb	John	w	28	1852	Minn	Laborer
LS	Bader	Teller	w	17	1863	Canada	Waitress
LS	Gorman	Annie	w	22	1858	Pennsylvania	Waitress
LS	Shears	Ann	w	52	1828	New York	
LS		Tedia	w	22	1858	Canada	
LS	Norton	Charles	w	57	1823	New York	Laborer
LS		Roxanne	w	42	1838	New York	Keeping House
LS		Harry	w	12	1868	Michigan	

LS: Lakeside Hotel
Race: W-White, M-Mulatto, B-Black

1880 Federal Census for Florence Township,
Goodhue County, State of Minnesota
Taken June 9 and 11th, 1880 by O. P. Francisco

Last Name	First Name	Race	Age	Born	Birth Place	Occupation
Larson (aka Loken)	Ole	w	52	1828	Norway	Laborer
	Martia	w	42	1838	Norway	Keeping House
	Lars	w	12	1868	Norway	
	Jennie	w	10	1870	Minnesota	
	Sevorina	w	7	1873	Minnesota	
	Otto	w	6	1874	Minnesota	
	Henry C.	w	4	1876	Minnesota	
Evert	Henry		30	1850	Mecklenburg	Farmer
	Augusta		21	1859	Minnesota	
	Emma		2	1878	Minnesota	
Krelberg	John	w	24	1856	New York	Laborer
	Marta	w	20	1860	Hanover	Keeping House
	Henry	w	2	1878	Minnesota	
Gerken	John	w	65	1815	Hanover	Laborer
	Margaret	w	48	1832	Hanover	Keeping House
	Joseph	w	16	1864	Hanover	Herder
Lubeck	John	w	50	1830	Mecklenburg	Laborer
	Augusta	w	30	1850	Mecklenburg	Keeping House
	Fred	w	7	1873	Minnesota	
	Dolly	w	4	1876	Minnesota	
	Ada	w	2	1878	Minnesota	
Bartels	Jacob	w	27	1853	Hanover	Laborer
	Caroline	w	24	1856	Prussia	Keeping House
	Martha	w	1	1879	Minnesota	
Haller	Engelbert	w	47	1833	Wurttemberg	Carpenter
	Carrie	w	13	1867	Minnesota	Keeping House
	Alfred	w	11	1869	Minnesota	
Markmann	John	w	40	1840	Prussia	Laborer
	Friedrica	w	31	1849	Prussia	Laborer
	William	w	9	1871	Minnesota	
	Annie	w	6	1874	Minnesota	
	Sophia	w	4	1876	Minnesota	
Schloerstein	Wolf	w	63	1817	Austria	Laborer
	Mary	w	66	1814	Austria	Keeping House
Kells	James	w	24	1856	Wisconsin	Laborer
	Tracy	w	23	1857	Austria	Keeping House

1880 Federal Census for Florence Township, Goodhue County, State of Minnesota

Taken June 9 and 11th, 1880 by O. P. Francisco

Last Name	First Name	Race	Age	Born	Birth Place	Occupation
Zimmerman	Christ	w	52	1828	Switzerland	Laborer
	Kate	w	47	1833	Prussia	Keeping House
Bremer	Joseph	w	47	1833	Mecklenburg	Farmer
	Dora	w	39	1841	Mecklenburg	Keeping House
Herder	Chas F.	w	47	1833	Prussia	Farmer
	Mary	w	49	1831	Prussia	Keeping House
	Lewis	w	20	1860	Minnesota	Farm Worker
	Carrie	w	18	1862	Minnesota	
	William	w	16	1864	Minnesota	
	Eddie	w	13	1867	Minnesota	
	Emelia	w	11	1869	Minnesota	
	Herman	w	5	1875	Minnesota	
	Lydia	w	1	1879	Minnesota	
Kohn	Elsie	w	59	1821	Mecklenburg	Keeping House
Sperl	Annie	w	50	1830	Austria	Keeping House
	Emanuel	w	11	1869	Minnesota	Herder
Hawkinson	Ole	w	38	1842	Sweden	Laborer
	Ellen	w	42	1838	Sweden	Keeping House
	Mary	w	10	1870	Sweden	
	Andrew	w	7	1873	Sweden	
	Eddie	w	4	1876	Sweden	
	Alfred	w	1	1879	Minnesota	
Anderson	Herder	w	25	1855	Sweden	
Peterson	Chas	w	6	1874	Sweden	
	Peter	w	26	1854	Sweden	Stone Mill Work
Goss	Charles	w	46	1834	Straslund, Prussia	Laborer
	Caroline	w	43	1837	Straslund, Prussia	Keeping House
	Chas	w	13	1867	Straslund, Prussia	Herder
	Annie	w	9	1871	Straslund, Prussia	
Peterson	Chas	w	45	1835	Sweden	Laborer
	Fiat	w	39	1841	Sweden	Keeping House
	Emil	w	10	1870	Sweden	
	Arvede	w	7	1873	Sweden	
	Helmut	w	5	1875	Sweden	
	Helmer	w	3	1877	Sweden	
	Lissette	w	1	1879	Sweden	

LS: Lakeside Hotel
Race: W-White, M-Mulatto, B-Black

1880 Federal Census for Florence Township, Goodhue County, State of Minnesota

Taken June 9 and 11th, 1880 by O. P. Francisco

Last Name	First Name	Race	Age	Born	Birth Place	Occupation
Paulson	Arylist	w	35	1845	Sweden	
Bartels	George	w	53	1827	Hanover	Laborer
	Katy	w	52	1828	Hanover	Keeping House
	Henry	w	12	1868	Hanover	Herder
Evensen	Even	w	45	1835	Norway	Laborer
	Lena	w	50	1830	Norway	Keeping House
	Louis	w	15	1865	Norway	
	Ole	w	5	1875	Minnesota	
Koch	William	w	29	1851	Mecklenburg	Laborer
	Mina	w	29	1851	Mecklenburg	
	Charles	w	2	1878	Illinois	
Krelberg	Henry	w	50	1830	Mecklenburg	Laborer
	Dorothea	w	40	1840	Mecklenburg	Keeping House
	Henry	w	16	1864	Mecklenburg	Laborer
Wurtz	John F.	w	38	1842	New York	Teacher
	Emily P.	w	33	1847	Michigan	Keeping House
	Edith W.	w	5	1875	Minnesota	
	Annie	w	2	1878	Minnesota	
	Ella	w	7m	1879	Minnesota	
Schenach	Emanuel	w	56	1824	Tyrol	Wagon Maker
	Ameliana	w	50	1830	Tyrol	Keeping House
	Victoria	w	17	1863	Minnesota	
	John	w	15	1865	Minnesota	
Muller	Henry	w	64	1816	Mecklenburg	Laborer
	Doris	w	62	1818	Mecklenburg	
Bahr	John	w	68	1812	Saxony-Coburg	
	Julia	w	64	1816	Saxony-Meininger	Keeping House
Schenach	Godfried	w	58	1822	Tyrol	Laborer
	Annie	w	49	1831	Tyrol	Keeping House
	Engelbert	w	17	1863	Minnesota	R.R. Worker
Ackerman	Michael	w	44	1836	Bavaria	Carpenter
	Margaret	w	51	1829	Hanover	Keeping House
	Annie	w	19	1861	Minnesota	
	Edward	w	17	1863	Minnesota	

LS: Lakeside Hotel
Race: W-White, M-Mulatto, B-Black

1880 Federal Census for Florence Township, Goodhue County, State of Minnesota

Taken June 9 and 11th, 1880 by O. P. Francisco

Last Name	First Name	Race	Age	Born	Birth Place	Occupation
Hunecke	Henry	w	47	1833	Prussia	Carpenter
	Louisa	w	48	1832	Mecklenburg	Keeping House
	Lena	w	21	1859	Minnesota	Servant
	Louisa	w	16	1864	Minnesota	
	Eddie	w	14	1866	Minnesota	
Johnson	Hans	w	38	1842	Norway	Farmer
	Gurina	w	32	1848	Norway	Keeping House
	Annie M	w	14	1866	Norway	
	Johnnie	w	11	1869	Minnesota	
	Elisa M	w	8	1872	Minnesota	
	George	w	6	1874	Minnesota	
	Henry	w	2	1878	Minnesota	
	Maude	w	4mo	1880	Minnesota	
	Jacob	w	19	1861	Minnesota	
Hunecke	John	w	48	1832	Prussia	Farmer
	Caroline	w	48	1832	Mecklenburg	Keeping House
Friedericks	Christ	w	52	1828	Mecklenburg	Farmer
	Sophia	w	54	1826	Mecklenburg	Keeping House
	Herman	w	15	1865	Mecklenburg	
Smith	Dora	w	78	1802	Mecklenburg	
Dammann	Peter	w	33	1847	Germany	Laborer
	Rebecca	w	42	1838	Germany	Keeping House
Poppe	Katie	w	14	1866	New York	
	Annie	w	12	1868	Massachusetts	
Dammann	Annie	w	73	1807	Germany	
	1880 Frontenac			41	Houses	
				168	Residents	
				x	Lakeside Hotel	

LS: Lakeside Hotel
Race: W-White, M-Mulatto, B-Black

Last Name	First Name	Race	Age	Born	Birth Place		
Herder	C.F.	w	52	1833	Germany		
	Mary	w	54	1831	Germany		
	Edna	w	18	1867	Minn		
	Herman	w	10	1875	Minn		
	Lizzie	w	6	1879	Minn		
Bremer	Joseph	w	51	1834	Germany		
	Dora	w	44	1841	Germany		
	Fred	w	12	1873	Minn		
	Dora	w	9	1876	Minn		
Church	G.	w	64	1821	Germany		
	Anna	w	54	1831	Germany		
Ackerman	Michael	w	50	1835	Germany		
	Marg	w	57	1828	Germany		
	Anna	w	24	1861	Minn		
	Geo	w	10	1875	Germany		
Hunecke	Henry	w	53	1832	Germany		
	Louisa	w	54	1831	Germany		
	Louisa	w	21	1864	Minn		
	Ed	w	19	1866	Minn		
Haller	Engelbert	w	57	1828	Germany		
	Carrie	w	18	1867	Minn		
	Alfred	w	16	1869	Minn		
Gense	William	w	32	1853	Germany		
	Sophie	w	28	1857	Germany		
	Henry	w	12	1873	Germany		
	Anna	w	9	1876	Germany		
	Minnie	w	5	1880	Germany		
	Martha	w	10m	1884	Minn		
Schenach	Emmanuel	w	61	1824	Germany		
	Anna	w	55	1830	Germany		
	Dora	w	22	1863	Minn		
	John	w	21	1864	Minn		
Kohn	Eliza	w	68	1817	Germany		
	H.	w	22	1863	Germany		

Race: W-White, M-Mulatto, B-Black

1885 Minnesota State Census as of May 1, 1885
Post Office: Frontenac, Assessor: I. G. Munger

Last Name	First Name	Race	Age	Born	Birth Place		
Bartels	George	w	57	1828	Germany		
	Kate	w	56	1829	Germany		
	Geo	w	22	1863	Germany		
	Henry	w	17	1868	Germany		
Krelberg	John	w	28	1857	Germany		
	Martha	w	24	1861	Germany		
	Henry	w	7	1878	New York		
	Kate	w	3	1882	Minn		
Meyer	Minnie	w	44	1841	Germany		
	Geo	w	25	1860	Ohio		
	Kate	w	19	1866	Illinois		
	Fred	w	21	1864	Illinois		
	Mina	w	16	1869	Illinois		
	Bertha	w	11	1874	Illinois		
Possehl	John	w	35	1850	Germany		
	Augusta	w	35	1850	Germany		
	Clara	w	8	1877	Germany		
	Augusta	w	6	1879	Germany		
	Paul	w	3	1882	Germany		
	Lucy	w	9m	1884	Minn		
Schloerstein	Wolf	w	65	1820	Germany		
	Mary	w	73	1812	Germany		
Sperl	Maris	w	55	1830	Germany		
	M.	w	16	1869	Minn		
Hawkinson	Ole	w	44	1841	Sweden		
	Ellen	w	47	1838	Sweden		
	Mary	w	15	1870	Sweden		
	Andrew	w	13	1872	Sweden		
	Eddie	w	10	1875	Sweden		
	Alf	w	6	1879	Minn		
Strupe	Carl	w	55	1830	Germany		
	Sophia	w	44	1841	Germany		
	Henry	w	11	1874	Germany		
	Frank	w	5	1880	Germany		
	Albert	w	2	1883	Germany		

Race: W-White, M-Mulatto, B-Black

1885 Minnesota State Census as of May 1, 1885
Post Office: Frontenac, Assessor: I. G. Munger

Last Name	First Name	Race	Age	Born	Birth Place		
Johnson	Hans	W	43	1842	Norway		
	Gurena	W	39	1846	Norway		
	Mary	W	18	1867	Norway		
	John	W	15	1870	Minn		
	Lisa	W	13	1872	Minn		
	George	W	10	1875	Minn		
	Henry	W	7	1878	Minn		
	Maud	W	5	1880	Minn		
	Elizabeth	W	2	1883	Minn		
	Linda	W	3mo	1885	Minn		
Johnson	Olaf	W	37	1848	Sweden		
Muller	Henry	W	69	1816	Germany		
	Charlotte	W	55	1830	Germany		
Carstenson	Ole	W	57	1828	Norway		
	Olena	W	56	1829	Norway		
	Casper	W	21	1864	Norway		
	Minnie	W	19	1866	Norway		
	Tornel	W	16	1869	Norway		
	John	W	13	1872	Wisconsin		
Lester	William	W	28	1857	Iowa		
	Lena	W	27	1858	Norway		
Koch	W	W	35	1850	Germany		
	Minnie	W	32	1853	Germany		
	Charles	W	7	1878	Illinois		
	Herman	W	2	1883	Minn		
Olson	Carl	W	48	1837	Norway		
	Carrie	W	52	1833	Norway		
	Lucy (Louis Carlson)	W	21	1864	Norway		
	Anna	W	18	1867	Norway		
	Romtry (Ragna)	W	15	1870	Minn		
Paulson	Hans	W	24	1861	Norway		
Lubeck	John	W	63	1822	Germany		
	Augusta	W	33	1852	Germany		
	Eda	W	7	1878	Minn		
	Paulina	W	5	1880	Minn		
	Wm	W	2	1883	Minn		
	Augusta	W	8m	1884	Minn		

Race: W-White, M-Mulatto, B-Black

1885 Minnesota State Census as of May 1, 1885
Post Office: Frontenac, Assessor: I. G. Munger

Last Name	First Name	Race	Age	Born	Birth Place		
Gerken	John	w	60	1825	Germany		
	Marg	w	53	1832	Germany		
	Joseph	w	21	1864	Germany		
Haga	Ole	w	37	1848	Norway		
	Albertina	w	35	1850	Norway		
	Lars	w	11	1874	Norway		
	Martin	w	5	1880	Norway		
	Maria	w	3	1882	Norway		
	Ole	w	2	1883	Norway		
Gulbrandson	Peter	w	25	1860	Norway		
(Gilbertson)	Carolina	w	24	1861	Norway		
	Carolina	w	1	1884	Minn		
Olsen	Gulbrand	w	68	1817	Norway		
	Patrolina	w	57	1828	Norway		
Larson	Ole	w	50	1835	Norway		
aka Loken	Martha	w	44	1841	Norway		
	Hans	w	25	1860	Norway		
	Ole	w	21	1864	Norway		
	Mary	w	19	1866	Norway		
	Lars	w	17	1868	Norway		
	Jeannie	w	15	1870	Minn		
	Sabrina	w	11	1874	Minn		
	Otto	w	9	1876	Minn		
	John	w	7	1878	Minn		
	Henry	w	6	1879	Minn		
	George	w	4	1881	Minn		
	Hilmer	w	2	1883	Minn		
Lester	James	w	27	1858	Iowa		
	Anna	w	23	1862	Norway		
	Walter	w	4	1881	Minn		
	Richard	w	2	1883	Minn		
	Arthur	w	4m	1885	Minn		
Dammann	Peter	w	37	1848	Germany		
	Rebecca	w	47	1838	Germany		
Poppe	Kathy	w	20	1865	New York		
Poppe	Mary	w	17	1868	Massachusetts		

Race: W-White, M-Mulatto, B-Black

1885 Minnesota State Census as of May 1, 1885
Post Office: Frontenac, Assessor: I. G. Munger

Last Name	First Name	Race	Age	Born	Birth Place		
Dammann	John	w	40	1845	Germany		
	Anna	w	24	1861	Germany		
	Henry	w	4	1881	Germany		
	Harris	w	2	1883	Germany		
	Anna	w	3mo	1885	Minn		
Hunecke	John	w	53	1832	Germany		
	Carolina	w	53	1832	Germany		
Kells	James	w	28	1857	Wisconson		
	Tracy	w	24	1861	Germany		
	D. F.	w	10m	1884	Minnesota		
Reinhard	Jessie	w	17	1868	Minnesota		
Garrard	Israel	w		1885	Ohio		
	1885 Frontenac						
				36	Houses		
				12	Residents		
				x	Lakeside Hotel		

Last Name	First Name	Race	Age	Born	Birth Place	Occupation	
Kingsley	Armin	w	64	1831	New York	Miller	
	Matilda	w	51	1844	Vermont		
	Fred	w	32	1863	Minn	Miller	
	Bertha	w	29	1866	Minnesota		
	Arthur B.	w	16	1879	Minnesota		
Westervelt	Julia A.	w	82	1813	Mass		
	Mary	w	47	1848	Mass		
Garrard	Israel	w	70	1825	Ohio	Lawyer	
Garrard	G.W.	w	32	1863	New York	Farmer	
	V. H.	w	31	1864	New York		
	B.M.	w	2	1893	New York		
Allen	Hannah	b	35	1860	New York		
Allen	F. K.	b	55	1840	New York	Coachman	
Harris	Leona	b	23	1872	Minnesota		
Schenach	John	w	30	1865	Minnesota	Laborer	
	Mary	w	28	1867	Minnesota		
	Emmanuel	w	71	1824	Germany	Wagon Maker	
	Dora	w	33	1862	Minnesota		
Possehl	John	w	45	1850	Germany	Laborer	
	Augusta	w	45	1850	Germany		
	Clara	w	18	1877	Germany		
	Augusta	w	15	1880	Germany		
	Carl	w	13	1882	Germany		
	Louis	w	11	1884	Minnesota		
Hunecke	Edward	w	29	1866	Minnesota	Carpenter	
	Katie	w	28	1867	New York		
	Edwin	w	1	1894	Minnesota		
Dammann	Peter	w	48	1847	Germany	Laborer	
	Rebecca	w	60	1835	Germany		
Gohrke	Chas	w	32	1863	Germany	Laborer	
	Minnie	w	27	1868	Germany		
	Lillie	w	4	1891	Minnesota		
	Lizzie	w	2	1893	Minnesota		
Sepke	Ella	w	12	1883	Minnesota		
	Mary	w	10	1885	Minnesota		

1895 Minnesota State Census, June 1895
Florence Township, Goodhue County

	Last Name	First Name	Race	Age	Born	Birth Place	Occupation
LS	Brunner	John	W	41	1854	Switzerland	Hotel Keeper
LS		Louise	W	31	1864	Minnesota	
LS		Aleda	W	4	1891	Dacotah	
LS		Ann	W	2	1893	Wisconsin	
LS	Gerken	Joseph	W	31	1864	Germany	Hotel Clerk
LS	Lubeck	Edith	W	17	1878	Minnesota	
LS	Poppe	Mary	W	28	1867	Massachusetts	
LS	Gense	Minnie	W	15	1880	Germany	
	Carlson	Lewis	W	30	1865	Norway	Farmer
		Carrie	W	25	1870	Missouri	
	Oleson	Carl	W	57	1838	Norway	Laborer
	Strupp	Henry	W	21	1874	Germany	Laborer
	Kells	James	W	38	1857	Wisconsin	Agent
		Theresa	W	37	1858	Germany	
		Daisy	W	10	1885	Minnesota	
		Edna	W	9	1886	Minnesota	
		Alfred	W	6	1889	Minnesota	
	Olson	Hans	W	33	1862	Norway	Quarryman
		Anna	W	32	1863	Norway	
		Violet	W	8	1887	Minnesota	
		Hennrietta	W	5	1890	Minnesota	
		Clara	W	3	1892	Minnesota	
		Harry	W	1	1894	Minnesota	
	Larson	Ole	W	65	1830	Norway	Quarryman
		Martha	W	55	1840	Norway	
		Otto	W	20	1875	Minnesota	
		John	W	19	1876	Minnesota	
		Henry	W	16	1879	Minnesota	
		George	W	14	1881	Minnesota	
		Hilmar	W	12	1883	Minnesota	
	Gerken	John	W	74	1821	Germany	
		Margaret	W	62	1833	Germany	
	Hunecke	John	W	60	1835	Germany	Laborer
		Carrie	W	53	1842	Germany	

1895 Minnesota State Census, June 1895
Florence Township, Goodhue County

Last Name	First Name	Race	Age	Born	Birth Place	Occupation	
Lubeck	John	w	73	1822	Germany		
	Augusta	w	44	1851	Germany		
	Edith	w	17	1878	Minnesota		
	Pauline	w	14	1881	Minnesota		
	Willie	w	12	1883	Minnesota		
	Augusta	w	10	1885	Minnesota		
	John	w	8	1887	Minnesota		
	Lena	w	6	1889	Minnesota		
	Daisy	w	1mo	1895	Minnesota		
Gilbertson	Peter	w	34	1861	Norway	Laborer	
	Caroline	w	31	1864	Norway		
	John	w	11	1884	Minnesota		
	Arthur	w	6	1889	Minnesota		
	Lilly	w	3	1892	Minnesota		
	Edna	w	1	1894	Minnesota		
Haga	Ole	w	47	1848	Norway		
	L.	w	45	1850	Norway		
	Ian	w	21	1874	Norway		
	Mary	w	13	1882	Minnesota		
	Ole	w	11	1884	Minnesota		
	Matilda	w	6	1889	Minnesota		
Oleson	Ole W.	w	38	1857	Norway	Quarryman	
	Anna	w	26	1869	Norway		
	Bertha	w	2	1893	Minnesota		
	Norman	w	1	1894	Minnesota		
Hanson	Gus	w	24	1871	Norway	Quarryman	
Strupp	Charles	w	63	1832	Germany	Laborer	
	Sophie	w	54	1841	Germany		
	Albert	w	11	1884	Germany		
Friedericks	Sophia	w	76	1819	Germany		
Bartels	George	w	32	1863	Germany	Carpenter	
	Minnie	w	26	1869	Illinois		
	Rueben	w	1	1894	Minnesota		

1895 Minnesota State Census, June 1895
Florence Township, Goodhue County

Last Name	First Name	Race	Age	Born	Birth Place	Occupation	
Muller	Henry	w	79	1816	Germany		
Bartels	Henry	w	29	1866	Germany	Carpenter	
	Nellie	w	26	1869	Germany		
	Millie	w	7	1888	Minnesota		
	Harris	w	3	1892	Minnesota		
	Edna	w	1	1894	Minnesota		
	George	w	67	1828	Germany		
Hausman	C.M.	w	71	1824	Germany		
	Catherine	w	68	1827	Germany		
	Eva	w	40	1855	New York		
Schloerstein	Wolf	w	80	1815	Germany		
Carstensen	Ole	w	65	1830	Norway	Carpenter	
	Olina	w	64	1831	Norway		
	Casper	w	33	1862	Norway	Stone Cutter	
	Sevena	w	35	1860	Norway		
	Minnie	w	27	1868	Norway		
	Torval	w	24	1871	Norway	Stone Cutter	
	John	w	21	1874	Wisconsin	Stone Cutter	
Herder	Charles	w	53	1842	Germany	Farmer	
	Mary	w	65	1830	Germany		
	Merkl	w	28	1867	Minnesota	Farmer	
Bremer	Joseph	w	66	1829	Germany	Farmer	
	Joanna	w	54	1841	Germany		
Lubeck	Fred	w	22	1873	Minnesota	Farmer	
	Dora	w	19	1876	Minnesota		
Schenach	Anna	w	65	1830	Germany		
Hunecke	Henry	w	62	1833	Germany		
Gense	Wm	w	44	1851	Germany	R.R. Worker	
	Sophia	w	40	1855	Germany		
	Anna	w	19	1876	Germany		
	Minnie	w	15	1880	Germany		
	Martha	w	10	1885	Minnesota		
	Carrie	w	4	1891	Minnesota		
	1895 Frontenac			36	Houses		
				135	Residents		
				x	Lakeside		

LS: Lakeside Hotel
Race: W-White, M-Mulatto, B-Black

1900 Federal Census, as of June 1st, 1900 Florence Township, Goodhue County, Minnesota

Enumerated by me on the 11th day of June 1900, Louis Carlson

Last Name	First Name	Age	Born	Birth place	Occupation	Years Married	Children Born	Children Living	Immigrated	Own or Rent	Free or Mtg	Farm or Home
Bartels	Henry	32	1867	Germany	Carpenter	12			1872			
	Nettie	31	1869	Germany		12	3	3	1885			
	Millie	11	1889	Minnesota								
	Harry	8	1892	Minnesota								
	Edna	6	1894	Minnesota								
Bartels	George	34	1862	Germany	Carpenter	10			1872			
	Minnie	29	1869	Illinois		10	4	2				
	Rueben	5	1884	Minnesota								
	Richmond	1	1889	Minnesota								
Friedericks	John	60	1840	Germany	Laborer				1859			
Schenach	John	35	1865	Germany	Laborer							
	Mary	33	1866	Minnesota			1	0				
	Emmanuel	75	1835	Germany			3	2				
Hunecke	Henry	68	1940	Germany	Carpenter				1862			
	Mary	56	1965	Germany								
Kinglsey	Armin D.	69	1830	New York	Miller	22	7	4		o	m	h
	Fred R.	36	1863	Minnesota	Miller							
	Bertha	34	1865	Minnesota								
Bremer	Joachim	65	1834	Germany	Farmer	32			1866	o	m	f
	Dora	58	1841	Germany		32	0	0	1868			
	Fred D.			Minnesota	Farm labor							
Carlson	Louis	35	1864	Norway	Farmer	8			1870	r	f	f
	Carrie	30	1870	Missouri		8	2	2				
	Raymond L.	4	1896	Minnesota								
	Winfred F.	1	1899	Minnesota								
Hausman	Carl	76	1823	Germany		48			1849	o	f	h
	Catherine	73	1826	Germany		48	10	5	1850			
	Eva	47	1852	New York								
Friedericks	Henry	29	1871	Minnesota	Day laborer	6				r	f	h
	Hilda H.	26	1874	Sweden	Dress maker	6	1	1	1892			
	Florence	4	1895	Minnesota								

LS: Lakeside Hotel

1900 Federal Census, as of June 1st, 1900 Florence Township, Goodhue County, Minnesota
Enumerated by me on the 11th day of June 1900, Louis Carlson

Last Name	First Name	Age	Born	Birth place	Occupation	Years Married	Children Born	Children Living	Immigrated	Own or Rent	Free or Mtg	Farm or Home
Garrard	Israel	74	1825	Ohio	Land Lord	11	2	2		o	f	h
Meyer	Katie	34	1865	Illinois	Clerk Dry Goods							
	Bertha	24	1876	Illinois	House Keeper							
Westervelt	Julia	86	1813	Mass		42	5	3		o	f	h
	Mary C.	52	1847	Mass								
Erickson	Erich	60	1839	Norway	Lay Reader	25			1878	o	f	h
	Millie	51	1849	Norway		25	0	0	1878			
Haga	Ole	53	1847	Norway	Day laborer	31			1881	o	f	h
	Albertine	50	1850	Norway		21	5	4	1881			
	Larz	25	1875	Norway	Teamster				1881			
	Ole	16	1883	Minnesota	Farm Laborer							
	Matilda	11	1899	Minnesota								
Olson	Ole W.	37	1862	Norway	Stone cutter	9			1883	o	m	h
	Anna	30	1869	Norway		9	6	6	1890			
	Bertha	7	1892	Minnesota								
	Norman	5	1894	Minnesota								
	Lizabeth	3	1896	Minnesota								
	Hulda	2	1897	Minnesota								
	Selma	1	1899	Minnesota								
	Roy	6m	1900	Minnesota								
Hine	Louis	26	1874	Germany	Laborer, Quarry	4			1882	r	f	h
	Grace	20	1879	Indiana		4						
Friedericks	Sophia	72	1827	Germany		26	5	2	1867			
Gilbertson	Petter	39	1861	Norway	Laborer, Quarry	16			1882	o	m	h
	Caroline	40	1860	Norway		16	7	6	1883			
	Arthur	11	1889	Minnesota								
	Lilly	8	1892	Minnesota								
	Edna	6	1894	Minnesota								
	Linda	3	1897	Minnesota								
	Raymond	3	1897	Minnesota								

1900 Federal Census, as of June 1st, 1900 Florence Township, Goodhue County, Minnesota

Enumerated by me on the 11th day of June 1900, Louis Carlson

	Last Name	First Name	Age	Born	Birth place	Occupation	Years Married	Children Born	Children Living	Immigrated	Own or Rent	Free or Mtg	Farm or Home
	Carstenson	Casper	36	1863	Norway	Stone Cutter	1			1872	r	f	h
		Mary	32	1867	Mass		1	0	0				
	Olson	Carl	62	1837	Norway					1869	o	f	h
	Lubeck	John	79	1821	Germany		27			1870	o	f	h
		Gusta	49	1851	Germany		27	10	9	1870			
		William	17	1882	Minnesota								
		Gusta	15	1884	Minnesota	Nurse							
		Johnie	13	1886	Minnesota								
		Caroline	10	1889	Minnesota								
		Daisy	6	1893	Minnesota								
LS	Hall	John	52	1847	Ireland	Land Lord Hotel					r	f	h
LS	Ketchel	Ermannia	22	1877	Minnesota	Clerk							
LS	Hanna	Marvin	37	1863	Iowa	Hotel clerk							
LS	Alexander	William	37	1863	Scotland	Cook Hotel				1875			
LS	Mattison	Emma	26	1874	Sweden	Servant				1898			
LS	Feiery	Bessey	23	1876	Minnesota	Servant							
LS		Maggie	28	1872	Minnesota	Servant							
	Dammann	Petter	53	1847	Germany	Laborer	26			1865	o	f	h
		Rebecka	65	1834	Germany		40	3	2	1853			
	Gerken	Johannes	36	1863	Germany	Laborer	3			1866	o	f	h
		Mary	23	1876	Minnesota		3						
		Margaret	66	1833	Germany		25	1	1	1866			
	Hunecke	John	65	1834	Germany		40			1852			
		Caroline	64	1835	Germany		40	0					
	Bolang	Ole	45	1854	Norway	Livery	24			1882	r	f	h
		Martha	46	1853	Norway		24	8	4	1882			
		Christine	15	1884	Minnesota								
		Edith	13	1887	Minnesota								
		Alfred	10	1890	Wisconsin								
		Rudolf	3	1897	Minnesota								

LS: Lakeside Hotel

1900 Federal Census, as of June 1st, 1900 Florence Township, Goodhue County, Minnesota
Enumerated by me on the 11th day of June 1900, Louis Carlson

Last Name	First Name	Age	Born	Birth place	Occupation	Years Married	Children Born	Children Living	Immigrated	Own or Rent	Free or Mtg	Farm or Home
Strupe	Henry	25	1874	Germany	Farm Laborer	4			1884	r	f	h
	Dora	24	1876	Minnesota		4	3	3				
	George	3	1896	Minnesota								
	Laura	1	1898	Minnesota								
	Begamin	7mo	1899	Minnesota								
Carstenson	Ole	72	1828	Norway		45			1870	o	f	h
	Olena	70	1829	Norway		45	8	7	1870			
	Tarvel	30	1869	Norway	Stone cutter				1870			
	John	28	1872	Wisconsin	Stone cutter							
Herder	Carl F.	67	1832	Germany	Land Loard	43			1857	o	f	h
	Mary D.	69	1830	Germany		43	9	9	1857			
Dammann	John	52	1848	Germany	R. R. Laborer	22			1884	r	f	h
	Annie	40	1859	Germany		22	6	5	1884			
	Annie	15	1884	Minnesota								
	Mary	13	1887	Minnesota								
	Emma	10	1890	Minnesota								
Gense	William	49	1851	Germany	R. R. Laborer	26			1882	o	f	h
	Sophia	45	1854	Germany		26	5	5	1882			
	Carrie	9	1890	Minnesota								
Gohrke	Charles	37	1863	Germany	Blacksmith	10			1882	o	f	h
	Minnie	30	1869	Germany		10	2	2	1882			
	Lily	9	1891	Minnesota								
	Lizzie	7	1893	Minnesota								
Sepke	Mary	14	1885	Minnesota								
Struppe	Carl	68	1832	Germany	Day Laborer	35			1884	o	f	h
	Sophie	60	1840	Germany		35	8	4	1884			
	Albert	17	1883	Germany	Farm Laborer				1884			
	Charley	23	1876	Germany	Farm Laborer				1884			

LS: Lakeside Hotel

1900 Federal Census, as of June 1st, 1900 Florence Township, Goodhue County, Minnesota

Enumerated by me on the 11th day of June 1900, Louis Carlson

Last Name	First Name	Age	Born	Birth place	Occupation	Years Married	Children Born	Children Living	Immigrated	Own or Rent	Free or Mtg	Farm or Home
Possehl	John	50	1850	Germany	Day Laborer	25			1882	o	f	h
	Augusta	49	1850	Germany		25	4	4	1882			
	Clara	23	1877	Germany					1882			
	Paul	18	1881	Germany	Day Laborer				1882			
	Louis	15	1885	Minnesota								
Larson	Ole	72	1828	Norway		41			1869	o	f	h
aka Loken	Martha	59	1840	Norway		41	13	12				
	George	19	1881	Minnesota	Farm Laborer							
	Anton H.	17	1883	Minnesota	Farm Laborer							
	Tena	7	1892	Wisconsin								
	Lars	55	1845	Norway	Laborer, Quarry				1869			
Olson	Hans	39	1860	Norway	Laborer, Quarry	13			1869	o	m	h
	Annette	38	1862	Norway		13	5	4				
	Violet	13	1886	Minnesota								
	Hennrietta	11	1888	Minnesota								
	Clara	8	1891	Minnesota								
	Harry	6	1893	Minnesota								
Gilbertson	Gilbert	84	1816	Norway					1882			
Hunecke	Edward	34	1865	Minnesota	Carpenter	7						
	Katie	34	1865	New York		7	2	2				
	Edwin M	6	1894	Minnesota								
	Walter J.	4	1896	Minnesota								
Garrard	George W.	36	1863	New York	Contractor Stone	10				o	f	h
	Virginia H.	36	1864	New York		10	3	3				
	Beulah M.	7	1893	New York								
	Evelyn D.	3	1896	Minnesota								
	Catherine W.	1	1898	Minnesota								
Lubeck	Edith	21	1878	Minnesota	House Keeper							
	1900 Frontenac		37	Houses								
			147	Residents								
			x	Lakeside Hotel								

Photo Album

John Hull Underwood

Photographer

~~~~~

1885 Frontenac, Minnesota

Courtesy of Lake City, Minnesota

Historical Society

The label below was often on the back of the
John Hull Underwood photographs.

Lake Pepin Scenery---Frontenac Views.

No ....

J. HULL UNDERWOOD, Photo.

Underwood frequently indicated
the season and the year
along with a title of the picture.

Pulling Ashore   Autumn 1885

Landing   Autumn 1885

On the Shore   *November 1885*

Lakeside North Bay, Point no Point   *November 1885*

Waiting   November 1885

The Return   November 1885

After every storm, there comes such calm   *November 1885*

St. Hubert's Lodge   *Autumn 1885*

Waiting for the Carriage   *Autumn 1885*

On the Porch of Winona Cottage   *Autumn 1885*

At the Gate   Autumn 1885

Autumn 1885

On the Porch of Virginia Cottage

Lakeside from the Plateau   *Autumn 1885*

A visit to the Artistry Den

St. Hubert's Lodge   *November 1885*

Lakeside Hotel in background

November 1885

Bird's Point, Head of the Lake

Ice cutting on the lake

Ice Harvest - Cutting

Ice Harvest - Loading

Ice Harvest - Hauling

Ice Harvest - Storing

Ice Harvest-The Last Load   *Winter 1885*

Lakeside in Winter

Winona Cottage in Winter

St. Hubert's Lodge   Winter 1885

Dacotah Cottage – Snow drifts and Evergreens   Winter 1885

Shadows on the Snow　　　　　　　　　　*Winter 1885*

Out for a Sleigh Ride　　　　　　　　　　*Winter 1885*

40 Degrees Below Zero   Winter 1885

Road on the Lake   Winter 1885

Dining Room in England

Photo Album
Edith and Anna Garrard,
Photographers

~~~~~

1899 Frontenac, Minnesota

Courtesy of Webster Collection

Edith and Anna,

daughters of

Lewis and Florence Garrard,

compiled and sketched this album

to commemorate their

August and September 1899

visit to Frontenac, Minnesota

Host for visit - Uncle Israel

Aug
29,
1899

→ Gen. David G.

...nis Hurd

Our Hosts.

1854

The first
view
of Lake Pepin.

1894

Beauty that fades not
with years.

A Glimpse of
St. Huberts.

Another view?

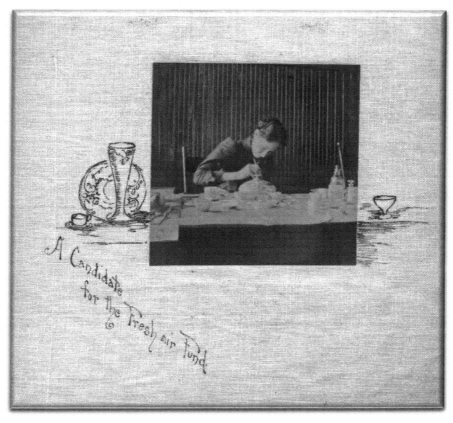

A Candidate
for the Fresh air fund.

A Sweep of Beach.

Tourists Examining Old Ruins.

A Bit of Forest Primeval on the Wisconsin Shore.

"View thro' the Hole in
— Nature's Curtain —

A Pepin Cup Defender?

Students of Ichthyology.

On the Hotel piazza.

Puzzle : Find The Ladies. —

Hilarious Tourists

The Rescue —

The First View of "Lakeside."

Gambolling
on
their native
heath.

Other Gamblers

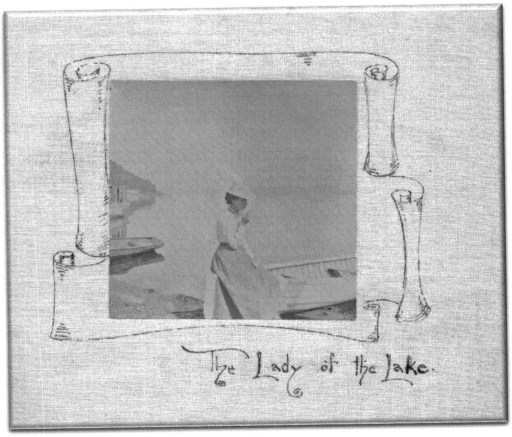

The Lady of the Lake.

With Feet Privileges.

CUBA LIBRE

322

House Boat
on the River

Preparing for a Sketch.

A Mushroom Expert.

On the Highway.

Strange Bird seen by Our Boatman while Crossing the Lake.

When Nature Smiles.

Poetry
and
Prose.

Thro' sandburrs to the Ferry.

The Kodaker
Kodaked.

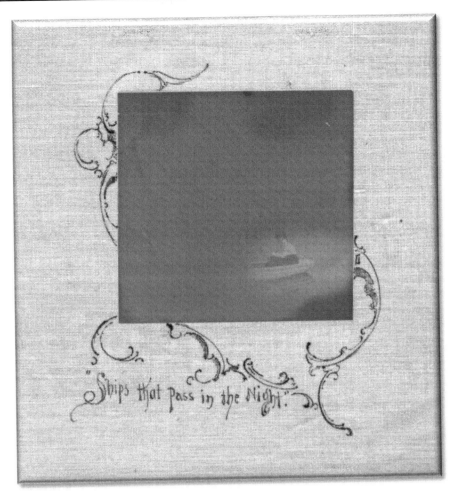

"Ships that Pass in the Night."

"The Stealer Stooping Beach-ward,"

Up Fern Creek.

Sep 1.
1899.

Fern Creek.

A Dog on Good foreground

Point No. Point.

Nectar and
Ambrosia

Ripe Plums and
Cold Water.

A Good Story
by a good fellow.

1858 and 1859

Garrard Letters

~~~~~

Two letters are printed.

1858 Lewis Garrard to his mother
Sarah Bella McLean

1859 Israel Garrard to his brother
Lewis Garrard

Following each copy of an original letter is
a transcription along with notable highlights.

Letters are courtesy of
Southern Minnesota Historical Center,
Memorial Library, Minnesota State University,
Mankato, Minnesota.

These two letters are only a sample of an extensive
donation of documents
made to the Memorial Library in 1973
by Florence Wilson Baker and Edith Garrard Wilson.

Chapelwood. Oct. 10th 1858.

Dear Lewis   Sunday Night.

I wrote to you last Sunday but since then I have had several letters from you and we have had a visit of three days from Mr. Westervelt, so that I will not longer delay writing to you.

Mr. W. & I spent the time very industriously and made up a bill of Dry goods & Groceries amounting to over 1500.00 almost all of it payable in 60 days. I also gave him $400.00 to enable him to pay the freight bills, and settle the bills at Galena. The Company's investment amounts thus to about 2000.00. I hope the most of it will be disposed of in the payment of debts due by us, so that you and I can retire at the end of winter. Mr. Westervelt I think would do very well to continue in it. He is not absorbed as we are in Farm Management.

I think that the amount of goods will make it advisable to open the store down at the Wauhrae. Let the firm be Westervelt & Co. I am not in favor of our name being used in the store. It would be better to have the Mercantile name simply E. Westervelt.

I have told Judge McLean and John both of the difficulty I had in getting Howard to do any valuable service, + indeed gave them a full

account with my opinion that I would not be able
to do any thing with him. The Judge is now supporting
all the rest of the family, and says that Hancock is
big enough to earn a living and must do it. that he
must never expect another dollar. that he must take an
axe and make a living chopping wood if in no other
way. That I dont wish to add to the Judges troubles
and, he will try what effect a letter of advice from me
and perhaps one from his father will have on him.

Mr Westervelt was looking well and
feeling well and I hope had as pleasant a no is
as was compatible with the amount of work we did

I send you a letter for Mr Schneider
from her husband who has lately got back here. He
says he could not sell his property in Germany +
that none of those could who are coming out. they will
be able to do so this winter + will be on in the spring
I told him that there was no work for him up
at Lake Pepin in the winter, and as he can get
good work at the Pork Houses at that season he
wishes his wife + the children to come down. Of
course you will send off Adam and Barbara at
the same time. They should box up their things +
take Deck passage to St Louis + from there to
Cincinnati by boat. I will have to advance them
money to get back with but that is better than
having them at the farm all winter. He says he
will pay me back all the money, at the rate of
$ ___ per month.

He and Pohl are bad investments. Pohl ought not to
be trusted a dollar's worth at the store. He must
be charged 2.50 per month now sent as soon as his
wife quits working for me in the Boarding House. He is
to be charged 2.50 per week boarding for himself for
all the time he has been there. He will have to settle
all their bills before he gets his deed if there is any
balance against him on his wifes wages account.

I have no doubt you have had
a hard time during Mr W's absence; but it is a
good training and you will do your work easier here
after for it. Mr W & I had a talk on the subject
of my going back this fall and we concluded that
there was nothing of sufficient importance to occasion
my return. You and he know my interests as well
as I do and have full authority to attend to my
trainers, dispose of my men, horses, cattle, building material &c, &c. It is out of the question for
me to go up there to relieve you of your duties and
responsibilities there unless you can come down here
and attend to what work I have before me here
for the next month or more. I will very gladly
exchange the duty of raising money for any thing
that ever fell to my lot at Lake Pepin. You
don't need me up there and will not until
the patents are issued on the strip and are
at the Land office. This will be during the
winter I suppose.

I would like very much to see my

friend Gallagher, & to go with him over the town site
and our lands, but the business of getting him to move
his mill down from Grey Cloud you and Mr Welch
tirolt can attend to. You can afford to be liberal
with him for he is a complete master of logging, rafting
milling &c in all its branches, and an energetic capable
man in every way, and a noble fellow and particular
friend of mine. He is a man that can be trusted.

Mr Wood's condition and the expected
births in the family prevented me from bringing him
out, so that I have another trip to New York and back
to make this fall.

Dodd did not succeed in getting the
loan for you. I have had enquiries made in those
places most likely to afford the funds, but so far without
success. While Mr W was here I had no chance to attend
to this matter but tomorrow will give my whole time to
it until it is accomplished.

I am also trying to find a purchaser
for some of Kennard's lots. Henshaw the Cabinet maker
purchased lately the lot on the Whitewater canal west of
our lease to Harding Johnson. 210 feet on the canal and
120 feet deep to the alley at 100 per foot. 1/6 cash
balance in 1.2.3.4.5 years with 6 per cent interest. He
will put up a large Cabinet manufactory on it. It is
a fair enough sale, and its advantage to us in the improve
ment of that vacant lot will be very great.

[November, 1858?]

The Baker's had a sale on Freeman Street lately. The lots went low, from 26, to 36 dollars per foot. The Orphan Asylum is looking for ground, having sold their place on Elm St to the City for $150,000. We have offered them the 280 feet on Freeman next to Orr's for 200.00 per foot.

There are some things you have written for which I have not sent you. First you have written for socks, (dark color). I don't know whether you mean cotton or woolen. If woolen, there are some that will suit you among our goods. Second. There is a book called the "Students Vade mecum", a large book about the size of a small law book. Do you want that. Do you want a "Dispensation book" giving the formulas of preparing medicines, or a book which indicates the remedies for given diseases. When you write about these books I will send you up the histories which you wrote for and which I have forgotten. I sent Beach's family medicine in the Box containing Mr DeGraw's things.

There is a box, a keg of pork, a keg of fish, a keg of molasses I suppose for Madison Hancriow. t bill of the freight on them should be sent to me for collection off of the Dr.

I made some enquires for money yesterday, without success. I will not neglect any opportunity of getting what you need

By Express I sent you today a package containing $500.00 received from Kennon to be paid to the Jenkins boys. I wish you would attend to this without delay. They ought to take a good deal of grain on account of the balance. They have a note of mine. Take a receipt for the money and also endorse it on the back of the note & let one of them sign the endorsement. Do the same with the amount of goods they get.

John McLean sent Reinwald a pair of pantaloons by Express the other day. It was done under the mistaken impression that I had shipped all of our goods.

Nathaniel received a fee of $1000.00 for his argument of the Chicago R. R. Depot case. I have no doubt he has a first rate legal mind. Stanbery has given him a share in some of his most important business.

Mother and the Judge are as usual. I wish we could induce them to spend their summers at Lake Pepin instead of Clifadwood. Jeps affair stands in the same condition.

Affectionately yr Brother
Israel Garrard

Chapelwood Oct 10, 1858

Sunday night

Dear Lewis

I wrote to you last Sunday but since then I have had several letters from you and we have had a visit of three days from Mr. Westervelt, so that I will no longer delay writing to you.

Mr. W and I spent the time very industriously and made up a bill of dry goods & groceries amounting to over $1,500.00 almost all of it payable in 60 days. I also gave him $400.00 to enable him to pay the freight bills, and settle the bills at Galina. The company's investment accumulates this to about $2,000.00. I hope the most of it will be disposed of in payment of debts due us, so that you and I can repay at the end of the winter. Mr. Westervelt I think will do very well to continue in it. He is not absorbed as we are in farm management.

I think the amount of goods will make it advisable to open the store down at the warehouse. Let the firm be Westervelt & Co. I am not in favor of our name being used in the store. It would be better to have the Mercantile name simply E. Westervelt.

I have told Judge McLean and John both of the difficulty I have getting Hancock to do any valuable service and in deed, gave them a full account with my opinion that I would not be able to do anything with him. The Judge is now supporting all the rest of the family, and says that Hancock is big enough to earn a living and must do it. That he must never expect another dollar. That he must take an axe and make a living chopping wood if in no other way. I don't wish to add to the Judge's troubles, and, so will try what a letter of advice from me and perhaps one from his father will have on him.

Mr. Westervelt was looking well and feeling well and I hope had a pleasant a visit as was compatible with the amount of work we did.

I send you a letter of Mrs. Schneider from her husband who has lately got back here. He says he could not sell his property in Germany and that none of them could who are coming out. They will not be able to do so this winter and will be on in the spring. I told him that there was no work for him up at Lake Pepin in the winter and as he can get good work at the Pork Houses in that season he wishes his wife and children to come down. Of course, you will send off Adam and Barbara at the same time. They should box up their things and take deck passage to St. Louis and from there to Cincinnati by boat. I will have to advance them money to get back with but that is better than having them at the farm all winter. He says he will pay me back all the money at the rate of $_____ per month.

He and Pohl are bad investments. Pohl ought not to be trusted a dollars' worth at the store. He must be charged $2.50 per month room rent as soon as his wife quits working for me at the boarding house. He is to be charged $2.50 per week boarding for himself for all the time he has been there. He will have to settle all these bills before he gets a deed if there is any balance against him on his wife's wages account.

339

I have no doubt you have had a hard time during Mr. W. absence; but it is a good training and you will do your work easier here after for it. Mr. W. and I have had a talk on the subject of my going back this fall and we concluded that there was nothing of sufficient importance to occasion my return. You and he know my interests as well as I do and have full authority to attend to my business, dispose of my men, horses and cattle, building material & etc. It is out of the question for me to go there to relieve you of your duties and responsibilities there unless you can come down here and attend to what work I have before me here for the next month or more. I will very gladly exchange the duty of raising money for anything that ever fell to my lot at Lake Pepin. You don't need me up there and will not until patents are issued on the script and are at the Land Office. This will be during the winter, I suppose.

I would like very much to see my friend Galligher & to go with him over the town site and over the lands, but that business of getting him to move his mill from down from Grey Cloud you and Mr. Westervelt can attend to. You can afford to be liberal with him for he is a complete master of logging, rafting and milling & all its branches, and an energetic capable man in every way and a noble fellow and particular friend of mine. He is a man that can be trusted.

Mr. Wood's condition and the expected birth in the family prevented me from bringing Kate out, so that I have another trip to New York and back to make this fall.

Dodd did not succeed in getting the loan for you. I have had inquiries made in those places most likely to afford the funds, but so far without success. While Mr. W. was here I had no chance to attend to this matter but tomorrow will give my whole time to it until it is accomplished.

(Cincinnati, Ohio news and references not transcribed)

Israel Garrard (in Ohio) to Lewis Garrard (in Minnesota) on Oct 10, 1858

Highlights in the letter:

1)   Israel is in Chapelwood, which is the name of the house in Cincinnati, Ohio.
Lewis is in village of Westervelt.

2)   Evert Westervelt visited Israel in Cincinnati for three days the week of October 3, 1858.

3)   Westervelt and Israel made up a list for village store supplies and ordered $1,500 worth of dry goods and groceries.

4)   The two-story warehouse was built in the summer of 1858. Israel suggested part of the warehouse be used as a store.

         Name of store owner: - Westervelt & Co.
         Name of Mercantile store: - E. Westervelt

5)   Schneiders are: Jacob Schneider and Dorothea Schneider (nee Shale, first marriage Katzenberger). Adam and Barbara are Dorothea's children.

     a)   In winter of 1858, Jacob is in Cincinnati working. Jacob sends letter to his wife in the village of Westervelt.

     b)   Jacob cannot sell his property in Germany.

     c)   Other hopeful emigrants cannot sell their property either and will come in the spring.

     d)   Because there is no work for Jacob Schneider in Lake Pepin, Israel told Jacob there is no work at Lake Pepin in the winter and suggests that he work in Pork (slaughter) House in Cincinnati

     e)   Israel doesn't want them at farm all winter. This would be the Waconia farm.

     f)   Israel will loan money to pay for Jacob's wife and children to come to Cincinnati.

6)   The Boarding house is active and Israel says Mrs. Pohl working "for me."
This confirms that the boarding house, later known as Winona Cottage, belongs to Israel, and is functioning in 1858.

7)   Pohl's

     a)   Mrs. Pohl is working at boarding house

     b)   Mr. Pohl is not a good investment and Israel doesn't trust him, so no credit is to be given at the store.

     c)   Mr. Pohl must pay room and board when his wife is no longer working for Israel.

     d)   Mr. Pohl room rent will be $2.50 per month. His boarding will be $2.50 per week.

8)   Israel will not be visiting Lake Pepin during the rest of 1858. Lewis Garrard and Evert Westervelt will take care of business. Israel asks Lewis to care for the men, horses, cattle, and building material. Therefore, Lewis was the manager of the Garrard interests in Israel's absence. Israel was not in Lake Pepin area very often at this time.

9)   Israel writes of a mill and a person called Galligher. No information was found and no known mill was built at this time.

Waconia July 10th 1857

Dear Mother

Your welcome letter of the 21st & 23rd ult. came yesterday; but doubtless would have come sooner had the _county_ been stated. You all seem to be enjoying yourselves in the usual way, in visiting, gardening removing fences &c. It is singular how every change either in adding to or taking from is an improvement. However I am glad to hear of these things as they afford employment to poor people, are innocent a ~~very expensive~~ not very expensive. I am impatient to hear of the extension of the house over the basin with patent spiral stairway to the water &c. You have yet much to do; indeed your work is scarcely more than commenced.

I wish while you have the spirit of progress on you, you would come & help me a little. I have three miles of fence to build this coming year. About the place here I have adopted the Clifton style of fence & like it pretty well save that it is protection neither against dogs nor chickens.

I have several breaking teams at work turning over the prairie sod for next years commencement in tillage. I will have a large farm if _____ can be procured in time to be of use to me. I wish you could get out of Clifton ideas & spend the same amount here so as to have worthy return — both for cash & thought outlay. One fault with Minnesota is the bright sky & glare; though there are not near the white limestone roads & dust of your vicinity. The crops are growing finely & the prospect is cheering for the farmers. This state agriculturally viewed is in the first rank as we have none of the mishaps the papers report of the more southern latitudes.

Our county convention was held on Friday & I was one of the two delegates from this township. The principal object was to nominate delegates to the State convention which on the 20th nominates the Gov. & other state officers & two congressmen. Of course the fall campaign was the great topic & prospective candidates, & their friends were busy manufacturing popularity. Many of the _____ of the county are polite enough to say they wish me ____ to the legislature. What the sequel is to be I cannot well say but the chance is good for my recep.. Already those who fear me are telling lies about me, but this is to be expected. I am also a little disgusted with the profession of some who pretend to be my friends & yet are the meanest of hypocrites. Of course I do not tell them that I understand them, but shall try to use them for some purpose – After this year I think it will be well to drop politics as far as my own advancement is concerned & attend only to my personal business. Perhaps many do not know that I am of more importance to the party than might seem at first sight, on account of the prospective value of my lands & the amount of capital I will have invested; which will make me the richest farmer in the county — my brothers excepted who may exceed me there or are all fairly started

It will be an exceedingly great disappointment to me if you do not come out here — if but for a day or two. To own so much property village & county & to have so many means of enjoyment at command, is but poor satisfaction when I think you may never see them. Indeed I consider it almost a duty for you to see what we are doing. You know Minnesota as yet only as the dream or travels & my means & try to think & believe it all that we say it is.

will you mention to Israel that we need a tittle or two for the sitting room but not to buy any; as Mike the cabinet-maker can make one for me.

I suppose you will be soon leaving Chapelwood. What arrangement do you make in leaving the house & servants. When does any body go to. You say Aunt Ruhamah has gone to Philada. Has Ben gone to Mifflin. I suppose Israel has told you that he will fit up a house for his friends as mine is too small for but two or three besides myself.

The sun is broiling hot & the corn grows beautifully. Animal & vegetable life are in full & sudden vigor. A month ago one would have thought our crops threatened failure; but this is a peculiar climate & quick when once its qualities of development are at work. I am very anxious to have a talk with you & with all of you. I have been deprived this pleasure now a great while.

Love to all

Lewis.

Waconia, July 10, 1859

Dear Mother,

Your welcome letter of the 21st and 23rd alt. came yesterday but doubtless would have come sooner had the county been stated. You all seem to be enjoying yourselves in the usual way in visiting, gardening, securing fences, etc. It is singular how every change either in adding to or taking from is an improvement. However, I am glad to hear of these things as they afford employment to poor people are innocent. I am impatient to hear of the extension of the house over the basin with patent spiral stairway to the water etc. You have yet much to do; indeed your work is scarcely more than commenced. I wish while you have the spirit of progress on you would come & help me a little. I have three miles of fence to build this coming year. About the place here, I have adopted the Clifton Style of fence & like it pretty well save that it is protection neither against dogs nor chickens.

I have several breaking teams at work turning over the prairie sod for the next year's commencement in tillage. I will have a large farm if money can be procured in time to be of use to me. I wish you could get out of Clifton ideas and spend the same amount here so as to have worthy return both for cash and thought outlay. One fault with Minnesota is the bright sky and glare; though these are not worse than the white limestone roads and dust of your vicinity. The crops are growing finely & the prospect is cheering for the farmers. This state agriculturally viewed is in the first rank as has none of the mishaps the papers refer to in more southern latitudes.

Our county convention was held on Friday. I was one of the two delegates from the Township. The principal object was to nominate delegates to the state convention which is the 20th, nominated Gov. and other state officers & two congressman. Of course, the fall campaign was the great topic & prospective candidates and their friends are busy manufacturing popularity. Many of the substantial men of the county are polite enough to say they wish me to go to the legislature. What the sequel is to be I cannot once say but this chance is good for accept. Already those who fear me are telling lies about me, but this is to be expected. I am also a little disgusted with the propositions of some who pretend to be my friends & yet are the most hypocrite. Of course, I do not tell them that I understand them, but shall try to use them for some purpose. After this year I think it will be well to drop politics so far as my own advancement is concerned & attend only to my personal business. Perhaps many do not know that I am of more importance to the party than might seem at first sight, or account of the prospective value of my lands and the amount of capital I will have invested; which will make me the richest farmer in the county - my brother excepted who may exceed me when we are all fairly started.

It will be an exceedingly great disappointment to me if you do not come out here if but for a day or two. To own so much property village & county & to have so many means of enjoyment at command is but poor satisfaction when I think you may never see them. Indeed, I consider it almost a duty for you to see what we are doing. You know Minnesota as yet only as the drain on Israel's and my account & to think & believe it all we say it is.

Will you mention to Israel that we need a table or two for the sitting room but not to buy any; as Mike the cabinet maker can make one for me?

I suppose you will be soon leaving Chapelwood. What arrangements do you make in leaving the house & servants? Where does everybody go to? You say Aunt Ruhannah has gone to Philip who has gone to Mexico.

I suppose Israel has told you that he will fix up a house for his friends as mine is too small for but two or three more beside myself.

The sun is boiling hot & the corn grows beautifully. Animal and vegetable life are in full & sudden vigor. A month ago, we would have thought our crops threatened failure, but this is a peculiar climate & quick when once its qualities of development are at work. I am very anxious to have a talk with you & with all of you. I gave been deprived the pleasure now a great while.

Love to all   Lewis.

Highlights in this letter:

1) Lewis identifies this letter as being written at Waconia.

   At the time this letter was written, Lewis was not in Dacotah Cottage house yet but temporarily staying at Waconia Farm.

2) In this letter, Lewis identifies the distinctive fencing around the lots as Clifton Style.

   Fence design has cross boards on the top half with horizontal boards on the bottom half.

   Clifton is the name of the Cincinnati, Ohio, neighborhood where Justice John and Sarah Bella McLean live.

3) Mike the cabinet maker would have been Michael Ackerman, the carpenter.

4) "I suppose Israel has told you that he will fix up a house for his friends as mine is too small for but two or three more beside myself."

   This refers to a guest house that Israel plans to build, probably on St. Hubert's block, because more room for guests is needed.

5) "I have several breaking teams at work turning over the prairie sod for the next year's commencement in tillage." Waconia Farm land is being prepared for cultivation and Lewis is overseeing the process.

6) …."mention to Israel that we need a table or two for the sitting room.'

   Could mean that that Lewis and Israel shared a home or that Waconia Farm requires a table or two.

7) Israel will be staying with his brother Lewis when he visits to oversee additions being made to St. Hubert's Lodge.

8) Letter written in 1859. Sarah Bella McLean came to Frontenac in 1862, three years later. Sarah Bella came one year after her husband, Justice McLean, died in 1861.

9) County Convention

   Less than a year after arriving in village of Westervelt, Lewis is a township delegate and is being encouraged to be a county delegate.

Frontenac Tour Guide

~~~~~

Consider removing the Tour Guide
pages to create a convenient guide.

1894 Plat Map with Location Identifiers

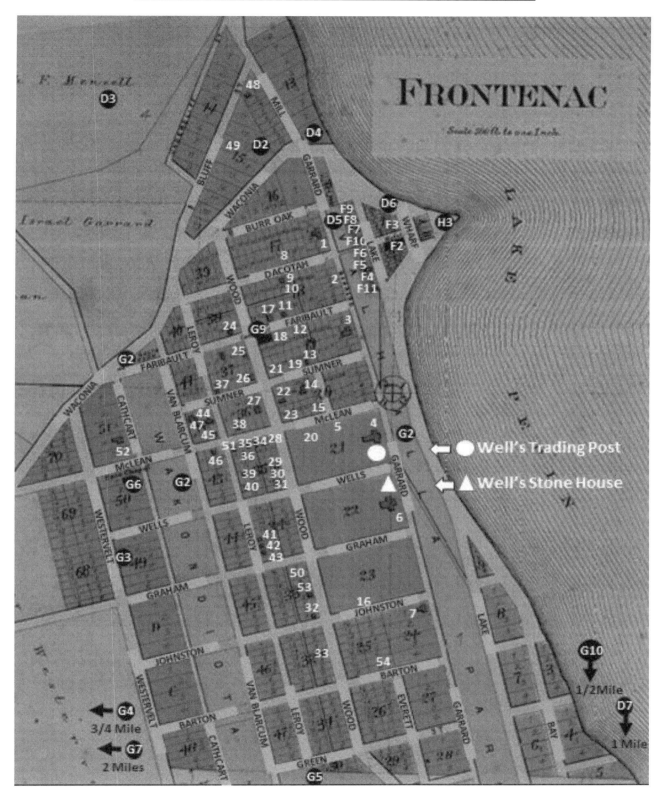

1894 Plat of Frontenac with House, Park, and Business Location Identifiers

Section E: Pioneers & Their Homes - Houses 1 - 14

E#	Block	Lots	2018 Status	House Name	2018 Addr	On Street	Between	1870 Owner	1870 Family Residents	1870 Profession	Born	Where born
1	17	1-13	Exists	Dacotah Cottage	28743	Garrard	Burr Oak / Dacotah	Sarah Bella McLean	Vacant			
1.1	18	2	Moved Exists		28819	Garrard	Dacotah / Faribault	Jacob Schneider 1861-1865	Already Moved		1831	Hessen-Darmstadt
2	18	7	Moved Gone	Pine Cottage	Mid Block	North side of Faribault	Manypenny / Garrard	Sarah Bella McLean	George Burmeister	Miller	1839	Prussia
3	19	1-9	Exists	Winona Cottage	28895	Garrard	Faribault / Sumner	Israel Garrard	Boarding House			
4	21	All	Exists	St. Hubert's Lodge	29055	Garrard	McLean / Wells	Israel Garrard	Israel Garrard / Hans Johnson	Lawyer / Laborer	1826 / 1842	Kentucky / Norway
5	21	NE corner	Moved Gone		29055	Garrard	McLean / Wells	Israel Garrard	Buildings on St. Hubert's block			
6	22	All	Exists	Locust Lodge	29133	Garrard	Wells / Graham	Evert Westervelt	Evert Westervelt	Farmer (1st yr)	1813	New York
7	24	1	Exists	Greystone	29277	Garrard	Johnston / Barton	Sarah Bella McLean	James Davidson	Lumber Man	1831	Pennsylvania
8	17	10	Gone		34921	Dacotah	Manypenny / Wood	Elam Miller	Elam Miller	Plasterer Mason	1836	Mississippi
9	18	23	Exists	Honey Bee	34962	Dacotah	Manypenny / Wood	Nicholaus Poppe	Nicholaus Poppe	Laborer	1824	Hanover
10	18	S 23	Gone		S. of 34962	Dacotah	Manypenny / Wood	Nicholaus Poppe	Christ Christianson	Laborer	1834	Norway
11	18	S 10-11	Exists		34921	Faribault	Manypenny / Wood	John Gerken	John Gerken	Laborer	1826	Hanover
12	19	22	Moved Gone	The Poplars	28891	Manypenny	Faribault / Sumner	Israel Garrard	Karsten Stuhr	Laborer	1837	Hanover
13	19	10, 11	Gone		E. of 34911	Sumner	Manypenny / Wood	Israel Garrard / Evert Westervelt	Community Buildings			
14	20	20-23	Exists	Parsonage	28597	Manypenny	McLean / Sumner	Sarah Bella McLean	Jacob Van Eschew	Clergy Man	1828	Switzerland

Section E: Pioneers & Their Homes - Houses 15 - 28

E#	Block	Lots	2018 Status	House Name	2018 Addr	On Street	Between	1870 Owner	1870 Family Residents	1870 Profession	Born	Where born
15	20	10-13	Burned Gone	Community Church		N Side of McLean	Manypenny Wood	Sarah Bella McLean				
16	23		Gone		Mid Block	N Side of Johnston	Garrard Wood	Sarah Bella McLean	Nicholas Christ	Laborer	1843	Prussia
17	18	12	Burned Gone		34903	Faribault	Manypenny Wood	John Hunecke	John Hunecke	Tailor	1832	Westfalen, Prussia
18	19	20	Gone		Mid Block	S Side of Faribault	Manypenny Wood	August John Lubeck Heirs	Carl C. Steffenhagen	Retired	1803	Prussia
19	19	12	Exists		34911	Sumner	Manypenny Wood	Engelbert Schenach	Engelbert Schenach	Laborer	1832	Tyrol, Austria
20	21	West End	Gone			S Side McLean	Garrard Wood	Israel Garrard	St. Hubert's Shop			
21	19	14-16	Moved Exists	Kittle House	NE Corner	Sumner & Wood	Manypenny Wood	Israel Garrard	Ole Larson Loken / Carl Olson	Laborer / Laborer	1828 / 1838	Norway / Norway
22	20	17-19	Exists		28960	Wood	McLean Sumner	Englebert Haller	Engelbert Haller	Carpenter	1833	Wurtemberg
23	20	14-16	Moved Gone		34879	McLean	Manypenny Wood	Martin Schlunt	Boarding house / Martin Schlunt	Boarding	1828	Wurtemberg
24	38	1-3	Moved Exists		Mid Block	N Side of Faribault	Wood LeRoy	Israel Garrard	Christopher John Steffenhagen	Farmer	1824	Mecklenburg
25	37	10-12	Gone		Opposite 28900	Wood	Faribault Sumner	Henry Hunecke	Henry Hunecke	Carpenter	1834	Prussia
26	37	1-3	Exists		28929	Wood	Faribault Sumner	Michael Ackerman	Michael Ackerman	Carpenter	1835	Bavaria
27	36	1-2	Exists	Frontenac Hotel, aka Schneider Hotel	28971	Wood	McLean Sumner	Jacob Schneider	Jacob Schneider / Claus Hauschild / Christ Brinkman	Hotel keeper / Laborer / Laborer	1831 / 1832 / 1833	Hessen-Darmstadt / Hanover / Hanover
28	35	6	Gone		SW Corner	Wood & McLean	McLean Wells	John Hager	John Hager	Laborer	1833	Bavaria

Section E: Pioneers & Their Homes - Houses 29 - 43

E#	Block	Lots	2018 Status	House Name	2018 Addr	On Street	Between	1870 Owner	1870 Family Residents	1870 Profession	Born	Where born
29	35	7,8	Exists	Post Office	29039	Wood	McLean Wells	Henry Lorentzen	Henry Lorentzen	Postmaster & Notary	1821	Hamburg
30	35	9	Gone		29055	Wood	McLean Wells	Henry Isensee	John Olson	Boot & Shoe Maker	1815	Norway
31	35	10	Exists		29065	Wood	McLean Wells	John Friedericks	John Friedericks / Johannes Gerken	Laborer / Laborer	1840 / 1824	Mecklenburg / Hanover
32	33	7-8	Exists		29255	Johnston	Wood LeRoy	John Seba	John Seba	Laborer	1829	Hanover
33	32	4	Moved Exists		29289	Wood	Johnston Barton	Israel Garrard	Josiah Batchelder	Boat Builder	1833	Maine
34	35	5	Exists		34844	McLean	Wood LeRoy	Gottfried Schenach	Gottfried Schenach	Blacksmith	1825	Tyrol, Austria
35	35	4	Exists		34832	McLean	Wood LeRoy	Emmanuel Schenach	Emmanuel Schenach	Wagon Maker	1825	Tyrol, Austria
36	35	2-3	Moved Gone		S. side McLean	West of Alley	Wood LeRoy	Henry Muller	Henry Muller	Laborer	1815	Mecklenburg
37	37	6	Exists		34805	Sumner	Wood LeRoy	Joseph Weich	Joseph Weich / John Vierengel	Carpenter / Musician	1804 / 1842	Baden / Bavaria
38	36	5	Gone		North side	McLean	Wood LeRoy	John Bahr	John Bahr	Turner of Wood	1811	Hanover
39	35	15	Gone		N. of 29050	LeRoy	McLean Wells	Joachim Koehn	Joachim Koehn	Laborer	1838	Mecklenburg
40	35	14	Exists		29050	Leroy	McLean Wells	Christ Friedericks	Christ Friedericks	Laborer	1827	Mecklenburg
41	34	12	Gone		N. of 29136	LeRoy	Wells Graham	John Markmann	John Markmann	Laborer	1841	Prussia
42	34	11	Gone		29136	LeRoy	Wells Graham	Wolfgang Schloerstein	Wolfgang Schloerstein	Laborer	1816	Austria
43	34	10	Gone		S. of 29136	LeRoy	Wells Graham	Mary Ann Sperl	Mary Ann Sperl	Housekeeper	1845	Austria

Section E: Pioneers & Their Homes - Houses 44 - 54

E#	Block	Lots	2018 Status	House Name	2018 Addr	On Street	Between	1870 Owner	1870 Family Residents	1870 Profession	Born	Where born
44	42	N 1/2 of 1,2	Exists		34778	Sumner	Van Blarcum LeRoy	Carl Peters	Joachim Bremer	Laborer	1831	Mecklenburg
45	42	S 1/2 of 1,2	Gone		34783	McLean	Van Blarcum LeRoy	Israel Garrard	Barn			
46	43	3-4	Gone			South Side of McLean	Van Blarcum LeRoy	Charles F. Herder	Charles F. Herder	Farmer	1833	Prussia
47	42	3-4	Exists		28964	Van Blarcum	McLean Sumner	Frontenac Mission	Vacant			
48*	15	1-3, 11	Gone		28535	Lake Ave Way	Waconia Bluff	Ole (Larson) Loken	Ole (Larson) Loken	Quarryman	1828	Norway
49*	15	13	Moved Exists		W. of 28535	Lake Ave Way	Waconia Bluff	Evert Westervelt	James Lester Annie (Loken) Lester	Quarryman	1856 1861	Iowa Norway
50*	33	1,2	Gone		34850	Graham	Wood LeRoy	Hans Olson	Hans Olson	Quarryman	1860	Norway
51*	35	1,2	Exists		34808	McLean	Wood LeRoy	George Bartels, Jr	George Bartels, Jr	Carpenter	1862	Hanover
52*	51	4	Gone		34661	McLean (CR 2)	Cathcart Waconia	Nathanial Collins McLean	Nathanial Collins McLean	Stock Raiser	1818	Ohio
53*	33	6	Gone		28790	Wood	Johnston Graham	Ole Haga	Ole Haga	Quarryman	1847	Norway
54	25	7,8	Moved Exists	Virginia Cottage	Mid Block	N. Barton	Garrard Wood	James A. Owens	James A. Owens	Clerk for Garrards	1839	Pennsylvania

* 19th Century Frontenac Homes NOT on the 1870 Overlook Picture

1995 Aerial with 1870 Building and Shoreline Locations

Section D: Building the Village

ID	Status	NAME	Plat Map Location Description	2018 Street # (Approx)	2018 Street	Begin Year	End year	Yrs Exist in 2018
D2	Gone	Saw Mill	West of Mill Street, Between Waconia and Bluff	28589	Lake Avenue Way	1856	1871	15
D3	Gone	Quarry	NW of Undercliff Street		Frontenac State Park	1858	1920	62
D4	Gone	Lime Kiln	East of Garrard Avenue North of Waconia, Block 13	SE of Lake Ave Way Bridge	Lake Avenue Way	1858	1871	13
D5	Gone	Brewery	West of Lake Street, Block 11	SW of 28725	Lake Avenue Way	1860	1864	4
D6	Gone	Wharf	North Border of Block 1	28776	Lake Avenue Way	1867	1900	33
D7	Gone	Flour Mill	Head of Sand Point Trail	Near Hwy 61	County Road 2 Blvd	1866	1912	46

Section F: Lakeside Complex

ID	Status	NAME	Plat Map Location Description	2018 Street # (Approx)	2018 Street	Begin Year	End year	Yrs Exist in 2018
F2	Exists	Lakeside Hotel	South of Agate Street West of Wharf Street	28796	Lake Avenue Way	1858	*	160
F3	Gone	Pavilion	North of Agate Street West of Wharf Street	28793	Lake Avenue Way	1859	1997	138
F4	Gone	Stable	East of Lake Street	28813	Lake Avenue Way	1867	1976	109
F5	Exists	Kittle House (Grapevine)	West of Lake Street, Block 11	28775	Lake Avenue Way	1865	*	153
F6	Moved Exists	Virginia Cottage	West of Lake Street, Block 11	N. of 28775	Lake Avenue Way	1865	*	153
F7	Gone	Lakeside Shop	West of Lake Street, Block 11	28745	Lake Avenue Way	1869	1975	106
F8	Gone	Poplars Cottage	West of Lake Street, Block 11	S. of 28725	Lake Avenue Way	1863	1997	134
F9	Gone	Fern Cottage	West of Lake Street, Block 11	28725	Lake Avenue Way	1860	2009	149
F10	Gone	Pine Cottage	West of Lake Street, Block 11	28745	Lake Avenue Way	1858	1949	91

Aerial of Frontenac Plain from Lake Pepin Looking West

Section G: Village Life

ID	Status	NAME	Plat Map Location Description	2018 Street # (Approx)	2018 Street	Begin Year	End year	Yrs Exist in 2018
G2		Frontenac Parks						
	Gone	Eclipse Park	Intersection of Waconia & Bluff. Area now in Frontenac State Park			1857	1859	2
	Exists	Delta Park	Bordered by Waconia, (N), Faribault (S), & Van Blarcum (W)		North of Wakondiota Park	1857	*	161
	Exists	Valhalla Park	Bordered by Waconia (N), Ludlow (S), Garrard (E), & Lake (W)		Garrard, Lake	1857	*	161
	Exists	Wakondiota Park	Bordered by Faribault (N), Winona (S), Van Blarcum (E), Cathcart (W)		Van Blarcum	1857	*	161
G3	Moved Exists	Frontenac School	Westervelt Avenue Way	29118	Westervelt Way	1869	1958	89
G4	Exists	Waconia Farm	McLean across from Waconia Cliff	29750	County Road #2	1850	*	168
G5	Exists	Frontenac Cemetery	West of Wood, South of Green St.		South Extension	1867	*	151
G6	Exists	Christ Episcopal Church	Southeast Corner of McLean and Westervelt Avenue	34660	McLean, County Road #2	1868	*	150
G7	Gone	Dakota Park	West of Territorial Rd		South of CR #2	1871	1941	70
G9	Gone	German Methodist & Norwegian Lutheran Church	SE Corner of Faribault & Wood	W. of 34894	Faribault	1888	1975	87
G10	Exists	Villa Maria Academy	South of Winona Avenue	29847	County Road #2	1891	2018	127

Section H: Mississippi River & Lake Pepin

ID	Status	NAME	Plat Map Location Description	2018 Street # (Approx)	2018 Street	Begin Year	End year	Yrs Exist in 2018
H3	Gone	Lighthouse	Frontenac Point, East of Block A & B			1871	1877	6

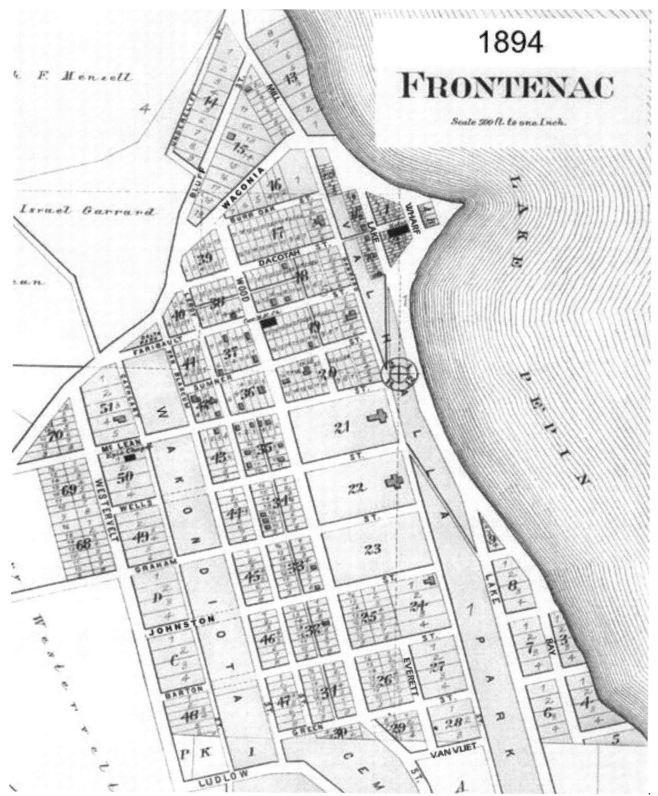

The 1894 Frontenac Plat Map

The locations of buildings are indicated on this map by
overhead view icons that approximate the size and shape of the buildings.

ADDENDUM – for Personal Notes

ADDENDUM – for Personal Notes

Name Index

Name Index

Name Index

Name Index

Name Index

SCHAEFER
Mathilda, 128
SCHAFER
Agatha, 184
SCHENACH
Annastasia (Schretter), 191, 192, 193
Bertha Elizabeth Ruth, 195
Catherine L., 190
Clara, 194
Edmund Martin, 195
Elenor (Ariel) (Hellah), 190
Ellen Mary (Furney), 191, 192, 193
Emily Marie, 195
Emmanuel, 191, 192, 193
Engelbert, 78, 190, 194
Francis (Frank) Joseph, 195
Frederick, 195
Gottfried, 190
John, 191, 192, 193
Joseph, 190, 191, 194
Josephine, 191
Julia Theresa (Quigley), 195
Louis G., 194
Maria (Mary) Sophia Henrietta (Friedericks), 78, 194
Maria Theresia (Feineler), 190, 191, 194
Marianne (Anna) (Berktold), 190
Mary, 191, 192, 193
Mary Ann (Taggert), 195
Son, 192
Victoria, 191
SCHERF
Alydia Louise (Johnson), 197
Carolina Johanna Maria (Steffenhagen), 60, 196, 208
Carolyn Augusta, 60, 76, 196
Charles Martin, 136, 196
Christina (Schmidt), 196
Clara (Olson), 172, 197
Cortland Herman, 197
Emma Emelia, 196

SCHERF
Etta Mina, 197
Harrison Herman, 172, 197
Herman, 60, 196, 208
Jeannette Hermina, 197
Katherine L. (Krelberg), 136, 196
Martin, 196
William Frederic, 197
SCHILLING
Charles Phillip, 132
Freda Marie (Koehn), 132
SCHLOER
Charles Cleveland, 144
Joseph Michael, 171
Tena Golilda (Nelson), 144
Violet (Olson), 171
SCHLOERSTEIN
Mary Ann (Maria), 198, 206
Mary Barbara, 124, 198, 206
Theresa, 124, 198
Wolfgang, 124, 198, 206
SCHLUND
Frank, 199
Josephine (Schlunt), 199
SCHLUNT
Anna B. (Barger), 199
Anna M., 199
Casper, 199
Frank, 199
Ida (Rothnick), 199
Ida Agnes (Hoffman), 200
Joseph R., 200
Josephine, 199
Josephine (Koester), 200
Josephine (Schupp), 199
Margaret, 200
Martin, 199
Martin Reinhart, 200
Mary, 199
Matilda, 200
Veronica, 200
SCHMIDT
(No Given Name.), 79
Albert, 195

SCHMIDT
Anna (Steffenhagen), 216
Bertha Elizabeth Ruth (Schenach), 195
Christina, 196
Doris, 79
Edward, 216
Sophia, 78, 79
SCHMITZ
Maria (Koch), 127
Sebastian, 127
SCHNEIDER
Albert, 123
Annie H., 122
Carrie F., 122
Clarence Chester, 123
Dorothea (Shale), 37, 98, 119, 121, 122, 201, 205
Henry C., 122
Jakob, 119, 201, 205
Mary Barbara, 201
Minnie C., 122
Walter J., 122
William J., 123
SCHRETTER
Annastasia, 191, 192, 193
SCHUELER
Sophia Christina Elizabeth, 52, 53, 108, 111
SCHULTE
Anna Mar. Cathr. Elisabeth, 106, 108, 110, 111
Eva Gertrude (Poepelbaum), 106
Gaudens Gaudentius, 106
SCHUMACHER
(No Given Name.), 218
Johanne Sophie Magdalene, 213
Louisa, 130, 131
Mary Jeanette (Steffenhagen), 218
SCHUNK
Molly, 58
SCHUPP
Josephine, 199

Name Index

Name Index

Made in United States
Orlando, FL
17 December 2023

41295436R00209

Genealogy of a Village

~~~~~~~

19ᵗʰ Century Frontenac, Minnesota

Lorry Wendland

Dedicated

To all who have contributed to the

Spirit of Old Frontenac